THE HEART & SOUL
OF THE
NEXT GENERATION

EXTRAORDINARY STORIES
OF ORDINARY TEENS

Michael J. Bradley, Ed.D.

HARBOR PRESS

GIG HARBOR, WA

Library of Congress Cataloging-in-Publication Data

Bradley, Michael J., 1951–
    The heart & soul of the next generation: extraordinary stories of ordinary
    teens/Michael J. Bradley.
        p. cm.
    ISBN 0-936197-53-6 (alk. paper)
        978-0-936197-53-1 (alk. paper)
    Teenagers—United States—Biography. 2. Adolescent psychotherapy—United
    States—Case studies. I. Title.

HQ796.B68614 2007
305.235'0973—dc22   2005052704

THE HEART & SOUL OF THE NEXT GENERATION
Extraordinary Stories of Ordinary Teens

Printed in the United States of America
10   9   8   7   6   5   4   3   2   1

Harbor Press, Inc.
P.O. Box 1656
Gig Harbor, WA 98335

HARBOR PRESS and the nautilus shell design are registered trademarks of Harbor
Press, Inc.

To all of the teenage heroes and heroines
I have known, who have taught me so much,
and who continue to teach me today.

Visit Dr. Bradley on the Internet
and subscribe to his free e-newsletter.

www.docmikebradley.com

CONTENTS

ACKNOWLEDGMENTS

First, to those who have shaped my own heart and soul, and so shaped my work, the best I can do is to say, "Thank you" to Bonnie Arena, Pete Bradley, Tony Chunn, Ginny Harvey-Dawson, Joe Ducette, Mattie Gershenfeld, Barry Kayes, Fred Hanna, Terry Longren, Father Michael McCarthy, Father John Riley, Chuck Schrader, Gene Stivers, and Pat Williams.

Second, once again I owe an inadequate thank you to my other family, that wonderful team at Harbor Press. Over the years, each member has pushed on through great challenges and terrible losses to make our books happen. Such is the way with people who see their work as something much more than a job.

To Peg Booth, the determined publicist and promoter of our books: You bring the passion of a lioness caretaking her cub as you pound on doors to get our work known. Thank you for being so tenacious.

To Harry Lynn, the steadfast publisher of these works: An entrepreneur once told me with some awe how he found one of our books in an airport bookstore, something this successful businessman viewed as the ultimate marketing achievement. "Your publisher must be amazing to get that done," he marveled. What he didn't say was, "After all, you're no Doctor Phil." Thank you for being so smart.

To Sandy McWilliams, the patient publicity director and spiritual voice of these books: If the caring and compassion in these stories ever become human, they would become you. Thank you for being so wise.

To Debby Young, the gentle editor and skilled seamstress of my writing: Your edits are always right on the money and make my jumbled thoughts speak so much better. Thank you for being so articulate.

Finally, thanks to the folks to whom I owe debts I can never repay, people who are heroes to me every day. To my daughter Sarah, who is my joy: In working so hard to become the wonderful girl that you are, you have become my inspiration. Without you, our family would be without its life and energy.

To my son Ross, who is my courage: I still cannot tell you how much I love and admire who you are. I stand in awe of how you quietly move in to soothe and heal people in pain with empathy and humor. Without you, our family would be without its compassion and laughter.

And to my wife Cindy, who is my heart and my vision. Without you, our family would not be. You are the best person I will ever know. Thank you.

INTRODUCTION

During my 30-year career as an adolescent psychologist, this book gathered dust on a back shelf inside my brain, blocked by some vague frustration, waiting for something to push me to my keyboard. Then one evening, while on a panel at a seminar on adolescence, I found myself suddenly haunted by the faces of some of the kids you are about to meet. As people spoke of various teen struggles, these teenage faces in my head began to powerfully answer some of their most poignant questions. "Yes," I silently exclaimed, "Ronald, man, you should be here to answer *that* question. And Susan, *geez*, your story would get a standing ovation." As their unforgettable faces began to fade, I vowed to finally write this book that I had struggled with for so long.

After that night, the words flew out of me. I think that's partly because the stories of the kids you are about to meet have been repressed far too long inside my files, and inside my heart. Many times, I'd try to pull out these most special memories, dust them off, and verbally share them with others, but I'd always find that my voice would fail. My spoken words could never convey the essence of these kids or their struggles, losses, and victories. After each telling, I'd shake my head, frustrated at my poor offerings of such profound people. Like a colorblind artist, I had no way of conveying the rich hues, the subtle textures, or the inspiring character of these *human beings.* Yes, *human beings,* not just *teenagers,* but complex *people,* folks like us who dream, feel pain, get scared, love, succeed, fail, strive to do better, and then fail again. But more often than you might think, they also triumph heroically, in ways that might reassure those adults who fear for the future of our world.

Many could dispute their hero status. One could argue that these kids were not the student council presidents or football stars, and, to my knowledge, not one went to West Point or Harvard. But this book is not about the heroism of the athlete, soldier, or scholar, or even the struggle of the physically challenged kid. For we can all see that heroism, and have some sense of what those accomplishments are about. The heroics you'll experience in this book are all invisible. No parades, no honors, not even one medal gets awarded here. In fact, most of the kids you'll meet had no idea of their own valor, no concept of their courage under fire, of the teenage bravery most adults would envy. If confronted, they would all vehemently deny being special. I think it was that humility and ordinariness that most endeared these kids to me.

Each of the chapters that follow comes from a drawer where I've kept the files of extraordinary, ordinary kids I've known. Since most of these people could not be located, some of their identifying data have been changed to protect their identities. But of the clients whom I was able to contact, all gave me permission to use their stories, though sometimes without a smile. Whether their memories brought them sadness or joy, each was anxious to help others who are now facing similar challenges not to hurt so much. Isn't that the way of heroes?

Some stories tell of very dramatic situations that most kids are lucky enough never to face, like abuse, addiction, and death. Others are about more common problems that many teens confront daily like bullying, divorce, and rejection. But each story offers some wisdom, some nugget of gold that the rest of us, old and young, can use in our own lives as we fight the same fights, using their examples as models for ourselves to help us triumph in the end, as these kids did.

These adolescents were very special in another way. They offered powerful words and insights about experiences common to most teenagers, things that most adolescents cannot or will not share, fragile self-revelations bravely offered by vulnerable kids whose peers usually stay silent to protect themselves from a confusing and hostile world. Some were able to disclose directly and fluently; others spoke powerfully without saying a word. But if you look closely, you'll even know what the silent ones said.

These stories were mostly recorded as they unfolded, with conversations captured exactly as they occurred either in tapes (used for training and teaching) or in a reconstruction of my elaborate notes. In my early therapist years, I discovered that being able to replay a client's exact words was a very powerful tool. Not having the best memory, I developed a system of blindly writing extensive shorthand notes during therapy sessions so that I would not lose critical words, thoughts, or observations. Afterwards, I would add my own impressions to these texts, and then put the special ones away like fine wines of experience. They were stored with a hope that one day they might be taken out, shared, and savored so that the pain, struggles, and triumphs of these heroes might become helpful to the rest of us, whether adolescent or adult.

For the teenage reader, I hope that these stories do at least two things. First, I hope they *teach*. Most kids tell me that they learn best about how to deal with challenges by listening to other teens. Ideas can come alive and become real through the words of a peer. It's like how watching a friend struggle with drugs can become the best anti-drug program you'll ever see. Second, I hope these stories *inspire*. I can't tell you how many times I've walked into my office at 10 AM feeling overwhelmed and sorry for myself, and walked out at 10 PM feeling confident and lucky. The only thing that happened in my life during those twelve hours was a thing called inspiration. Like that day when a teen fighting to survive cancer taught me how to stand up to a challenge I thought I couldn't handle. He did this just by telling me his story.

To the adult reader, my hope is that these pages become a kind of canvas, a painting through which the lives of adolescents take on their true depth of color, conveying a real sense of what it's like to be a teen today and in many ways, a teen at any time. Far too often, we only view teenagers in black and white snapshots that discount them as simple children. We assume that their unwillingness or inability to talk implies that they don't experience life as we do, that they don't *really* feel pain or joy, fear or hope. Whether a parent or principal, a counselor or cop, I believe that the kids you will meet here will teach or re-teach us all that teens feel life *at least as intensely* as adults, and that they struggle mightily with powerful issues of morality, character, and courage in battles that we adults too often never see. In knowing this, perhaps we can maintain a respectful empathy for the kids we love and care for, and then our next generation can better rely upon us. That's my greatest hope of all.

Whether an adult or a teen, I have one last wish for you: that this book become an engaging journey through that amazing chapter of life called adolescence. I hope that these pages come alive, making you see, hear, and feel what I get to experience daily in working with teenagers: maddening frustration, raucous laughter, paralyzing fear, wondrous hope, overwhelming sadness, and almost always, that odd, quiet joy of victory.

That list of wishes makes it finally clear to me why these stories were so difficult to share for so long a time. Because in chatting about these kids over the years, I never did their stories justice; my depictions were such poor representations of their poignant struggles and profound character. But now I can relax. For their own words do a much better job, and it is their own words that you are about to hear.

So if you are ready, turn the page and I'll let some of the next generation speak directly to you. I suspect that when you've said goodbye to the twentieth teen, you will feel much better about the hearts and souls of the next generation. But first, be sure that you really want to take this ride called adolescence. Because once you start, it can get a little scary. And it's really, really hard to get off.

I know. I never did.

1

HEROICALLY ORDINARY

Matt's Story

In spite of their numerous and unprecedented challenges, most contemporary teenagers quietly muddle through this crazy world to become fine people. Many days, I'm unsure of how that's possible, but the research assures me that it's true. I suppose that, like everyone else, my eye is always drawn to those kids grabbing the TV spotlights, the ones doing the self-destructive things that the adult world seems to push upon them, such as sex, drugs, and violence.

Whenever I think of all those good kids who quietly fly below our radar, Matthew always pops into my head. He could have been the poster boy for ordinary teenagers. Not tall, but not short; not fat, but not skinny; not particularly athletic, but not especially clumsy; not Track 1 in school, but not Track 4. He was not lots of things—he was just ordinary. That's what he most disliked about himself—the fact that he was just a face in the crowd, and not the popular, heroic figure he dreamed of being. He was about to learn that "popular" and "heroic" are often words that don't always belong together.

~

"Fourteen," he corrected with a sigh. "I'm *fourteen*, not thirteen. I don't know why my dad put that on my form there. He keeps thinking that I'm younger than I am. I guess I act younger or something—but I'm

fourteen. Maybe if I played football or did drugs, he'd remember how old I am."

That comment made me look up from Matt's paperwork, which was extensive. The three months of reports from a host of doctors and hospitals all spoke of a yet-undiagnosed stomach problem that caused Matt substantial pain, mostly in the mornings. The final report speculated that his illness might be emotionally based, which is how he came to reluctantly sit before me. "The doctors, I know what they're all thinking. They're thinking that I make this up to get out of school. They're wrong. I'm not in love with school, but I don't hate it either, not that much. And if I wanted to ditch school, I'd make up a better symptom than gut pain. Do you know what kinds of things doctors do to you when you have gut pain? Those tests would convince any kid faking it to go back to school—trust me."

Matt looked uncomfortable, as if anticipating another lousy doctor experience. I tried to reassure him. "Well, trust *me*," I smiled, "I've had both kinds of tests, and the tests I give are a *whole* lot better." Matt's eyes got big. "You mean . . . you . . . *do* tests like that?" "No, no," I explained, "I'm sorry. That was a bad joke. Any tests I give are just done with words or pictures or puzzles. I never stick anything in anybody, OK?"

As Matt nodded, I took in his picture. A pleasant, open, but worried face; average 14-year-old height and weight, although a little on the chunky side; rumpled, sandy hair; one ripped, untied sneaker; and a death-themed, heavy-metal-band shirt and a huge spiked bracelet, both of which looked comically out of place on this boy. As if he were reading my mind, Matt shifted uneasily and took off the massive bracelet. He held it and rubbed his wrist like the band was something he had been forced to wear, and was glad to finally have off.

"So, you were saying," I continued, "that your dad can't remember how old you are, because . . . you don't do, well, *unusual* things?" "It's not my dad's fault," Matt explained, "My dad's great. He's a really nice guy. He works two jobs for us and he never complains or gets mad or anything. He's yelled at me, like, twice in my life that I can remember, and once was when I let the refrigerator fall down the basement steps, so that hardly counts." Without pausing to explain the refrigerator catastrophe, he went on. "It's me, not my dad. I'm, like, so . . . boring, and . . . I don't know, so . . . *ordinary*, that no one really remembers me." He thought for a minute. "It's like I'm not there a lot even when I am," he summarized matter-of-factly.

Those words set off a rush of reactions in me: My stomach suddenly recalled that same empty feeling of being a nobody teen. My head couldn't remember ever hearing a kid describe that so well, and my heart worried that he might feel badly about himself. But he claimed that he didn't. "It's like at school. I don't get teased or bullied—much—you know, just the usual stuff. And I do OK with grades, so, no, I'm not *down* on myself. It's just that I'm not *up* on myself either. I mean, like, lots of kids, they're somebody. They're, like, football players or student council types or real smart or real popular—you know, the cool kids. I don't mind that I'm not like any of that. Only sometimes, it feels . . . funny."

Matt put his bracelet on and off a few times without speaking, like he was trying to figure out how to make it fit him. "Can I ask what you're thinking?" I asked. "Sure," he answered, and then he added, "Um, do you want me to just keep on talking, because . . . I'm not sure I know what you want to hear." "Matt," I explained, "in here, whatever you think and say is a lot more important than whatever I think or say. So it would be great if you just said whatever goes through your brain, OK?" "OK," he shrugged, "but it's kind of . . . embarrassing because I don't have anything, like, smart to say, and I don't think I've got any big problems, so what I think about is probably pretty boring. By the way," he diverted, "what the heck is that?"

He was pointing to a plaque on my wall that read: ORDER OF THE GOOD TIME, NOVA SCOTIA. I answered hurriedly, trying to get back to his thoughts. "Oh, that's a neat thing I was given by some wonderful folks in Canada. That was an idea started by the explorer Samuel de Champlain in 1606. In their second winter in the wilderness, when his team of explorers was sick and scared and sad, he somehow knew that keeping their spirits up would help them survive those terrible days. So he started a kind of club to boost their morale by having these special dinners and processions, where they would make a big deal out of nothing to try and feel better. It's weird because now, 400 years later, scientists are just beginning to understand how important good morale is in fighting diseases. But, Matt, if it's OK, I'd like to get back to talking about your own morale, and your own thoughts."

Matt nodded approvingly at the plaque. "Cool," he said, "*Very* cool." He turned back to me. "OK, what I was thinking before was about how at school, there's these teachers that I like a whole lot, and I don't think they can remember my name. And sometimes . . . well, this just happened again today . . . when I was trying to talk with them, you know, trying to hang out with them a little bit, one of the cool kids walks up—he's a basketball star—and, well, the teachers just started to talk over me to the cool kid—like I wasn't there anymore, like I just vanished in the middle of my sentence. But I understand, you know, 'cause I wasn't saying anything important, and the cool kid, he's talking about the game on Friday and all. I couldn't compete with that. I never can compete because there's nothing special about me that would make anybody interested in me. That's what I mean about not being there. Even my parents, I think they're bored with me sometimes. That's why I joke with them about doing drugs—but I never would." He put his bracelet down, giving up on it, and rolling his eyes. "Maybe I should," he added.

In spite of his words, Matt was not feeling sorry for himself, nor was he fishing for sympathy. He was simply narrating his ordinary life as he saw it. "Do you want to know what I'm thinking again?" he asked. When I laughed and nodded, he seemed pleased. "I was thinking about how I need to be more than I am, but I don't know how. You know what I'm great at? I'm great at seeing both sides of an argument. I'm *too* good at it. When we debate things at school, or if my friends are having a fight, when I hear one side I think, 'Yeah, that's right.' And then when I hear the other side I think, 'Yeah, that's right, too.' Both sides can't be right but I have a hard time sticking to one side. I'm lousy at having an opinion. I'm *fantastic* at being neutral," he added sarcastically.

"Matt," I asked, "have you ever thought that maybe there are *too* many people in the world who have *too* many opinions that they are *too* sure of? Have you ever considered that perhaps it's wonderful for you to be honest enough to say that there's much that you are unsure of, to say that you value both sides of things, that you don't believe that you have all of the answers?"

Matt was riveted for a moment. Then he asked, "Do you think this stuff is what makes my stomach hurt?" Without trying to be funny I answered, "I have no idea. . ." and before I could finish my sentence, we both burst out laughing.

For the next few sessions we continued pretty much like that. I warned him that his therapy would be a kind of search mission, getting him to talk his thoughts out to see if there was anything there that might explain his gut pain, but nothing seemed to come close. I became a little frustrated, concerned that I wasn't helping, and worried that his symptoms were worsening, not improving. But Matt seemed to enjoy talking more and more, as if he had years of ready-to-share thoughts stored up.

One day he brought a thought in the door with him. "You know, I never realized how much I hate being plain and ordinary." He paused, and then warned, "This next part is *real* embarrassing. Sometimes . . . well, *lots* of times I have this daydream at school where I'm this hero-warrior guy who . . . who . . . I can't even say it," he blushed, ". . . where I'm this, like, hero who rescues the school from these terrorists who try to blow up the building with everyone in it. Isn't that *insane*?" he asked, not able to look at me. "Yep," I nodded, "I'm afraid that's pretty bizarre. Now, if you had rescued your school from *communist commandos*, like *I* did when *I* was fantasizing at school, now *that* would be OK. But, *terrorists*? Yeah, that's pretty insane."

He looked up at me inquisitively without laughing. So I answered his unasked question. "And, no, I'm not making that up to help you feel better, Matt. That's *my* embarrassing truth. And I'll go you one better. Even today at age 54, I still sometimes daydream about being a hero. Not as often as in 8th grade, though. Of course, back then I had the cool kids that I needed to impress, and more importantly, I had the gorgeous Francine Leotta that I needed to rescue from the godless killers. And we both know how incredibly adoring she would have been then. Unfortunately, the commies never showed, the cool kids never saw me as their hero, and Francine never got to show her adoration. So, tell me, how's *your* counterterrorist thing working out?"

This time he laughed loudly. "You're really not making that up?" he giggled. "I wish I was," I admitted, "but the truth is, I suspect that most kids have fantasies like that. I think lots of us want to be heroes, and I also think that's great. Because we all *can* be heroes—maybe not the terrorist/commando-fighter-type heroes, but *everyday* heroes. Like the hungry, exhausted cop on the news the other night who found the strength to chuckle-up the lost, crying 4-year-old, making him feel safe until his mom got there; or a teacher I knew who had the worst day of her year, who I watched patiently set her own pain aside to lend a comforting ear to an upset student; or that *plain, ordinary* 14-year-old young man who was nice to that kid who got bullied a few weeks back." Matt blushed again. "My mom told you? Well, I didn't go fight the jerks or anything. That was no big deal. That's not being a real hero."

"It is to me," I answered firmly. "Matt, I've met a couple of those war-type heroes. And they tell me that *their* heroes are ordinary folks like that cop, the teacher, and *you*—people who have a set of values and act on them, even though they're tired or angry or scared. One war hero told me that his heroism was a crazy, one-time thing that he thought didn't mean much. He wanted to be more of an everyday hero like those *plain, ordinary* people, like you." Matt shook his head, my words tumbling uselessly out of his ears.

"Look, Matt, I'm not telling you to *feel* a certain way—you have to feel what you feel. I am asking that you think, that you take another look at what being ordinary means." As he sat and thought, I had an idea. "If you and your mom say it's OK, the war hero guy I mentioned might be willing to chat with you about this stuff, if you want."

Two weeks later, Matt walked slowly into the room like he was thinking hard thoughts. He looked older to me. "I met Mr. Moore [the decorated war hero]," he said. "You knew that he's a teacher at my school, right? Well, guess what? Nobody there knows about him being a hero. He made me promise that I wouldn't tell anyone—he doesn't want people to know. You know what he said? He said that what he did when he got his medal was *not* how he wants to be known. He said he used to be like some guy who's mean to his wife and kids, and runs into a burning building to save someone, and then goes back home and is mean to his wife and kids. He said everyone calls that guy a hero, and thinks that he's great, but he's not, really. Just because you do one special thing, he said, that doesn't make you a hero." Matt sat and thought about that before going on.

"He said that *his* hero was his sergeant who never got any big medals or anything, but who, every day, just took care of his men, trying to keep them safe, and joking with them to keep their spirits up and stuff, even when he was more tired and sick and scared than they were. The sergeant always worried about his guys, talking to them about going back to school, and not drinking, and stuff. Mr. Moore said that when he got his medal he wanted to rip it off and give it to his sergeant, that the sergeant deserved it a lot more, but that the sergeant will probably never get one because he's the kind of hero that people never know about. Then he said that the sergeant didn't care about getting medals, just about being a good person. And not just on one day, but on every day, especially on those days that were real bad."

Matt mulled his own words for a while. "Mr. Moore, he said that his goal now was to try and be a hero like that sergeant, to be caring and patient and helping with his wife and kids, and to the kids at school, and to people he doesn't even know." Then Matt quizzically shook his head. "You know what else he said? He said that if someone ever gave him a medal for that stuff, he'd *hate* it. Because, he said, he needs to do this *quietly*, just for himself. That part I don't understand. I think I need to ask him about that. Why would you *not* want to get respected, you know, stand out in the crowd and be seen as cool?" Although he directed his question at me, I just shrugged. Some answers are best found on our own.

That night, Matt's mom called to cancel his next session. Tearfully, she told me that Matt's gut pain had finally been diagnosed.

He had a very rare and very vicious form of cancer that he might not survive. "The doctor," she sniffled on the phone, "told us that Matt's pain had to have been severe." Then her guilt washed over her like a tidal wave. *"All this time. . ."* she sobbed, *". . . all this time we wondered if he was making this up to try and miss school . . . and he just kept going, day after day, even though he hurt so bad . . . and no one was listening. . ."*

The word hero popped into my head.

I went to see Matt at the hospital. His mom had warned me that he would be terribly nauseous and weak from the treatments, and that he had lost his hair, and so maybe he would not want company. While I waited for him to come back from a treatment, the nurses asked if I was related to Matt. When I explained who I was, two of them looked at each other and then asked if I could keep a secret. They told me that from day one on the ward, as sick as he was, Matt seemed to make it his business to help the other kids on the pediatrics floor, especially the two who had no parents to visit them. He had created a club where all of the kids in that hospital were instant members, and they would all pool their treats—candy, popcorn, pudding—whatever. Every day, when most of the parents weren't around, the kids who could walk or "wheelchair" would march around the ward, playing silly songs on homemade instruments like box drums and hair comb harmonicas, and they'd visit the rooms of the ones who couldn't get out of bed. And there they'd sing more silly songs and eat their treats. This worked so well as a morale booster that the nurses had vowed to keep the idea going even after Matt left. They had never, ever seen a 14-year-old boy do anything like that.

My look of amazement caused one nurse to say, "Wait—here's the weird part. Matt made us swear not to tell anyone, *including his parents*, about these great things that he's done. He calls his club the ORDER OF THE COOL TIME." Her eyes misted a bit. "He's so sick and he's doing this wonderful thing for everyone else. Why on earth does he not want anyone to know?" she asked me.

I knew that Matt would want me to just shrug like I had no idea, so I did. The mist in my own eyes wanted to tell them the truth or, better yet, to give him a medal. But he would have hated that. That's just the way those ordinary heroes are.

~

As of this writing, Matthew is doing OK. He said that some time must pass before they'll really know that he's won his cancer battle. He told me that straight-up, still not looking for any sympathy. Just telling it like it is.

Most adolescents wrestle painfully with their dread of ordinariness, trying to find some way to break away, to be different, to be special—to be heroes. Some become provocative, acting out as a way of defining themselves as apart from others. Most just struggle quietly and bravely, doing the right things, being good people, and feeling lost and unimportant.

Not unlike de Champlain, the explorer, Matt blazed a trail that I asked his permission to share so that others might learn from his struggle. (He was uneasy with my telling his story, but he relented when he decided that it might help someone else.) He discovered a few things about heroism and ordinariness that all of us, teens and adults, might consider.

He found that true heroism is not one deed, but a view of the world that says, "This place is not about me." It is a quiet but steely belief that sees its best expression in the ordinary world, by ordinary people, and not on ball fields by great athletes, or on battlefields by great warriors. In its finest hour, heroism appears as compassion, not as competition—as creating, not as killing. It is a thing for silent, private pride, not raucous, public acclaim.

Matthew has already won his battle of the ordinary. He's found his path to heroism—in embracing that simple ordinariness of himself and others, and then seeing how each day presents heroic opportunities for each of us. And if you ever doubt that, I'd suggest a visit to that hospital to see the precious smiles of those small, scared, hurting members of the ORDER OF THE COOL TIME.

2

WHEN A FAMILY DIES

Ty's Story

Myths about contemporary adolescents profoundly affect our view of kids, and profoundly influence their lives. For example, today's teens are portrayed as terribly violent, to a point where kids see themselves as more threatening than any prior generation. Yet they are half as violent as their parents were when they were teens. Today's teens are described as selfish and self-centered. Yet this is the most giving generation we've ever recorded. But perhaps most erroneously and most sadly, teens are seen as largely immune to the effects of divorce in their families. Many feuding couples negotiate temporary "cease-fires" to postpone their splits until their kids are teenagers, because, as everyone knows, teenagers aren't hurt by divorce like young children, right? After all, when they are given the news, they mostly just shrug their shoulders, and say, "Whatever."

That's pretty much what Tiffany did when she was 15 and her parents split. Her mom told me that Ty (pronounced "tie") would hardly talk about it with them, saying only, "Just leave me out of the custody crap, OK?" She had already listened to the part about how Mom and Dad would be so much happier in separate homes, and then they would be so much nicer to their kids. She also listened to the part about how hardly anything would change because Dad was hardly there anyway, and when he was there they fought a lot. So then the divorce would help the kids be happier, too. She politely listened to all the parts, and then said, "Yeah, OK, whatever. Can I go now? I've got lots of homework." She wasn't upset at all, was she?

The large mural project in the foyer at the teen drop-in/crisis center was having a crisis of its own. The volunteer artists were yelling and accusing each other of ruining it. Something about the perspective wasn't working. As the squabble ran on, a girl timidly opened the front door, walked in behind the crowd of squawking art critics and studied the work. She was a big girl, pretty much a head higher than her peers, and not the body type you see on the cheering squads. She seemed to have done everything she could to make her appearance as bad as she could, as if she took up where nature left off in trying to make her a misfit: rumpled, bushy, red hair, oversized jeans hanging off of an oversized body, and tattered, orange Mickey Mouse flip-flops on a freezing February day. I wondered if she was protesting the fact that adolescent girls simply aren't allowed to have less-than-perfect bodies in today's world.

She did know painting. Waiting for a pause in the artistic ruckus, Ty said, "Well, if you guys don't mind an opinion, there is a way you could merge the two angles into one. Look," she instructed, "if you draw a fantasy transition here, and then go to a black background . . ." The crowd was impressed. "What's your name?" one kid asked. When she climbed out of her artist role, her initially confident voice was suddenly barely audible. "Uh, Tiffany," she mumbled apologetically, "but . . . I hate that name, so I call myself Ty. Actually, I hate that name, too, but I, like, ran out of options." Only the two adults in the group laughed. The kids just started staring at each other or at the floor. Partly to break the uneasiness, I welcomed Ty to the center and asked her to have a seat in the office. She looked horrified. "Oh, I'm not here 'cause I need help or anything," she hurriedly explained, "I'm just looking to volunteer some time to fulfill my community service requirement at school. I'm sort of a counselor to all of my friends, so I thought I would be good here." She looked crestfallen when I explained that we'd love to have her, but that the peer counselors must first complete a training program that would not fit with her deadline. "But, hey," I added, "we sure could use an art crisis counselor. Can you help us out?" "Sure," she said. But her eyes suggested that she was looking for a different form of expression. Or perhaps just for someone to listen.

In the following days, the mural magically began to transform into a work so wonderful that visitors came just to see that wall. But Ty was never anywhere to be found when most of us were there. The security log showed that she was timing her visits to only work when the building was nearly empty, later at night. Wondering what that was about, I swung by the center at 10 P.M. one evening, and sure enough, there she was, completely absorbed in her work.

"Don't jump," I cautioned as I came up behind her, "It's just me," but she startled anyway, and immediately started to pack up her brushes. "I'm . . . I'm sorry," she mumbled. "For what?" I asked, "I'm the one who scared you half to death." She seemed apologetic for taking up space in the world. "Ty, please," I asked, "Can you just hang out for a minute?" She stopped packing, but wouldn't look at me, as if she was being disciplined. "Look, I'm sorry," I said, "I mean, if you'd rather leave, that's OK, too, it's just that . . . well, if you'd like to chat . . . what I meant was that . . ." I stopped talking and took an exaggerated breath. "How about if I come in the front door again and maybe then I can talk in a way that makes sense?"

She didn't even smile. "Ty," I said, "please excuse my pushiness, but when I look and act like you, it's usually because I've got things on my mind that I think no one wants to hear, or will make people mad, or make them hate me, or something like that. You just seem all tied up in knots. What's up?" She looked like she was about to cry, when headlights suddenly flooded through the front door glass, and her very angry father burst in. "TIFFANY!" he yelled. "You were due home over *an hour ago, GODDAMMIT*. Your mother is in a freakin' panic. Why didn't you answer your goddamn phone? Is this where you've been every night all week? What the hell are you doing?"

"I'm sorry," she mumbled again to the floor, but then she looked at me. "I'd better not come back here . . ." "Mister, um, Feldman, is it?" I interrupted, "I think this is my fault. Ty is trying to fulfill a school requirement by doing this mural and . . ." I stammered when I realized that he was rolling his eyes because I called his daughter "Ty." ". . . and . . . I wasn't clear with her about when she should do this." I turned to Ty. "It is late . . . um . . ." I didn't know which name to call her, so I didn't use any, ". . . so maybe we should work out a schedule with your dad so he knows when to expect you home."

No one spoke for a moment, and then Ty quietly told the floor, "My father doesn't live in my house anymore." Dad's face turned even redder. *"That's not the point here, Tiffany,"* he said through gritted teeth. *"The point is that. . ."* and he launched into a litany of Ty's recent failings. But Ty knew exactly what the real point was. And now, so did I.

The next evening I ambushed Ty at her beautiful mural again, but she didn't jump. She might have been expecting me. "The kids here are so glad you joined us, Ty," I said. "You see, my idea for the mural was a scene of Elvis Presley riding a winged tiger and fighting Bruce Lee." I watched Ty suck in her cheeks so as not to laugh, so I added ". . . on a velvet art Confederate battle flag background with those pulsating mini-lights in it." She laughed a loud, halting, piecemeal laugh, covering her mouth like someone trying hard to not spit food out. Or like someone who had not laughed in a very long time.

When she stopped laughing and went back to painting, I decided to see if her window might stay open. "So, when did your dad leave?" I asked. Her brush never stopped moving. "Last month," she said. "They told me and my brother that they're . . ." she flipped her head and dropped her voice to imitate them, ". . . moving in different directions, and that we'll all be *so much happier* if they split up." Then she just snorted disgustedly and widened her eyes at hearing that line again, as if it sounded even dumber this time. "We're smart kids so, *naturally*, we understood," she said, nodding sarcastically. "Actually," she added quietly, "I have no idea if my little [13-year-old] brother understood. He hasn't said word one about the whole mess." "And have you gotten past word one?" I asked. "Oh, sure," she said, "my two friends are 'divorced' too, so they understand. I can talk to them." She picked up a rag to fix some error on the painting. "But it's weird, you know, talking to them? We all talk like photographs, not like paintings. You see, photographs show the *what* of something, you know, like an event or a person. Paintings should go *past* the what, and make a lot more happen inside the person watching. When my friends and I talk, we talk about the money problems, and the embarrassment of our dads getting girlfriends, like, immediately, and of our moms being basket cases—that's like the *what*. But we never talk like paintings."

"What would a painting of a divorce look like?" I asked. She thought for a bit. "I don't know how anybody could paint that," she said. "It's, like, a thousand different things, and it's probably very different for different people." She kept repainting and correcting one corner, trying to get it perfect. "The other night, we had 'family dinner' night. The counselor my family is seeing suggested this. We see the counselor because my parents say that they're going to have an *'amicable'* divorce, which, you know, is where the kids don't get hurt?" She shook her head. "Anyway, once a week, we all sit down to eat dinner together to, quote, remind us that we're still a family, unquote, even though we're not, even though my father lives in another place with his new girlfriend and her kids, even though everybody is sick to their stomachs all the time. It's *bizarre!* We sit and pretend that we're something we're not. They talk all this stupid stuff to me like, '*How was your day, dear?*' I feel like sayin', '*Oh, just hunky, Dad. And how are things at your office, Father? You know, that office where your new girlfriend works? My, you are SOOO hardworking—away from Mom for only 2 weeks and you've got a girlfriend already. Do you get to hook up with her in the back room where I used to nap when I was too sick to go to school?*"

She stepped back from her painting, annoyed and stymied by some defect that only she could see in the corner. But it was her pain, not her paint that frustrated her. Ty's head dropped. "The truth is I don't want to say anything to them. I . . . ." she sighed, "I had this weird experience, like I was going insane. I was sitting there at the table when they were talking all that stupid talk, and suddenly I felt like I was zooming away from them, like an out-of-body experience. I was there, but I wasn't. They were all just getting smaller and farther away, and their voices sounded like they were in a tunnel. I felt like I was going to throw up, but I didn't. It was like my whole body was nauseous. And . . . empty—*so horribly, horribly empty.*"

She began to cry just as she had laughed: loud, halting, and piecemeal. I wanted to hug her, but shrinks can't do that anymore. So we both just stood helpless, feeling that terrible, gaping hole that her shattered family had left inside of her. *They* needed to be there to hug her. But they were gone, each warping away into their own separate spaces, no longer anchored by a bond of love between the parents. With no one to hold her, she slowly sank to the floor, and I sat as close as I could.

Her crying slowly quieted and sounded more normal, like a storm that settles into a soft rain. Finally, she looked up with swollen eyes and said, "I'm sorry, I'm sorry." I feigned outrage. *"WILL YOU PLEASE STOP APOLOGIZING WHEN I'VE GOT NO IDEA WHAT YOU'RE APOLOGIZING FOR?!"* She laughed again. But this time, as with her crying, laughter became easier for her. "I guess I don't feel like my feelings are OK," she sniffled. "You think?" I joked. Ty nodded and laughed, rummaging for some unpainted rag to wipe her nose. "I guess I do need to see a counselor before I become a counselor," she said. "Can you see me?" she asked. "If it's OK with your folks, sure," I answered.

We sat and stared out the front door a while. She sighed a huge sigh and said, "God, I'm so tired."

In our counseling sessions in the weeks that followed, Ty spoke powerfully and painfully about the death of her family. But no matter how much I badgered, she refused to allow her parents to attend, or to be direct with them in their family counseling sessions. In one of our last meetings, Ty used dark words to paint an adolescent's picture of divorce that too many teens know all too well.

"They look like children to me now," she said of her parents, "like they became my older brother and sister. You know, nice, and family and all, but crazy—like they're just older teenagers who like to think that they're all grown up, but they're not. All my life they talked to me about honoring my commitments and being disciplined and stuff, and then they do this? I'm not allowed to quit dance class because I, quote, made a commitment, but they can quit their family? How do you make yourself vulnerable to people who can't run their own lives? No, it would be just too weird to tell them the truth. They couldn't handle it. They can't even really face what they're doing to themselves."

She sat and thought a bit, her eyes welling up. "We used to go to this funky vacation place in the mountains every summer since I can remember. My brother and I used to make fun of it until our folks would say, 'OK, let's go to a new place.' But we'd always tell them that we knew that *they* loved it there, so we'd go one more year, just for them. But the truth was that my brother and I loved that place, even though it was kind of dumb. We loved it 'cause it was *our family's place*, you know? We always had great times there, sometimes just all of us laughing at how silly the whole town was." Her head sank as she cut to the pain of her memory. "I always thought that they knew that my brother and I really *did* want to go there, that it was a tradition that meant a whole lot to us, that it was, like, a symbol of our family, you know? Kind of funky, and silly, but *something that never went away, something you could always depend on being there, no matter what—something you know you could always come back to no matter how scary your own life was*." She looked up at me with a trembling face. "Now I think that they never knew any of that. If they did, they would never think of breaking up our family, would they?"

Two months after she first walked into the center, and on the day that the staff and kids dedicated the mural, Ty told the group that she was moving far away the next day. "I didn't want people here being sad, you know, 'cause there's already a lot of sadness here that you all help make better. Anyway, my mom, she doesn't make enough for us to afford to stay in our house now, so we're moving to live with my grandparents. So that means, you know. . ." The kids all stared at the floor just as they had the first time they met Ty. But this time, they were too sad to speak. With tears in her eyes, Ty gently unwrapped a painting she had brought with her. "If you guys want this, I painted this picture for other kids who come here whose families are splitting up. Maybe it will help them think that they're not so alone, you know? That's what . . ." her voice began to shake, ". . . that's what you guys did for me. And . . . that, well, it helped a lot. I don't want you guys to ever forget that what you do is important."

Now everyone was crying. One of the sniffling kids took Ty's painting and held it up. It pictured a little girl with bushy red hair planting flowers in a sunny garden. On the horizon behind was a terrible, threatening storm with ferocious claws of lightning that was tearing up other gardens and hurling other crying kids up into the air, shredding their flowers. It was headed her way. And as if the girl heard the thunder while she was planting, she was quietly calling, ". . . Mommy? . . . Daddy?"

No one was there to answer. But in the other corner on the horizon was the crisis center. And kids were holding the door open, calling for her to come in, offering shelter from the storm.

The group of kids stood stunned as they drank in Ty's painting. There was no noise for perhaps a minute. Knowing that half of these kids were from broken homes, and some were from families in conflict, my eyes jumped from one to the next to see their reactions to this poignant work. They seemed filled with recognition and remembrance of a special pain, old for some, new for others, and feared by the rest. Then, without a word and as if on cue, most of them slowly shuffled together and put their arms around one another as if to soften the hurt, perhaps to dilute the grief a bit. Even the two "wise guys" stood in silent, head-bowed respect to the shared anguish of this generation.

After the group hug ended, Ty said her individual goodbyes. She gifted everyone with unique farewells she had apparently prepared in advance, telling each something special about themselves. She looked so different to me. Even in this sad moment, the shy and awkward girl that we had met two months before was gone. In her place was an open, friendly, and strangely confident young woman, hugging these other kids to help them not feel so bad for her misfortune. There was magic in these connections, a magic that had helped her grow past the failings of her parents, to see a life beyond the death of her family. To find warmth, and purpose, and compassion—not by getting these things, but by giving them.

In her periodic notes to me, she pretty much confirmed this. She once wrote that working at the center with the other kids helped her realize that the divorce was her parents' failure and not her own: "I didn't do anything wrong," she wrote. "It was them, not me. Why did I act like I was bad? I have nothing to be ashamed of—*Duh!*"

Ty found other ways of giving that she says helped her a lot. When she moved to her grandparents' town, she immediately marched herself into the high school counseling center and helped them form their first-ever support group for teens of divorce which, of course, she led. She said that it made her feel a lot better whenever she could provide a little understanding for other scared kids running from that terrible storm in her painting. As she put it, "I seem to feel most safe when I give shelter to others."

Isn't that something a hero might say?

I don't know if any adolescent ever really recovers from the death of his family. The bleeding stops, and the wounds close, but the scars remain forever, bleak memorials to the overwhelming fear and loss that only a child can know, and rarely can verbalize. These are scars often hidden deep inside of an indifferent teenage body that shrugs and mumbles, "Whatever," when told that the family is no more. But like that defect in the corner of Ty's mural that only she could see, these are cuts that remain invisible to everyone but the victim for a long time. Then, later in life, they can become painfully visible, even crippling, when these children grow up and attempt to form families of their own.

Ty showed us a great way to heal these hurts. By reaching out to others and sharing their pain, she found relief from her own. Though she lost a lot in the divorce, she found a lot in its wake. She discovered much about herself: her skills, her compassion, her values, and most of all, her strength.

Although we've lost touch, I like to believe that some- where today Ty is raising kids of her own, gifting them with those best parts of herself that she found during those worst days of her life. And I'll bet that if her kids ever get to see her painting of divorce, they'll have no idea what it's about.

3

ORPHANED WITH PARENTS

Taylor's Story

The relationship between a teenager and her parents is powerful and mysterious. Yet for most of us, whether parent or teen, being in that relationship blinds us to its mystical nature. Much like not seeing a forest for its trees, we are so often bogged down in the day-to-day struggles of chores and grades and curfews that we rarely get to appreciate the magic that can exist in the unspoken bonds of trust and love between an adolescent and her mother and father.

Except, of course, when those bonds are not there. Then, often dramatically, we see the gaping, jagged hole that's left in the absence of the calming, centering, and healing influences of a close parent-to-teen connection. Kids who usually do the terrible things are kids who usually have no bonds with their parents.

Yet not all "unbonded" kids do bad things. Many, perhaps most, somehow find ways to overcome what experts see as overwhelming challenges to raise themselves into fine adults. How or why this happens, we don't know. But it really does happen.

Taylor felt the pain of the missing bonds inside herself, but she had no idea where that aching was coming from until she saw it thirty-thousand feet high in the sky. It's said that you can't miss what you never had, but I don't believe that anymore, not after knowing Taylor.

∼

The chaos in the terminal was incredible. The sudden thunderstorms had shut down the airport, cancelled many flights, and apparently knocked out the cooling system in the closed building. Packed with angry, frustrated travelers, the temperature and humidity soared along with the tempers of the sweating people. As I stood in a long line of flyers desperate to find alternate connecting flights, I unconsciously shook my head sadly as one man started berating the poor, helpless clerk, yelling and calling her names. I was debating whether to get involved when a clear, young voice behind me piped up saying, "I guess that's why they call these places 'terminals.'" For a moment there was silence, and then suddenly everyone around the voice started to laugh. The joke and the laughter spread up and down the line until everyone was smiling and pointing and looking back at the voice behind me. Even the jerk had to stop to find out why everyone was laughing. Perhaps thinking that he was the butt of the joke, he begrudgingly calmed himself, and then apologized.

"Well done," I said, turning to find what I assumed was a grown woman behind me. "I wish *I* had . . ." I stopped mid-sentence, startled to find an unusually small girl of perhaps 16 or 17 years, supporting herself on a large, multi-footed, metal cane. I started again, ". . . I wish I was as smart and funny as you. That guy makes me glad that they search us for weapons *before* we're allowed to talk to the poor clerks." She smiled shyly, just before I made her mad. "Look," I offered, obviously referencing her cane, "I'm sure everyone would be happy to let you move to the front of the line if . . ." "Don't do that, OK?" she said quickly and quietly. "Um, OK," I said awkwardly. I wanted to say more, like I was sorry or that I didn't mean to upset her, but I was afraid of making her feel worse. So I just turned back in line.

The walk to the new plane terminal seemed miles. After completing my hike, I hunkered down in the last seat at the gate. After about an hour, I saw my prior line buddy struggle into the same gate, puffing and sweating as she fought to handle her bags, her cane, and her dignity. She had apparently refused to ride in one of those handicapped-person golf carts, a thing that has tempted me more than once to fake a disease. She saw me, and instantly looked away. I had had enough. I got up and walked to her, even though she looked like she would run away if she could.

"Look, miss, I'm sorry I made you mad back there, and I understand about the disability thing—well, no, I *don't* understand about the disability thing, but that's not the point—anyway, they just announced that this flight will be delayed *four hours*, and I'm *NOT* going to sit here for four hours while you stand there and make me look like a jerk for not giving you my seat. So, if you have any decency, and I think that you do, you'll be a big person and help me out by taking my seat." I crossed my arms for a mock threatening effect. "*O-K?*" I added through gritted teeth, like a stern father might. "OK!" she laughed, "OK! Don't blow a gasket already."

As she settled in, she seemed happy that I sat on the floor next to her, like she was lonely and wanted to chat but didn't know what the rules were for adult speak. So I decided to help her out. "Please don't *you* blow a gasket with *me*," I asked, "but what's with the cane?" "Car accident," she said flatly. "Four years ago. Some damage to my spine. No biggie." "Maybe not to you," I said admiringly, wondering how her parents felt about that. That's when I first noticed the huge hole next to her.

"So where are your . . ." I dropped the word "parents," deciding to avoid possibly upsetting her again. ". . . um, destinations?" "Amsterdam," she said, "that is, if I ever make it first to Philadelphia for the flight. I'm going to a European study program for the fall semester." "Wow," I gushed, "that's great! At your age, getting to study in Europe? Fantastic!" "No biggie," she repeated. "Actually, I just came back from being in Europe for the summer. My school runs these programs there. My parents send me a lot." There was no bragging here—she was just reporting the news. But the hole next to her was getting larger.

When she reluctantly told me the name of her school, I knew that her world was privileged, at least if she wanted it to be. It was an elite boarding school for daughters of celebrities, senators, and the super-rich; a place that I happened to know about where more than one kid arrives for the first day of school by private jet. That picture of incredible indulgence always seemed sad to me in comparison with another that I hold close in my heart: one of my wife and I tearfully putting our own kids on a common yellow bus for their first day of school. Now, here next to me was the kid in that first picture. I wondered what her moneyed life was like. I worried for the sadness that seemed all about her. Somehow, she couldn't help but go to where I was thinking.

"My parents, they're hiking in the Antarctic now," she blurted. Mimicking my dumb style of humor she added, "That's the pole with the penguins." Her eyes were bright with her joke, but then they dimmed a bit when she heard me manipulate a little to learn about her family. "You don't like penguins?" I asked. "No," she said flatly, "I like penguins just fine. I would have loved to go, but . . . canes aren't allowed on trips like that, so, you know . . ."

A long silence settled into our corner of the airport. The scene of her parents going off on some dream trip without her hung heavily over us. She looked like she was sorry that she ever accepted my seat. I wanted to help her feel better, and I didn't even know her name.

"By the way," I said, "my name's Mike. I think penguins are cool." She smiled again, and pretended she was trapped in one of those forced introduction games. "*Heeelllooo,* my name is *Taylor. Very nice to meet you. I* will *NEVER* name any child of mine *Taylor. I think penguins are cool, too.*" She seemed only comfortable when clowning around or while talking of things outside of her personal world. So that's where we stayed while we awaited our plane. But as she spoke, I watched her eyes wander around the jammed room, resting only upon the clusters of families, watching the exhausted, exasperated parents patiently comforting their tired, cranky kids.

One large, sweaty, rumpled, baggy-eyed dad in particular held her gaze. He held a small girl who was apparently sick with a bad cold. He walked endlessly back and forth, holding his daughter gently in his big arms, with her head resting on his shoulder, softly rocking her and singing something inaudible to us, but comforting to his girl. In the middle of this airport madness, amidst the frantic bustle and ceaseless, pounding din, this father had magically created a special place—a peaceful, mystical garden where the ears of a sick little girl could hear only the soft lullaby of a loving parent as she drifted off to sleep, safe and secure from the insane world around her.

We both ended up staring silently at that beautiful picture, with me longing very much to hold my own family, and she . . . *"What?" I wondered, "What was she feeling?"* All she said was, "Do you have kids?" "Yes," I answered with a nodding sigh, suggesting how much I missed them. She never asked anything more about them.

The besieged airline counter clerk got on the loudspeaker and asked if anyone was willing to have their seats changed to allow families with small children to travel together, since their seats were scattered all over the plane due to the emergency bookings. As I got up to volunteer, I knew Taylor would be right there behind me.

"These must be penguin class seats," she joked as she ended up jammed next to me in the tiny seats at the very rear of the plane. "And I thought you were too intelligent to volunteer," I responded. I wanted to ask this wealthy girl why she was not comfortably curtained off up in first class, but my guess was that she would not tolerate being privileged like that, and wouldn't even like my asking the question.

Finally airborne, the plane settled into the soothing dusk of twilight aloft, the crying babies mostly drifting off to sleep, strangely calmed by the rhythmic throb of the engines. The dad we had both watched and admired was one row up, leaning back, resting his exhausted eyes, with his little girl sound asleep upon his chest. We listened in as the flight attendant tapped his shoulder and patiently explained that the girl needed to be belted into her own seat for her own safety. Dad tried to quietly argue a bit, but she was politely firm. He gently laid his girl down next to him, contorting himself to make her a soft pillow of his large, hairy, tattooed arm. Like other teenagers, Taylor groused, "That's ridiculous. They should just leave them alone." Then, unlike other teenagers, very softly she added, "He's a good father, isn't he?"

I decided to go way out on a limb. "Yeah, I'd guess so," I said, "but, you know, speaking as a dad, I think that there's nothing better in this world than holding your sleeping child, particularly when they're sick—or scared. I think most moms might say the same thing." Taylor said nothing, just breathing in the picture of that silly man and his runny-nosed daughter, bound together by unseen safety belts which were a thousand times stronger than the visible ones that had moved them apart. Then for a long time she looked out of the window at the soft pink and purple sky, as one star began to twinkle in the blue above.

She startled me with her words. She seemed to be talking to the horizon. "You know, I just realized that I can't ever remember my father *or* my mother ever holding me like that. Ever." I wasn't sure that she wanted me to have heard her, so I said nothing. This had to be a very hard thing for her to talk about. She turned to see if I had heard, and seeing that I had, she looked back to the sky and continued, "I'm, like, this orphan with parents. I thought that my nanny was my mother for a long time. I think I was, like, 6 when I found out who my mom was. That was when my nanny left. I was, like, mad at my mom, like, 'who is this lady telling me what to do?' And my father, well, his favorite joke is that he's never changed a diaper in his life, and never will, to include my mom's if she gets, you know, old. He's got two kids, you know, me and my brother, and he's, like, *proud* that he never had to change a diaper. He loves to tell everybody. My mom, she thinks that's a good joke, too." She shook her head, puffed her cheeks, and exhaled hard. "What's up with *that?*" she asked the moon, which had just popped onto the horizon.

The pink and purple sky slowly ebbed into a soft, comforting darkness to create a surreal dream world, one where Taylor could say things that she might never have said while stuck to the hard ground. "I think a lot about that stuff," she said. "I think about how I will do things differently for my own kids. I'll change their diapers, and they'll always know that *I'm* their mom. And I'm only marrying someone who *wants* to change their diapers, too—well, nobody *wants* to change diapers, but, you know what I mean." She didn't need to look at me to know that I knew exactly what she meant.

"All my life," she said, "I always felt like I was never home. I was always looking to go home, you know, but I never got there. School is not home, although that's where I live most of the time. And my parents have these houses all over the place, but they feel like hotels, not *home*. My grandmother's house, that feels like home sometimes, but I'm only there, like, one week every year." Taylor laughed a sad laugh: "My grandmom, she likes to say that her whole house could almost fit into my parents' bedroom. My kids, they're going to have a *home*, you know? It might be small and silly like Mom-Mom's, but that's where they're going to live until *they're* ready to leave. They're going to know that it will always be there for them, no matter what. And they're not ever going away to school unless they're older and they want to. And I'll always be there, no matter what."

She watched the night gently soothe the dusk to sleep outside of our plane, and she let me share her last thought, one that made me want to sit perfectly still to not screw up. "You know, it's not about the *house*. That could be big or small, or it could stay the same or it could change a lot. It's about the *home*. The home is the people inside of the house, loving each other, staying together, and being there for each other—forever. Even when they're not together, you know? You know?" I wondered who exactly she was asking outside of our window.

We looked across the aisle as the sick little girl started to whimper a bit, but still asleep. Dad reached over, unhooked her seat belt, and held her closely in his huge arms, breaking the rules once again, and not giving a damn. "I would not want to be the person who tells him that he can't hold his sick girl while she's having a bad dream," I said, half-jokingly. Taylor smiled, and then turned quickly back to her window. In its cloudy reflection, I saw tears in Taylor's eyes.

We sat saying little for the rest of that long trip. When she fell asleep, I pulled out my notebook and started to scrawl out what I had just experienced. I wrote about how this entitled, privileged girl made me remember another kid I had known years before who couldn't appear to be more different if he had tried. Yet Taylor was very much like a boy I had seen in a prison, a child who never really had any parents at all, but who, like Taylor, was somehow able to look back upon his shattered life and swear a blood oath that he would not have children unless his children would have parents—*real* parents; people who roll up their sleeves and dirty their hands working the soil of their children's lives; people who lovingly fight with them about drugs, and patiently hound them about school-work; people who effortlessly and endlessly hold their children when they're sick or scared, toddling or "teening," on the ground in daylight or thirty-thousand feet high in a dark night sky. The rich traveler and the poor prisoner both know the teenage pain of real parental love never felt, of real loving bonds never forged. And they both vowed to become adults better than what they had seen, to raise children knowing a security that they had never known.

I closed my notebook and made a silent plea to whomever it is that might listen in the darkness outside of windows at thirty-thousand feet: Please, *please* let these children have their dream. For I have been blessed to learn that in caretaking others, we heal ourselves. Please allow these kids to know the mending miracle of one day holding their own children, once scared or sick, now sleeping and sighing contentedly, safely cradled in their parents' loving arms, and safely bound to their parents' loving hearts.

When experts are asked to pick the single most important aspect of raising adolescents, we get weird and vague. We stumble around trying to find a way to describe the inde-scribable, to convey the mystical, to paint a picture of that which we see every day in our work, either in its affirming presence, or in its frightening absence. We use words like bonds, and connections, and closeness. But much like writers trying to describe breathtaking works of art, we get frustrated with our cruel inability to neatly package that emotion, that experience, and make it real for a listening audience.

Much to my surprise, Taylor stayed electronically in touch for a few years. Her notes sounded better and better to me, although it's so hard to see these things in letters. She told me that she saw a therapist for a while, and that it helped, even though that was an incredible compromise of her needs for independence and control. Her exact words were, "Once I stopped rolling my eyes at her [the therapist], she turned out to be pretty smart." I could hear Taylor's clowning voice saying those words, and they made me laugh.

She had brought her parents into a few sessions, and she said that even the therapist was appalled by their self-absorption, their inability to get outside of their own needs. But Taylor said that still helped a lot, letting her know that she was not nuts.

I never referenced her words in that plane years before. I wanted to, very much, but that's not how Taylor works. She never brought them up either, not directly. But one time, when she was about 20, she wrote a bit about guys that she had dated, about how she was patiently searching for "one who would change diapers someday . . . at 20, they're hard to find. Do you think that they ever grow up?" she asked.

Now, whenever I fly in those soft, twilight nights, I look for exhausted parents holding sleeping children, and I think of Taylor. And I think of the sleeping child that she will one day hold, thirty-thousand feet high in some other twilight sky—a child sighing, safe and secure in her mother's arms, closely bound to her mother's heroic heart, having no idea that things could be any other way.

4

WHEN HEROES FALL

Vincent's Story

Whenever it's said that respect is critical for successfully raising adolescents, all heads nod in vigorous agreement. But that's about where the consensus ends, for respect has many definitions. For some, respect means polite speech and manners. Others see it as a valuing of the innate worth of human beings. For many, respect is to be forcefully demanded by parents from their children. Yet others see it as a value first given, patiently and unconditionally, then quietly hoped for in return.

In working with adolescents, I've come to see their views of respect as encompassing parts of all of those definitions. To teenagers, respect is conveyed in words and manners, but it must be motivated by something much deeper. Most teens believe that it does imply a valuing of others, but also a valuing of self. They do believe that respect should be encouraged in children by their parents, but never demanded. Kids seem to intuitively know that respect—like love—can only be freely given, never forced.

The key to a teen's respect for her parents has to do with an upward-looking admiration, a recognition that the adults possess skills, values, and character that the teen does not, things that the teen admires and wishes to learn. When we ask kids to identify adults they do not respect, they point to people who rage, hit, cheat, and lie. When we ask teens which adults they do respect, almost invariably they identify folks who are moral, truthful, calm, and tolerant—especially in the face of provocations from others, especially provocations from the teens themselves.

Emotional control, humility, and living (versus preaching) a positive set of personal values builds parental connections with teens, golden bridges that carry wisdom from a parent to a child. Anger, criticism, and sarcasm corrode these conduits. Hypocrisy destroys them like a bomb.

Ironically, children are most dependent upon these parental bridges in their teen years, when the most advanced parts of their neurological and moral development occur. Adolescence is when future adults are truly being shaped, when children begin to assemble a set of values, moral-ethical codes to carry them through adulthood. This is not the time to blow up bridges.

Vincent had his bridge explode when he was halfway across, just when he was most dependent upon its massive strength, something he assumed would last forever. His recovery from that free-fall made him one of my heroes.

He was the boy whom Hollywood might cast as the 14-year-old son that everybody wants—well-spoken, hard-working, and so open and honest that you want to immediately rush in and help him not berate himself so much for making a mistake. With clear green eyes that distained any excuses, Vincent spoke softly of his failure with such shame and regret that he looked as if he had killed someone. "I can't explain this," he said while maintaining full eye contact, "it happened out of nowhere. I was at this party for my cousin. He just finished college. All the cousins were there, and the older ones were all drinking, along with two who were underage. They started saying that the younger ones—like me—that we were wimps because we weren't drinking. They kept trying to give us beer, and most of the night I refused, but then . . . I don't know, I guess I got kind of worn down by them. I go to this preppy school and everyone teases me because I never get in trouble or do anything bad. I think I'm real tired of that. Anyway, they took the keys to my uncle's van and kind of made us go with them to drink there . . . no, that's not really true," he corrected, "I went willingly. I was trying to act cool, I guess. They told T.J. to drive. He's only 15. He doesn't have a license or anything, and he had had a few beers, so he was driving crazy. The cops pulled us over on the expressway."

His bright green eyes filled with anger and disappointment with himself. "It's amazing that we didn't kill anybody. My dad, he was, like . . ." Vincent's voice disappeared into his shame as his father's image started to slowly fill the room. It was a huge image. "He, like, couldn't believe that I would do something like that. In the police station he didn't yell or punish me or nothing, even though the cops wanted him to, I think. He just stood there looking sad and disappointed, but he was still worried about me. He asked me if *I* was OK. I wish that he would've yelled and hit me or something—that would have been easier to take. Seeing how I let him down like that, it, just . . ." Vince's eyes kept talking although his voice could not. They spoke of the terrible anguish of a good kid who lets a loved parent down, who betrays the trust of someone much admired and respected, someone whose opinion means everything.

"Tell me about Dad," I asked softly. This quiet question was enough to finally bow Vincent's head. He slowly tore a candy wrapper into a thousand pieces as he spoke. "My dad, wow," he murmured, half to himself, "how do I tell you about my dad?" We listened to the paper tear for a while until he spoke. "My father is this amazing man. He had nothing when he was a kid—you know, had to pay his own way through college and everything. They were poor, like, live-in-the-projects-poor where there were gangs, and drug dealers, and all like that, and he managed to avoid all of that stuff. *He* never talks about those days. He's not, like, all about himself. I get the stories from his brothers and his friends. My dad was always the kid who'd rescue somebody, or stand up to the gangsters in the hallways or whatever. He took care of his family *even back then* when he was just a kid himself," here Vince looked back up at me, "like my age. He always worked jobs and gave the money to his father to help out. Then he goes on to build this big business and make a ton of money—not for him, you know, but for us, his family. He works crazy hard. He's always traveling and he never has any time to himself. And when he's not working, he's at our games and coaching or bugging us about our homework or whatever. I have four brothers, so that's a lot of time—a *lot* of time. I don't think he gets much sleep, but I can't remember ever hearing him complain or get nasty."

Vincent turned his gaze back to the floor, paused, and then leaned down to hurriedly pick up a tiny piece of candy wrapper that was there when he walked in. "I'm sorry," he apologized, "I'm making a mess." "Vince, it's OK," I laughed, "that wasn't even your trash." After a pause I added, "Do you think that maybe you're a little hard on yourself?" He stared back as if that was a strange thing to ask. "When I look at my dad, then, no, I'm not hard on myself. I want to be like him. He's my hero."

He was the man whom Hollywood might cast as the father that everybody wants. Clearly exhausted from his schedule, Vince's dad sat on the edge of his seat, shutting off his business cell phone for its non-stop ringing. He was filled only with worry, fear, and love for his son as I told him what I thought was going on with Vincent, which mostly was that he was a great kid who would likely be just fine. "In summary," I added, "my only concern for your son is that he's *too* good, at least in terms of his expectations and judgments of himself. He sees you pretty much as a god, as a heroic, perfect man who never makes any mistakes. That's a tough standard for Vince to match. It might help him ease up on himself a bit if you could share some of your own failures or shortcomings with him— that is," I joked, "assuming you've got some." Dad didn't laugh, and his eyes seemed to mist a bit, but he waved off my question as to why. "From the stress with the problem with his son," I told myself. But, still, something here bothered me.

Two years later, Vince's mom called, barely holding herself together. "Vincent asked to see you again," she said with a quivering voice. "Can you see him today? It's kind of urgent!" "What's going on?" I asked. "He said he'd rather tell you himself," she answered.

Vince walked in slowly and rigidly, as if he feared he might throw up. He sat down, red-eyed, ashen-faced, and shaking. Even after a two-year hiatus, we exchanged no pleasantries. He drew a deep breath and began in a disjointed fashion that slowly and sadly began to make sense. "I'm . . . older than when you last saw me. My voice sounds a lot like my father's now. People mix us up on the phone all the time. He has a special cell phone that he uses for work that no one else is supposed to touch—ever, he says, because it's so important for his business and only important people call that line. We were at the game on Sunday and he had to go to the bathroom. He left his phone in his jacket. It rang, and I answered because I was worried it might be real important."

He sat as if he were in some pain that no pill could relieve—shifting constantly, adjusting his position, his eyes flitting fearfully around the room. "When I said hello, I heard this woman's voice saying . . . saying . . ." His mouth could not release the actual words. ". . . saying, you know, sex stuff, about what she's wearing and stuff . . . It wasn't my mother." His head drooped down. "I said, 'Who is this?' and she laughed and said 'Well, it's not your wife, Frederick.' Then I asked again, '*Who* is this?' and she said, '*Oh my god!*' and hung up the phone.

"Then I saw that there had been a bunch of missed calls. I flipped through the list, and almost all of them were from the lady that just called. Then I flipped through the sent calls list, and there was her number, like, forever, like, for as far back as the list went. Then I checked his speed dial, and there was her number again." Vince looked up at me to see if I understood what he was saying, hoping that I would not make him put words to the awful truth he had discovered. I sighed and nodded.

"When he came back to our seats, I handed him the phone with her number on it and said, 'Who is she?' He looked like he was having a heart attack. He started making up some stupid story about how she was someone one of his partners knew, and how he was helping him out by talking to her and, well . . . just a stupid story. That's when I knew. If she were nobody to him, he'd have just yelled at me for touching his phone. But he didn't." Vince's brave, honest face collapsed into his hands. "So that's when I knew that he was lying. I even tested him by asking how many times he had talked to her. He said two. His phone said, like, two hundred." This big, strong, athletic 16-year-old began to cry like a small boy who wakes in the dark of the night, not knowing if his nightmare is only a dream. "That's the worst, you know? It's bad enough that he's screwing around on my mom, you know? But . . ." His crying grew into hard, shaking sobs. *"He kept changing his story around and . . . and each lie he told made it worse and worse and worse, like he was getting smaller and smaller and smaller . . . I've never, ever seen him look like that. So small, so small . . ."*

Vince took a few minutes to quiet himself. It looked like something deep inside of him was tearing and bleeding. "We left the game, and in the car he said, 'You're not going to say anything to Mom, are you? This will just cause her needless pain.' At first I said no, that I wouldn't tell her. Then I said, 'No, I'm not going to tell her—YOU ARE! AND YOU'RE GOING TO TELL HER TONIGHT!' I don't know where that came from." He paused and thought, and then wept again. "I do know where that came from. It came from what he always taught me: to be straight-up, to admit when you screw-up, take the consequences and move on. He always says that if you're doing something that you don't want your family to know about, then you need to ask yourself why." Vince laughed a soft, sad laugh. "Now what is all that? Just a bunch of bullshit lies, too?" His eyes squinted as if he was peering into a poisonous, frightening fog, and he asked me questions I could not answer: *"Who is he? Who is he?"*

Vincent shook his head, and then displayed the very courage and values that his fallen father had hoped to instill in this young man, things that Dad had lost somewhere. "Anyway, I'm not here for me. I need to know what to do about my family—my brothers and my mom. I'm the oldest and I've got to take care of them . . ." He asked a hundred family-centered questions about whether or how to tell his siblings, if divorce would be best for the family, and so on. After a bit I said, "Vincent, perhaps you are trying to do too much here? Maybe it's not your job to . . ." He cut me off. "Well, who else is there? My mom's a wreck. My 12-year-old brother has Down's syndrome. His heart is not in good shape. Who else is going to take care of the family now—my *father*?"

"I don't know," I answered. "Maybe we should ask him?"

For a moment on the following day, the perfect son and the perfect father sat together on the couch in my office. After the father sat next to the son, the son got up and moved to the chair furthest away. "We're finished," Vincent opened. "I want absolutely nothing to do with you. Maybe Mom says that she still loves you and wants to try to work it out, but I don't. You must have conned her into saying that. You get everybody to say what you want, don't you? You ALWAYS win, don't you? You're so good at the game, aren't you? *AREN'T YOU!?ANSWER ME, GODDAMMIT, AREN'T YOU?*"

Vince was right. Dad did look suddenly small. "Vincent, I—I don't know what to say . . ." Vince cut his father off. "WELL, THERE'S A FREAKIN' FIRST!" he yelled. "You ALWAYS know what to say. *ALL MY LIFE* you knew what to say. *Remember the last time we were here, in this office?* Do you know how big you looked to me then? I had messed up bad and you were calm and forgiving and understanding. You made me feel, like, in *awe* of you. Frankie [his cousin] got beat up by his dad for doing the same thing that I did, and he's gone crazy since then. What you did just made me work harder to do the right thing, and be a better person and . . ." Hearing his own words made Vince begin to scream. *"HOW THE HELL COULD YOU TAKE ALL THAT AWAY FROM ME? FOR SOME STUPID BITCH, TO HAVE SOME SEX? YOU WERE EVERYTHING TO ME, ALL I EVER WANTED TO BE. WHENEVER I WAS TIRED OR HURT OR SCARED IN A TOUGH GAME, TO GET ME THROUGH I'D ALWAYS THINK OF YOU, ABOUT HOW STRONG AND BRAVE YOU ARE—*I mean **WERE, GODDAMMIT . . . WERE!** *NOW WHO DO I USE TO GET ME THROUGH?"* As Vincent cried hard, his dad got up to go to him. The son leapt to his feet. ***"STAY THE HELL AWAY FROM ME!"*** he yelled.

They stood frozen there, separated by twelve inches that felt like twelve miles. Then the rage seemed to suddenly drain out of Vincent. He took a breath. "Dad," he said, almost softly, "I'm alone now. I'm on my own. It's over. What we had, what you taught me—it's all gone. I don't think we can ever get that back. I've got to do this on my own now."

Dad's strong head and muscled shoulders sagged heavily. His tears dropped hard to the floor. Slowly he turned and walked to the office door and put his hand on the knob. Then he turned back to try and face his boy, but could only face the floor. "I do remember the last time we were here. I remember the doctor talking about rebuilding trust, about getting past the flaws in people we love. He talked about understanding and forgiveness." Dad finally forced his eyes up to meet his son's. "Vincent, I need your forgiveness now. I don't deserve it, but I need it. The family needs it. I have no right to ask that of you, but I will anyway to try and save our family. You can take this as bullshit if you want, but the truth is that if I had to die now to erase this awful thing I've done, I'd chose to die—*happily*. Because now I can see this horror that I've caused, and it sickens me.

"I know we can't have what we had—I know that. But *what I told you* was not a bunch of crap—*I* was the bunch of crap. Those values, those ideals *are* worth struggling for, *worth dying for. I just wasn't up to the task of living them.* Please, whatever you decide about me, whatever you do, *don't* give up on those things. Yes, I am . . . flawed . . ." Dad paused and shook his head, ". . . terribly flawed. But please don't confuse my failure with the worth of the things that I've tried to teach you. Don't let my weakness cause you even more damage than it has." After a moment, he added, "If you ever want to talk more, let me know when and where and I'll be there. If not, I understand."

With that, Dad turned and left. Vincent stood staring at the door for a full minute, and then walked to the couch and sat where his father sat. He looked around the room, as if trying to see things from his father's perspective for a moment, and then leaned forward and held his head in his hands. "Now I'm totally confused," he sighed. He looked up at me, exhausted, but also clearer. "What my father said—did that make any sense to you?" he asked. But he knew that was really a question for himself. "That bastard," he said almost admiringly, shaking his head, "that bastard. In the middle of all this craziness, when I hate him the most, he says something really smart. God," he sighed, "just when things seem really clear, they get all messed up again." When he didn't speak for a while, I decided to.

"Maybe," I offered, "when things seem really clear is just when they're not? Maybe people can be very complex and contradictory, and so our relationships can be twice as complex and contradictory? Maybe reality is not black and white like we want it to be? Maybe good people aren't all good, and maybe bad people aren't all . . ." "Bad," Vince chimed in. Then he nodded, sat back, closed his eyes, and rested his head like this one very tough game was over. But he knew that his season had just begun.

In the following months, Vincent and his dad worked very hard, and rebuilt a relationship. Not the one that existed before, but a new and perhaps better one. The perfect son and the perfect dad disappeared, never to return. At first, I missed them a lot, since they were my fantasy of how perfect things might be for me one day, within my own life. Now in their place stood a normal son and a normal father, imperfect beings trying to do the right thing. Screwing up at times, sometimes terribly, but fighting their way through the pain to forgive and respect each other, and to love each other, as well.

I grew to like the new guys more.

The respect of an adolescent for an adult is a magnificent and fragile work of glass art. Hard to create, it's the product of ten thousand acts of caring, patience, and trust. Easy to smash, its beauty can be lost in one stupid, careless deed. Agonizingly difficult to rebuild, it never looks quite the same after the repair. But respect is so absolutely critical to raising children, that all adults must acknowledge our duty to build it and then to maintain it, no matter how great the effort, particularly when the glass lays shattered on the ground, crushed by our failures.

The irony is that we don't need to be perfect to hold kids' respect; we just need to be honest and humble, so that when we mess up, our failures can become strengthening lessons for the teens that look up to us. Imperfect adolescents can't really relate to gods who never screw up, but they can learn a great deal from human beings who, like them, make mistakes and who, unlike them, publicly admit their failings, apologize, and then strive to do better.

This is how we truly earn their respect. For kids know that being perfect is easier than being honest about imperfection.

5

WHEN WE LOSE, WE SOMETIMES FIND

Susan's Story

Death is the great irony of adolescence. Teens by their nature are so full of life, of everything yet to be. But these days, they are far too often visited by that dark angel of things that will never be. She frequently appears in the drunk driving death of a friend, or in the suicide of a classmate. But those are the adolescent death experiences that get all of the attention, and all of the sympathy. The teenage tragedy more common is the quiet, "Gee, that's a shame" loss of a parent. These seem to slip under our radar screens. Many of us look past the terrible sadness of a bereaved teen by saying things like, "Well, at least she's 15. It's not like a 5-year-old losing her mom." Having worked with too many of these wounded adolescents, I'm not so sure of that.

Most teenagers are blessed and cursed with insight and sensitivity that outrace their ability to communicate. Much like paralyzed adults, they are often tormented by a silent depth of emotion never even hinted at in a passive, seemingly uncaring, teenage face. Yet, in situations like losing a parent, a teen's emotional pain is at least as overwhelming as that of any child. And their fear is greater than any adult's.

Susan was the exception, a 15-year-old who could put powerful words to her experiences, sharing those very same feelings hopelessly trapped inside of thousands of teens who lose a parent every year. She became one of my heroes for, first, simply surviving her loss, but also for allowing her sometimes embarrassing, often bitter, and finally inspiring words to be shared here. Today, as a young woman and parent, she wanted her story to be told in the hope that her old voice might help other grieving kids feel not so totally alone, and perhaps help the rest of us to never discount their pain, no matter how arrogant they act.

"I'm, like, OK with all this, you know? I mean, just how much time can you spend thinking about this sh . . ., uh, stuff, you know, this cancer stuff. If she dies, she dies. There's nothing I can do about it. I'll survive—whatever. I'll be sad and all, but life goes on." Susan's 15-year-old panicked eyes betrayed her calm words about her mother's cancer.

I sat quiet for the moment, giving her a space to hear her thoughts. She looked so hard, and so brittle. Her face was sharp and drawn, with too much eye makeup. It looked like war paint. She was very slight. Too thin, really, with arms that shivered no matter how warm the room. At another time, on an easier road, her face would have been beautiful. But today it had a coldness that she could not shake off.

"I'm really pissed off that my aunt and mother are forcing me to come here, and I'm not coming back. No one understands. She's been sick and dying for like, forever, and I learned a long time ago that you just have to not think about it. Maybe that sounds cold to you, but too freakin' bad. I really don't care." She turned to face out the window away from me, and crossed her arms with a too-loud sigh.

As she silently stewed, I pictured the scrapbook of her life in my head. Age 5: Mom is diagnosed with breast cancer, hammered with radical mastectomy and life-sapping chemotherapy. Age 9: Mom's cancer recurs viciously. She undergoes more chemo, more surgery. Age 10: Dad runs off with someone half his age who has all of her parts. Age 12: Mom is told that there is little more that conventional treatment can do. She is also told to go die. She refuses. Mom finds a radical oncologist (cancer doctor) who puts her on extreme and experimental dosages of terrible drugs that keep the cancer at bay for five years while sucking the very life out of Mom.

From Susan's angry, silent face, the outline of her mother's warm, loving face slowly emerged, taking me back to a week earlier when Mom had bravely narrated these horrific events. "The truth is, Dr. Bradley, that I was glad when my husband left. The disgust in his eyes whenever he saw my mastectomy scars was too much for me to see. He's a health and fitness freak, you know, that perfect body guy? I think my cancer was the kind of thing he was always running away from in those marathons—like his own death, or illness, or maybe just aging. Our marriage was cooked the minute I got sick. I always knew in my heart that he was a little boy—a *gorgeous* little boy," she laughed, "but still a boy. It takes a man to go through this with a wife. He just wasn't up to that."

Mom's wisdom and strength was stunning, as was her control, to a point. Then her eyes suddenly filled with tears, and her breathing became labored as she continued. "I'm not willing to die yet. I just refuse, but I don't know how long this will work. I have to stay alive for a while longer. When you meet Susan, you'll know why. I know that Jessica, my 12-year-old, somehow will be OK. Jess is, well, I guess the word is resilient. I can picture a life for her after I'm gone, and I know she'll find her happiness again. But Susan is, well, you'll see what I mean when you meet her." Here Mom began crying. *"I can't leave her yet. She won't be OK."*

Mom's strength was suddenly gone. Her tears had used up her daily ration of energy, and her terrible disease was suddenly very visible. "Through years of counseling, prayer, and meditation, I've dealt with my own passing, and, God knows, I'm ready to go, for myself. This [the constant sickness from chemotherapy] is not being alive. I'm nauseous 24/7, I have no energy, and I can feel that *bitch*, my cancer, just waiting around every corner to get me. She [the cancer] has taken everything I ever loved away from me. I used to love to cook, you know, these great dinners. And now, even if I have the strength to lift pots, the smell of food makes me vomit." She paused and inhaled deeply to gather just enough life for another sentence. "So I'm about done. But Susan is not ready. She refuses to talk about this with me, my sister, or either of the therapists we've been to. Every day you can see her slipping further into this anger, this—*darkness* that will stay with her forever. It's taking her soul."

Mom paused again, but now she wrestled with what she saw as betraying her daughter. "She's becoming someone she's not." Mom's eyes filled with shame as she dropped them from mine, and she tore at her tissue. Her voice became very small. "Yesterday, when I got home from chemo, I sort of collapsed on the kitchen floor, and I conked out after throwing up a bit. I woke up to find Susan stepping over me to get something from the fridge. She . . . she . . . just got her soda, stepped back over me, and went to watch TV. She never said a word." Mom immediately looked up to plead for Susan. "That is NOT her. Susan is a sweet, loving, compassionate girl with a heart of gold. You'd have to know her to know how much pain she must be in to act so cold . . ."

Mom's face from the week before slowly faded back into Susan's as I suddenly realized that Susan was looking at me with an incredible sneer. "What are YOU staring at?" she snapped. "You," I answered flatly, "I was just picturing you stepping over your mom on the kitchen floor to get a soda." I waited for an explosion, but she was way past that. In a voice dripping with sarcasm she snickered, "My last shrink said that there is no one way to grieve a loss, so this is my way, OK? Just LEAVE IT ALONE." "I can't," I answered, "because while there is no one good way to grieve, there are lots of bad ways, and this is one of them. You're gonna' get whacked hard, Susan, harder than it has to be, if you don't trust someone . . ." Rising up from her seat, she cut me off. Her sappy, sarcastic voice was back. "I'm *so* sorry, but our time for this session is up. Perhaps we can continue this discussion at another time." As she sauntered out of my office, I awkwardly blurted something out: "Actually, I'm the sorry one, Susan. I'm sorry that you hurt so much and that I . . ." She spun on her heels. "DON'T YOU DARE FEEL SORRY FOR ME," she yelled, "YOU HAVE NO FREAKIN' RIGHT TO . . ." She stopped mid-sentence when she felt the tears in her eyes, turned furiously, and went out the door. *"You bastard,"* she muttered. *"You bastard."*

I had no idea why, but Susan showed up for our next appointment, offering no thoughts or questions about our last meeting, as if it never happened. For several sessions after that, we mostly just chatted back and forth, with her refusing to talk about her mom. But the softer Susan that Mom used to know began to emerge. She did care deeply about all sorts of things: her sister, her friends, even kids she tutored in a community service program at school.

Then one day she walked in as she never had before, looking exhausted, like she was very small and very lost in some big, scary place. Her swagger had disappeared along with her "war paint" makeup. She curled up in a small ball in the corner of the couch. Finally, she began to talk in a voice that I had not heard before. "Last night, I was up late. My grandpop [her mother's father] moved in last week, and I hate him. He's a PITA [pain-in-the-ass]. He's on me, like, non-stop about my attitude with my mom. Last night he yelled at me and told me to go to bed, so, of course, I wouldn't." Her words were the same, but today they held no arrogance. "He, like, moved in since Mom's, you know, whatever, has spread to her lungs and she can't walk the stairs now. Anyway, I was up at 3 A.M. and I heard them talking downstairs. I was sure they were trashing me, so I snuck down to listen in." She paused, and then buried her face in the pillow, as if about to speak words that she did not want anyone to hear. Especially herself.

"Mom was talking about how . . ." Susan's back started heaving with sobs that had no sounds. After a moment, she continued. ". . . about how scared she was to die. Not scared for her, but for *me*." I could barely hear what she was mumbling into that pillow, but I dared not move. "She was crying with her dad, saying how unfair this was, how God must have abandoned her since God shouldn't let her die when I'm so—so messed up. Then Mom said . . ." Here the heaving returned, but Susan pushed on. ". . . Mom said she could die in peace if she knew that I'd be OK." She lifted her face from the pillow, revealing a face twisted in pain. *"She's been going through all this pain and crazy treatment stuff just to stay alive a little bit longer—not for her, or for my sister, but FOR ME! THE ONE WHO'S BEEN HORRIBLE TO HER!"*

Finally, Susan's tears came to her. *"But I CAN'T be nice to her. She's DYING on me—she's leaving me. She's leaving me all alone."* Susan looked up at me and yelled: *"I DON'T EVEN KNOW HOW TO COOK CHICKEN."* Like a swelling cloudburst, she rocked and cried harder and harder for perhaps ten minutes, finally crying so hard that she began to gag. She grabbed a waste basket, stuck her face inside, threw up, and then produced an incredibly long and loud belch that was echoed even louder by the basket. After a pause, a new noise slowly emerged from the basket. Susan was softly *laughing*, and yet crying at the same time. Then her deep, "waste basket" voice quietly intoned, "And isn't *she* the delicate thing?"

Laughter just burst out of both of us, me on the couch and she still in the basket. She finally lifted her exhausted, tear-stained, vomit-encrusted face from the basket, looked at me, burped again, and laughed more. She made me flash back to a scene with my own daughter when she was a terribly sick, wonderfully courageous one-year-old. Both were babies, looking for love, safety, and relief from fear and pain.

"Pretty lame, huh?" she asked, "Yelling that I can't cook chicken? What's up with that?" As she wiped her face, she continued. "I guess I do know what's up with that," she sighed. "I feel so small, you know? I don't know how to do anything, how to live life. I've never even had a real boyfriend. Who's going to be there to get me through all that? I know this is real selfish of me—my mom's dying of cancer, my little sister is losing her mother, and all I can think about is me. But this just feels really *wrong*, you know? Like God's making this huge mistake? She's not supposed to die. She's supposed to be there—bugging me about homework, yelling at me not to have sex, smelling my breath when I come in from a party, but acting like she just wants a hug . . ." Susan paused, dropped her head, and cried again, but softly now. ". . . she's supposed to come to my wedding, to hold my baby, and—to tell me how proud she is of me, that I turned out great, you know?"

When she looked up with tears in her eyes and saw some in my own, it seemed to suddenly open a door for her. Seeing my tears made her think of another's. "I want to go now, OK? I'm not mad or anything, I just need to talk with my mom, like right now before I lose my nerve. OK?"

Susan's mom passed away five days later.

A memorial service was held for Mom at her synagogue, where a video tape captured Susan's words. After hearing many wonderful tributes, the audience murmured when a pale and shaking Susan walked haltingly to the stage to address the packed hall just as the ceremony was drawing to a close. Most had known about Susan's nasty reaction to her mom's illness. But they did not know about Susan.

"I'm here," she started in a very small, quaking voice, "to tell you about my mom. I'm not on the program or anything, because I didn't think I could do this. Now, I want to . . . but I still don't know if I can." She stopped, stared up at the ceiling, and took some deep breaths to fight for control. It felt as if the entire audience wanted to rush the stage to hug this girl. But this girl was suddenly a young woman. No one moved.

"I guess it's, like, no secret that I was a creep to my mom a lot. I think that made her feel real sad, and she probably hated that that's how you all thought of me and her, you know, together. So, as my gift to her, I wanted to tell you about my last week with my mom . . ." As tears stole her voice, a few of the audience ran up to hold her, but she waved them off. "I want to do this on my own," she said in a shivering voice. After a minute, she continued.

"Mom and I made up in that last week . . ." She sighed and rolled her eyes at herself. "I mean, I apologized to my mom for being such a little sh . . . um, you know what I mean." She smiled with glistening eyes as chuckles rippled through the gathering. The laughter seemed to calm her. "We spent, like, that whole last week together— me, and mom, and Jess. I took the whole week off from school, but I always cut so much that I don't think they noticed." Again, the audience laughed softly with Susan. "Jess and me, we moved into Mom's room. We'd just talk or eat or sleep or read no matter what time it was. It was weird . . . and, um, wonderful." Her sister started crying hard now. Susan asked if Jess wanted her to stop talking, but Jess shook her head no.

"Anyway, Mom, like, told us a zillion things that we never heard before, you know, about her life and stuff. She told us about who God was to her, and how she felt that he finally did answer her prayers because we were all together like that. I don't know if I believe that or not but . . . anyway, she told us about what she felt was important in life, what is really valuable. Not the *stuff,* you know, the *things* that everybody tries to buy, but the stuff *between* people, the love and the caring—like all of you being together here today." Here Susan bobbed her head with her mother's exact swagger that everyone knew and loved so much: "She's *lovin'* that." When the laughter faded, she continued. "She told us about boys, you know, like how to tell when someone really loves you." Susan's gaze accidentally fell on her father. When she saw him squirm, she quickly looked away, found me, nodded, and smiled. "*And* she told us how to cook chicken.

"Most of all, she said that now she felt like she wasn't really dying, that since we were all talkin', and close, and all, that she would live on forever inside Jess and me, and in our kids one day. I didn't know exactly what she meant then. I think I do now. So, please, don't be too sad or mad at God or whatever. Mom wouldn't want that. I don't want that for her, OK? What I want . . ." She stopped to think a moment. "What I want is that we all go home and, like, love the people we love, you know? Look, I almost lost my mom 'cause I was so stupid, so full of myself that . . ." She paused and smiled at the sad, sweet irony of her words. "Well, I *did* lose my mom . . . but, because I was losing her, I found her, you know?" She paused for her next thought. "Dr. Franks [the rabbi] asked if we wanted some memorial fund thing for my mom. If you want to do something for her, you don't have to give money, just don't be all stupid with each other, OK? Don't fight over dumb things, or just shut up and stop talking to each other. I think that would be the best memorial my mom could have. She'd think that was really cool. "

The profoundly wise young woman finally shrank back down to the shy teen, and she blushed. "Well, I guess that's all I have to say, I think. Thanks for listening. And . . . thanks . . . for caring about us." After staring uncomfortably at the group for a moment, she slowly turned away from the microphone as if she was leaving something unsaid. Then, suddenly, a teary-eyed but smiling young woman turned back to say what the teenager never could: "Mom, I love you."

~

Every single person I've ever worked with who confronted death in some way eventually came to one truth: The only thing that counts, the only aspect of our existence that has any real meaning, is our connection with those we love. Whether religious or atheist, young or old, the only real joys they held at the end of the road were their ties to the hearts of others; their only real regrets were those of love lost. That it is only in our relationships that we perhaps touch infinity.

Susan told me that today she has a beautiful young son who knows so much of a grandmother he never met that sometimes she forgets that he never knew her. As she spoke on with love, and wisdom, and strength about her life, her values, and her family, I knew how this son came to feel the love of his grandmother so very, very well.

6

THE KILLING BELIEF

Adam's Story

It is said that the death of a child is the worst of human tragedy. If horror can become more horrific, then losing that child to suicide is even worse. Such an event might be the most incomprehensible one we might ever know, an evil explosion of innocence that shreds the lives of everyone close by as effectively as a suicide bomber.

The incomprehensible is much more common than most think, an epidemic that has grown threefold from past generations. Every year about one in six teens seriously considers suicide. Every day, about 500 kids try to end their own lives. Thirteen succeed. Most years see almost 5,000 sets of shattered parents standing at gravesides saying goodbye to their children and wondering, why?

Answers to that question never seem to come to those who most deeply loved the one lost. Others more safely removed create explanations that help us to keep our emotional distance, and not get swept up in the terrible disquiet of that horror. We'll say things like "He thought that he couldn't stop using drugs" or "She felt like she was a loser"— arrogant, simple answers, quietly whispered since they might infuriate the ones most wounded who cannot accept that a simple thing could explain such a monstrous tragedy.

Ironically, those defensive, arrogant guesses hold the key to most of these pointless deaths: They involve a belief about self, a simple thing profoundly more powerful than even the weapons that kids use to end their lives. It's not the guns or ropes that kill—they are only the tragic tools used to violently complete a book of life that was abridged by a fatally false premise, a vicious, distorted belief such as the one that hunted Adam.

Adam was an astronaut on a doomed mission; a teenager lost in the dark oblivion, deep in a depression where the world seems devoid of any human meaning or warmth; where death by one's own hand seems to be the only sensible course of action. His was a more dramatic struggle than most but his journey tells the tale of self-destruction better than any, a story we all need to hear. Because Adam was, and is, our neighbor, our niece, or perhaps even our own child, separated from us not by light-years, but by dark beliefs—which create distances far greater and far more terrifying than any in the cosmos.

∾

Mom's phone call painted a picture of a boy slowly slipping out of the loving, life-sustaining grasp of everyone around him. Like someone drowning in front of his helpless family, 18-year-old Adam was becoming obsessed with dying. By age 16 he had already been through three hospitalizations, two serious suicide attempts, and a score of doctors. She told me about how bright he was, how he seemed somehow smarter than some of his therapists who often seemed baffled, or even angry during therapy sessions where he would appear to out-debate them about why he should live—or not.

Since Mom was a colleague, I tried to refer Adam elsewhere, but a terrified mother's love and fear smashed through my protests. "Michael," she said flatly, "I'm begging you—as a parent. I've got no one else to turn to, no place left to go. We've already been every-where. We're losing Adam. I can feel it." After a short silence, tears began to choke off her voice. "Lately he's begun pleading with us to let him kill himself. *He's begging for our permission to die.*" A freezing morning rain tracked down my windows as I blew my stuffy nose, washed my hands, and went to greet Adam for our first appointment. He was sitting stiffly in a waiting room chair, staring at me with blue, empty eyes as I approached. He stood and gave my hand one shake with a cool, soft grip, and then very quickly let go as if he were rationing his contacts with humans. He was very thin and slight, with a black, scraggly beard that looked like it did not belong on his young face, like a Halloween "Trick or Treater" with obviously fake whiskers. But there was nothing young or funny about his eyes. The closer I got, the wider and emptier they grew, matching the total lack of expression in his face. He seemed like a boy without a home, a child who belonged nowhere, one of those homeless dogs that roam mean city streets. Not angry, not sad, not begging for anything, just lost with no hope of ever being found. And not knowing what it is to be found. Or to hope.

I showed him into the office. He sat down efficiently, and proceeded to take charge. His voice was clear and flat, almost synthesized. He spoke words that would read as if they were challenging or arrogant or manipulative. But there was none of that in this boy. I had wished there was.

"I know you're supposed to give me the speech about confidentiality and all, but it's not necessary. My parents know everything I'm about to tell you. Feel free to tell them whatever you want. It won't make any difference. I'm going to kill myself and there's nothing anyone can do to stop that. It's time that everybody gets this." Then, without a trace of drama, he added, "I'm giving you thirty days."

Perhaps not coincidentally, I suddenly started to cough and choke loudly from my cold. Adam startled me with compassion. "Are you OK?" he asked. "Can I get you some water or something?" As I waved him off while coughing, he continued being nice. "That's a nasty cold. I just got over that myself. You must hate that choking thing—and you have to talk for your job."

I stared at him as I wiped my eyes and nose, trying to recover my dignity. "So why are you h . . . ?" I choked out in a raspy voice. Again, without arrogance, Adam began answering my question before I finished it. He had done therapy a lot. "For my mom. She's the only reason that I'm still alive. She begs me not to kill myself, and I do feel bad about how that will hurt her for a while. But I know that eventually she'll see that it was the right thing for me to do." When I sat quietly, he leaned forward a bit and played the rest of his cards.

"If she loved me, she'd let me go. If *she* wanted to die, I'd be sad, but I'd let *her* go if she really wanted to die. *I'd* never stop *her.* That's what you do if you truly love someone—do what's best for them. That's why I'm here. I need you to show my mom that it's best for me that I die. If you don't, I'll just kill myself anyway, and it will be worse for my mom.

"By the way," he continued, "if you try and have me committed again, I can talk my way out of the hospital. I know the game. If you guys try and force me into the hospital again, the most they can do is hold me for a couple of days, and then I'll kill myself the day I'm released. I hope I'm not making you mad. I mean I'm not, like, trying to threaten you or anything. I'm just telling you like it is." He did not seem to be threatening. He was just telling me like it is.

"Adam," I sighed, "I think this is a bad idea—my seeing you. There are many reasons that I should not be your therapist, reasons that can affect my judgment and so might hurt you. First, your mom is someone I know, someone I want to think well of me. If you kill yourself, I don't think she'll think great things about me. Second, if you blow your brains out, the professional circle your mom and I sort of hang out in might think I let you guys down. I'd hate that."

I paused for a few seconds before I laid down my last card, one I had hoped I would not regret. "The biggest problem might be that since I know your family, *I personally dislike how you behave.* I can't stand the way you sort of bully the people around you with this 'thirty days and I'm dead and you can't stop me' stuff. These are people who love you. Your mom seems like an OK lady to me, and you've got her hanging onto her sanity with her fingernails."

When he didn't answer, I ran on. "I also believe that you do not intend to bully people, that you really do think that you should die. That part confuses me, and I'd like you to tell me about that. But, first, I have to tell you that a part of me wants to smack you for the pain you've caused already, and for the forever nightmare you intend to put on the people who love you in thirty days. As your therapist, I'm supposed to be empathic, to understand how things feel from your point of view. I don't know if I can do that, since I see a horror coming for people I personally care about, and it's coming from your behavior. Maybe I'm not the right person for you."

Adam's eyes suddenly showed a small burst of energy. "I don't want to hurt anybody," he protested, "that's why I came here—to make my dying easier for them. But life is too painful for me. I don't belong here, in this world. There's no point in my trying. I know. I've tried a hundred times and it always ends up the same. The best that therapy ever does is to temporarily twist my thinking. I start to get confused about what's real, and I just end up staying alive a little longer just to suffer more. I KNOW how things will always be for me. I KNOW what's real. I want it to end. *It's unfair that all of you should make me stay here and suffer.*"

We both sat and stared for a while. Unprompted, he continued, but in a softer voice. "I've wanted to die since I was about nine or ten. I never belonged anywhere. Friends, school, jobs—nothing ever worked out for me, and I know it never will. I got bullied and laughed at a lot most of my life, but this is more than that. *I just don't belong here.* That's why I got bullied—*I'm different.* And I *know* that same stuff will happen for the rest of my life if I stay alive."

I studied his face and found no plea for sympathy or under-standing. "If you want to help me, then help me by seeing the logic in what I say, and help my parents to understand. If I had fatal cancer, and was in terrible pain, wouldn't they let me go? Can't they see that this is the same thing? I'm completely alone and mis-erable. Can't you see it? The last shrink told my parents and me to just accept that I'll be like, this loser for the rest of my life and to make the best of it. He was the only one who made sense."

"Adam," I asked, "is there any part of you, perhaps 10 percent or maybe just *1 percent* that thinks that it *might* be possible for you to have a life, to be mostly happy one day?"

Adam hated that question. I could see him wrestling terribly with himself. He so much wanted to be able to think that it was possible for him to have a life. But he could not overcome what all those beatings, losses, and failed attempts at living had powerfully and painstakingly built in him: *A belief that he should die.*

"Maybe 5 percent," he said. I pushed on. "Good. Now can you ever, ever recall being happy, or feeling that it was nice to be alive— maybe some holiday, or birthday, or just some nice memory?" Ever so softly, he nodded. "But I still don't see any of that ever happening in my future," he said. Yet now his voice spoke without quite the same conviction as before. "I still think that the way I see things is the way they really are, and that your 'happy 5 percent' talk is just a trick to make me stay alive and then only suffer longer." Then out of the blue he said, "But I don't think that you really dislike me."

When I laughed, Adam's immediate stiffening reminded me of how damaged he truly was. "Your instincts are good," I assured him. "I like you a lot. I hate what you're doing a lot. I think I'm beginning to understand why that 95 percent part of you wants to die. I can see where dying seems to make sense to that part. But that part is wrong."

He seemed calmer, so I put all my chips on one play. "Here's my offer. If, and only if, you can admit to just the *possibility* of having a life, I'll take your thirty-day deal. But not to convince your parents that you deserve to die, but to see if that tiny voice in you that wants to live can get a little louder and say that you can actually be mostly happy and sometimes miserable just like the rest of us. Whaddya' say?" He thought a bit, and then nodded like he was agreeing to a root canal.

Thirty days quickly ran into thirteen months. Trying to reshape Adam's deeply held beliefs about himself was like telling a funda-mentalist leader that his religion was all wrong. Like most of us, the passion and power of Adam's beliefs about himself lived in his emotional side, worlds and languages apart from his logic. In the game of life, our emotional beliefs are so powerful that they can overwhelm any contrary data that our logic might suggest. Listen to an album of songs about love lost, and you get the idea.

Adam *believed* that he could never be happy, and so that became his reality. He would experience some small victories of happiness by occasionally trying things. But these he found *upsetting* since they did not conform with his belief system, which would then label these success events as "meaningless" or "not enough." His was a closed system that effectively defied any therapeutic insight or change. Political strategists would be in awe of Adam's "spin" system.

But through the trench warfare of treatment, yard by agonizing yard, Adam's 5 percent "maybe I'm OK" side grew to perhaps 30 percent. Then the other 70 percent "I should die" side dug in and fought harder than it ever had. Perhaps as a result, the effects of his medicines suddenly shifted badly, and his death thoughts got a lot louder. He agreed to be hospitalized as he felt the bio-chemical aspects of his depression growing and urging him to die. But even then, Adam made it clear that his "clinical depression" was different from his "knowing" that he was fated to be a loser. He firmly predicted that when his meds were adjusted he would still believe that his life was hopeless. As always, his forecast was more accurate than AccuWeather's. The combined scientific skill of hundreds of meteorologists cannot compete with the power of a single human belief to predict the future. Only people can predict, and thus create, our future reality. And we do this with beliefs.

Just when Adam's forecast seemed darkest, two unanticipated storms burst into his life, two revelations that would cause even his own killer beliefs to pause. One afternoon on his way to the psychiatrist's office, his elevator got stuck between floors. He and a very pregnant woman were the only occupants. She had a panic attack. "She was screaming that there was no air," he said, amazed, "yelling that she couldn't breathe, that she was going to die—but it was like *only she was going to die.* I kept trying to tell her that if I was able to breathe, then she should be able to breathe too, right? It made no difference . . . the more scared she got, the harder it was for her to breathe. She was *so sure* that she was going to die that . . ." Adam paused and looked at me. "That she might have made it happen?" I asked flatly.

A week later, Adam had a life-altering insight provided by The Breed, a particularly vicious outlaw motorcycle gang. Since Adam's only relief from his torment was alcohol, he used to occasionally drink at a dive bar where he was known by the bouncers and patrons, a gathering that was not a lightweight, touchy-feely group of guys. One night, three Breed members walked in and eventually started to harass and grab the women there, even some of the girl-friends of boyfriends who just stood and watched. Adam was beside himself. "There were 50 guys in that bar, plus three big bouncers, and no one would say anything. I was amazed. I never thought that this stuff went on anymore. It was like some dumb old movie. One of the Breed had this girl by the wrists and she was crying and begging. So I stood up and said, 'Let her go.' The Breed guy, he lets her go, he turns to me and says, 'What the F__ did you just say?' Then, like, ten guys and two of the bouncers, they grabbed me and rushed me out the door yelling, 'He didn't say nothin'. He's sorry,' and they were yelling at *me*. 'Are you crazy?!' they said. 'That guy would kill you. Get the hell out now.' They stuffed me in my car, and I left, but I really, really wanted to go back. I fumed for about an hour, and then I did go back. I was going to get in that guy's face. When I got there, the Breed guys were gone. The guys in the bar thought that I was insane to come back.

"There were *50* of us, and *3* of them, and no one stands up to them? No one even calls the cops? This town has got a million bored cops who look for excuses to mess with punks. They pride themselves on having the quietest town in the county. I don't get it," he mused, "There's no way those 3 guys could stand up to 50. And I know that at least a couple of those 50 are guys that can fight, and *like* to fight. I don't understand this, and I can't stop thinking about it. Why can't I get it out of my head?"

If that Breed sociopath were in my office, I would have kissed him. "Adam," I said, "*think*. What was it that caused 50 strong young men to back down from 3?"

He sat a long time. Then he said, "I can't explain it." "OK, Adam," I said, "let's assume that just now, that was the 70 percent Adam answering. Can I ask that same question of the 30 percent Adam?"

Adam's face literally looked like clouds were lifting. He spoke haltingly: "They, the 50, they thought . . . they *believed* that the 3 could defeat them. It makes no sense, but that's . . . that's what they *felt—it's what they believed.* So . . . so the 50 were willing to let the 3 run their . . ." Adam looked straight at me. ". . . run their lives—hurt them, hurt the people they love, take their stuff, whatever. They just . . . they couldn't *see* that 50 beats 3 every time . . . they just . . . they went with a wrong belief instead of seeing . . . what was real."

"Good!" I almost yelled. "Now, Mr. 30 percent, what would have happened if you didn't leave that bar?" Adam shrugged. "Well, first, that guy would have broken my face. He was big, and I'm pretty scrawny. Second, I think that the bouncers would then have been forced to at least say something, and tell the Breed to leave. But they wouldn't go, so then . . . then I guess those 50 guys would have to decide if they were going to make a stand for that poor girl. And I think that they would have. I think that they would have fought for her even if they couldn't fight for themselves. At first, they'd be all upset and conflicted and scared, but once they stood up, I think they would have felt better. I know I'd feel better even if he knocked out some teeth and broke my nose, which he would have done. I know because whenever I took a stand with a bully, even when I got beat up, I still felt better."

"OK," I reviewed, "Is this what you said: First, the 50 guys had an incorrect belief that was running their lives. Second, if they were forced to look at that belief, they would see that it was wrong. Third, they would hate being forced to look at it, and that would make them upset—they'd rather just get bullied. Fourth, if they took a risk and challenged their belief, they'd feel better. Is that what you're saying?" Adam nodded with his eyes wide open, seeing exactly where this was going.

"Right," I said. "You can't stop thinking about this because *that bar is you.* The Breed is the 70 percent part, using an incorrect belief to bully you, calling you the worthless loser who should die. The 50 guys are your 30 percent part, knowing that this makes no sense but still caving in to the bully *only because the thought of changing, of challenging a belief feels so scary.*"

Adam stared at the coffee table as if he were laying out all the parts of a once-baffling 18-year-old puzzle, one that suddenly looked like it was solvable. "And you know who the girl is . . ." he said very softly, ". . . don't you? The girl . . . that terrified girl is *me*—back when I was small, getting pushed around and hurt. Just innocent, you know, not doing anything bad, just in the wrong place, at the wrong time—luck of the draw." He looked up at me with tears in his eyes, the first I had ever seen in all of our talks of pain and death, and he said, "I want both of us to be set free."

I sat forward and spoke very quietly. "Adam, listen closely: *Neither of you has to die to be free. All that has to happen is for those 50 guys, and your 30 percent part, to all stand up and say, "Let them go."*

Adam sat and thought. "You know," he said, "that little thought scares the crap out of me." "I hear you," I answered. "I know a guy who'd rather confront The Breed."

~

I've often heard intense suicidal depression described as a kind of cataract, a filter that distorts the world into something that it is not, a malignant editor that only allows bad things to get past, meticulously censoring out anything good or hopeful.

Adam's deadly editor was a belief—nothing more. That is an incredible thought to anyone trying to sort out why children take their own lives. It would seem more fitting to be able blame some terrible and complex disease or some chemical imbalance or some horrible life trauma. Yet usually it is a simple, erroneous, and deadly belief that pulls a trigger. For a belief of hopelessness can be a virus more fatal than many, and changing a belief can be a cure more frightening than dying.

Some kids think that they cannot survive losing a boyfriend. Others believe that the sun won't rise after failing algebra. A few predict that Dad will never approve of them. Many can't be gay. Most, like Adam, just knew that they were losers, that their luck would never change. And all of these kids, every single one of them, made happen what they believed would happen. They did not survive to believe differently.

Except for Adam. He survived. And, some would say, even flourished. His 30/70 ratio slowly but steadily shifted like an hourglass turned over. He started a free self-help group for young folks leaving mental hospitals, one that had no formal backing or supervision, and one that became more popular than the hospital's own. In our last chat, which was about 5 years after we first met, I learned that he was holding an "OK" job, had a few friends, bought a "bitchin'" car and was meeting so many girls that he had dumped two of them. He said that he was amazed at how "neurotic so many normal people are—I can't believe that I felt so inferior to everybody all those years."

He says that even 5 years later with all of these successes, his belief ratio is now about 70 percent "I'm OK," to 30 percent "I should die," the inverse of what it was before—not great, perhaps, but a clear majority. Five years does speak to the staying power of beliefs.

I sent a copy of this story to Adam to ask if he was OK with it. He wrote that he was, except for the part about him standing up to the Breed. "I know that happened," his note said, "but I wouldn't be real happy about some insane Breed guy reading this and somehow figuring out who I am. If I had to do it today, I definitely would not have gotten in that guy's face, I'd have snuck my cell phone out and dialed 911 . . . God, I must have been nuts!"

Adam was not nuts; he was just fighting for his life against a bad belief. And, in comparison, the Breed guy was not nearly as scary as his own killer creed. Many might call Adam a hero for confronting that lethal guy in the bar. But his real heroism occurred when he confronted that lethal belief in the office.

So the next time a pretty girl says she's ugly, or a popular boy says that nobody likes him, think of Adam. But mostly think of Adam when a kid says, "I want to die." Then don't say nice things like, "Sweetheart, you're gorgeous!" or "Son, you've got a million friends!" Most of all, don't say, "Oh, you don't want to die." These are caring words that rarely get past that vicious editor, and often, just make kids feel even worse. For with those words, we've given them a second problem: Now no one understands.

Instead, view those bad beliefs as bad food, and let those kids vomit them all out. Keep them talking by providing a caring, quiet ear so that on their own they might start to catch a glimpse of that deadly editor in their minds, the one who toils 24/7 under a red-lettered sign that says, BEWARE THE BELIEFS.

7

MISTER ORDINARY

Josh's Story

As different and unique as every adolescent is, each shares a secret, irresistible urge that connects all human beings: to find significance and meaning in life. At scattered times in our lives, we are all forced to confront our own eventual passing, and to then wonder, "What is life all about?" For most of us, that search is an endless adventure, a journey of experiences which shape our answers as we travel along. If we're lucky, we ultimately end up with some explanation of our existence, some reason to feel purposeful and important.

Teenagers are at the worst stage of that journey of experiences. They suffer from a new awareness of the fragility and finiteness of life, but they have fewer defenses than adults have to ward off the accompanying anxiety. Most of the time, teens are lucky enough not to have to think about these things. But often in the face of teenage tragedy, making sense of life can become an urgent, overwhelming, and very scary struggle that can produce feelings, questions, and worries that far outstrip most kids' abilities to communicate. That 15-year-old girl staring out the window and twirling her hair might be ecstatic, dreaming about a cute boy. Or she might be terrified, adrift in the incomprehensible concept of cosmic infinity, feeling suddenly small, hopeless, and inconsequential, unable to find her emotional way back home. Ask her what's on her mind, and she'll say, "Nothin'." She can suffer the agonies of the great philosophers and have no words to frame her feelings and thoughts—or she may not even have a clear awareness of exactly what she is struggling with. It can make kids feel very crazy, and very, very alone.

Where and how do you handle this at 15? As a teen, could you march yourself into a psychologist's office and say, "I'm here to find significance and meaning in my life, for I fear I'm going insane from the intractable nature of the cosmic questions, of my relationship with existence"? And even if kids could say that to us, how would we answer that question? Would we say, "Oh, you think too much" or "God loves you, go to sleep"? And would our answers help them in their quest or just give them the message to please shut up?

Just as many adults do when confronting life's issues, many kids distract themselves to avoid thinking about the big mysteries. Some do this by keeping their brains obsessed with activities, or addled with drugs. Most just push the thoughts out of their heads. But late at night, when a nearby death chases their sleep, the questions always await them, refusing to be quieted by the pat answers of parents, priests, or psychologists. These are questions that they must sort within themselves. Whether they ultimately find their answers in deism, existentialism, or anything in between, they must ultimately find their own answers. These are canons that cannot be copied. They only work as originals.

Josh was a 15-year-old who refused to distract himself with busyness or drugs to duck the eternal questions. He wanted to take them on straight-up, face-to-face. That courage made him a hero to me. But true heroes can pay painful, lonely prices.

The high school was different today; it was in pain. I could feel it as I climbed out of my car. I stopped, stood in the brilliant sunshine, and listened. Like a deafeningly silent spring in a beautiful, sad forest, there was no noise—no laughter, no music, none of the crazy cacophony of teenagers.

I was there as part of a team to help the school in dealing with the just-announced suicide of one of their students, the second one in three weeks. In the world of adolescent suicide, self-destruction can be a fatal virus that infects other kids, causing them to start to think the unthinkable. The team's job was to contain that virus by starting discussions, getting kids to talk out their feelings and questions, to help them vomit out those poisonous emotions that might otherwise lead them towards Dad's gun cabinet.

We started with a series of large assemblies to confirm the horrible news, and then broke into smaller groups where kids could talk. I wandered from one group to the next, listening to the quiet, bewildered thoughts that I've heard kids share too many times, when one boy caught my eye. He was sitting on the edge of his 10th grade group, half in and half out of his circle, both physically and emotionally. As I drew near, I finally was able to read the nametag that he had placed upside-down on his shirt. It read, "Josh," and had a small stick figure person drawn on it. The figure had its eyes closed and its hands over its ears.

As I watched him, Josh seemed to be shouting thoughts without saying a word. When one girl spoke, he rolled his eyes and shook his head, but very softly and carefully, as if he didn't want anyone to see. The girl was talking about her Christian faith, about how that helped her with crises like this. She said that she prayed that the student who suicided had accepted Jesus before his death so that he would be in heaven now. She said that suiciders cannot be admitted into heaven unless they repent before they die. Then a large, arrogant boy slumped and sighed mockingly and said that that was "so stupid, because there is no God and no heaven" and that the dead student now was "just a freakin' pile of dead tissue." I thought that Josh might agree with this, since I assumed that he was not religious himself. He gave me another of my endless adolescent surprises.

"And that's even dumber than what she said," he snapped at the arrogant kid. Immediately he looked scared and upset that his thought had popped out of his mind. "I don't mean, you know . . . I'm not saying that *you're* dumb . . ." The arrogant kid slowly rose up from his slump and stared menacingly at Josh. He was big and muscled. Josh was a much smaller, rounder boy with glasses. Trying to defuse the situation, the adult group monitor started to more politely restate what she thought Josh was trying to say when Josh cut her off. "What I meant was that neither of you *know* what happens when we die. You *think* you know, but *how* do you know? Nobody *knows*. We all just make stuff up to try and feel better, or . . ." here Josh looked quizzically at the arrogant kid, ". . . or worse, for some reason, I guess." Then he turned to the rest of the group. "But doesn't it bother you? Don't you all worry about this stuff too? Don't you all wonder what life is about, like, what it means?"

A silence set in that grew louder and louder. For a full minute, no one spoke. Josh searched each face for a response. No one would look back at him except for the arrogant kid who had never stopped glaring. "OK," Josh shrugged, "I guess you don't." Right on cue, the bell rang and everyone got up to leave. The arrogant kid circled far out of his way to bump hard into Josh, knocking his glasses crooked, and sarcastically saying, "*SSSOOORRRY!*" Josh just straightened his specs as if this was something that happened ten times a day. He slowly collected his books, pretending to be too busy to leave right after the arrogant kid. "Josh," I called, "Got a minute?" He happily came over to me, but was interested only in tracking the disappearing form of his bully. As I tried to ask him about his words, he saw that his bully was finally out of firing range. He cut me off and ran out. "Sorry," he called over his shoulder, "I'm late. Maybe another time?"

The next day I found Josh sitting alone in the lunchroom, reading a very boring, very complex book by Sigmund Freud that I had been forced to read in graduate school. He didn't see me approaching. "You must be kidding," I joked badly, "they make you read this stuff in high school?" Startled, he looked up like he was going to get hit. "N . . . no," he stammered, "I'm . . . I'm reading this because . . . because I *want* to." Then he looked annoyed and embarrassed, as if he had been caught reading a dirty book, and he closed it. I sat down and cut straight to the chase, guessing that he might prefer directness to small talk. "Josh, what do *you* think life is about?" I asked. His eyes studied mine for a moment before he spoke. He liked directness both ways. "So you think that I'm the next kid most likely to kill himself, the weirdo who asks crazy questions? Do you think that if a kid actually thinks about stuff, then he must be suicidal?" Now I was the embarrassed one. "Yes," I admitted, "that's part of why I sought you out. It's pretty rare to hear a 15-year-old talk like you did." When he heard me quote his age, he looked more annoyed. "*And* you pulled my records?" "Yes," I answered, "I was, and maybe am, concerned for you. But I also really want to know what you think." Then I waited. He was searching my eyes again. "I don't know," he answered flatly. "I don't know what life is all about, and that makes me crazy. I hate not knowing things. And *NOOOO*, I'm not suicidal." He paused a moment and continued. "But I am different. They . . ." here he opened his hands to the hundred kids laughing and yelling in the lunchroom, ". . . they are *completely* over the life and death questions from yesterday. They all knew *two* kids who thought that life was so pointless or painful or whatever that they preferred to be dead than alive, and all they do is act stupid, and *I'm* the weirdo!? They all just push these questions out of their heads and pretend that life makes sense, but I'm the one who has a doctor finding him in the lunchroom . . . where everybody can watch?"

Embarrassed again at my lack of forethought, I told Josh that I was sorry, and I moved on to chat with other kids, trying to cover the tracks of my stupidly putting him on public display. He watched me leave, and went back to hang out with Sigmund.

The next day we held voluntary groups for kids who wanted to talk some more about the suicides. Josh was not among the attendees. But as I left the room to get some water, I found him standing just outside the door apparently listening in. He spoke to me as if we were colleagues, as if nothing happened between us the day before. "That girl—the one in the red sweats—she's really been hurt by this, hasn't she?" When I said nothing, he continued. "She has no answers. When she talked about how she stopped believing in

God after her baby brother died, you could see how much she needs some explanation, some belief to make it all make sense, and that without one, she's really messed up. She's real sad and she feels like things won't ever get better, that life is pointless." He paused, and then glanced at me. "You know," he said, "she could be the next one [to suicide]."

I sat down in a chair next to him so that our eyes were level. "I'm asking again, Josh. What do you think life is about?" He never took his eyes or ears off of the group he was watching, but he answered softly. I thought that he was spying more as a worried observer than as a gossip. "Well, doc, I don't know what it's about. For me it's not about God or religion. Maybe there's a god, maybe not. I don't know, and I don't know how anyone really knows that. I hope that there is one, though. That would make things a lot easier for me. But, just saying that makes me worry that I could fool myself into religion just so I wouldn't have to worry, you know? That's what a lot of people do, I think. I mean, just on the face of it, religion doesn't work." When I looked quizzically at him, he turned to face me, slightly annoyed that now he had to stop monitoring the group.

"Look," he explained, "there's a hundred different religions with fifty different bibles, each saying that they and only they have the answers, that God only talks to them, that everybody else has a screwed-up view of God . . . and of *life*. And these people truly, truly believe only in what their priest or imam or rabbi or minister or whatever tells them. They'll die for that stuff. But if there are so many different views, and so many good people who deeply believe all those different views, then *who's right?* And if one is right, how can all those others be wrong? Maybe we create our own Gods. How do you know that you didn't create yours?"

Josh paused and studied my face again. I guessed that he was used to having people laugh, or leave, or lash out at him when he said things like that. But he was not agitating. He was searching. "Does that make you mad?" he asked. "Am I insulting you about your God?" "No," I answered, "but you are upsetting me a bit, because I don't really know, either. I have some beliefs, but you're right. I have no idea if they're actually correct or not." He moved closer to me. "Then how can you live your life?" he asked, "What guides you? Why stay alive? What is your life about?" I smiled at him while I shook my head. "Uh-uh, Josh, remember? I was smart enough to ask you first." Josh smiled his first smile at me.

"Yeah," he grinned, "I learned that trick a long time ago. OK. Here's more that I *don't* think life is about. I don't think it's about *stuff*, you know, like who gets the most toys. I don't think those people are really happy. I watch them in lots of places. The guys in the great cars? I think they're always worried about who's got a better car or a better seat at a baseball game. At the game I went to last week, I tried to figure out which seats had the happiest people. Most of the great-seat families looked pretty bad, screaming at their kids and at each other, and not talking very much. They did fix their hair a lot. The cheap seats had some unhappy people, too, but they had more really happy ones, where the parents were, like, hugging their kids, and laughing, and looking like they were just happy to be alive, to be with their families, you know? Not too much hair fixing there. So it's not about the stuff . . ."

Josh paused and furrowed his brow, as if he had just seen another important point in his data. "And it's not about partying, you know, drugs and girls and like that. Those kids act happy, but . . . in their eyes you see that . . . Anyway, I gotta' go," he said. From the end of the hall, he turned around, smiled again and yelled, "Next time, *I* ask *you* first!"

The following week I went back to the school for some follow-up talks. Josh was nowhere to be found. On my second day back, I asked the school counselor about him. She said that he had been suspended, "sort of," for *fighting.* "I know, I know," she said in response to my amazed look. "I can't really say much else about this. Maybe the principal can fill you in."

Reluctantly, the principal swore me to secrecy, and then told me a story. For some time, some kids in Josh's grade had been doing instant message/chat room "assassinations," where they would viciously go after the "loser" kids over the Internet, taunting and teasing and spreading horrible rumors about them. Apparently,

Josh had been monitoring this when he saw the I.M. jerks start to go after a "loser" girl who had recently been hospitalized for depression and suicidal thoughts. Late one night, this "fun" game got terribly out of hand and they got this girl so upset that she was threatening to shoot herself while online. The jerks were daring her to do it, saying that she was bluffing, that she didn't "have the [nerve] to do it." Josh called the police who called this girl's parents who found her sobbing at her computer with a loaded pistol on her lap. Josh became a hero to almost no one when he voluntarily ratted out the kids who were taunting this poor girl almost literally to death, a girl he barely knew. Of course, one of the jerks was his bully, who promptly pounded Josh at school, reportedly in front of other kids who cheered on the beating of the "f'ng snitch." The principal decided to send all the players in this bizarre drama home until she could sort it out.

The following day, Josh was allowed back in school. I found him walking slowly through the hall, head down, all alone as crowds of laughing, yelling kids zoomed all around him. He didn't seem surprised to see me. His face was still bruised, but the pummeling hadn't broken his sense of humor. "S'up, 'bro?" he said with a deep, swaggering voice. This soft, round, bespectacled kid talking like a gangster made me laugh out loud. "You Crips or Blood [gang types]?" I asked. "I was blood a few days ago," he answered, "but the ice finally got my nose to stop bleeding." I asked if he had a big drug buy going down, or if he could spare a few minutes. "Sure," he said, "my drug career here is all blown to hell anyway."

We sat on a bench outside. The bright sunlight made Josh squint and look down, but there seemed to be a lot of other pain wrinkling his face, as well. "You do know that you are a hero, right?" I said. "You do know that there's a good chance that you saved that girl's life?" Josh said nothing for a long time, digging the tips of his sneakers into the dirt. "I didn't really have a choice," he finally said. "It's not like I pained over turning in the pricks to the cops." His head went lower. "But this really hurts, you know? The few friends I used to have now can't be seen near me. I can't stand to go online anymore. I'm being blamed for every snitch thing that ever happened at school. I'm even getting fan mail. Here's the latest." He handed me a crumpled note that promised to "get" him for "narcing-out" [informing on] the bullies. "And, *NOOO,* I don't want to tell anyone about this. I think I'm probably leaving school, anyway. My parents said that they've had enough, that it's no longer up to me." After another pause, he added, "I guess they don't know how big a hero I am around here."

I felt like I wanted to give him something. "You're a hero to me, Josh. I don't think I could have done what you did." "I didn't do what I did for anybody else," he snapped, "it was just for me. I couldn't have lived with myself if I didn't do something. I don't know, maybe I was looking for a way to nail [his bully] without getting killed, and this was just real convenient, you know? Maybe I am just a 'f'ng snitch.'" He paused again. "Or maybe nothing is that pure? Maybe we do things for a bunch of reasons, not just one."

We sat and stared at the school, and listened to it for a bit. The backdrop of all that noise and activity seemed to give Josh a chance to step out of it and look back to see how he fit, and, perhaps, who he was. He heaved a great sigh. "I don't know if I'll be around for these chats anymore, not that I don't enjoy them. But if I'm reading my parents right, they're out now finding a new school for me to start on Monday. So there is one thing that I wanted to tell you." Josh suddenly looked 10 years older.

"With all of the crap that I've been through recently, what's really weird is that I think I do have a piece of an answer to that question you constantly nag about, you know, what I think life is about? I think that the answer is probably different for everyone, that we do sort of make up our own gods, and that we each have to find reasons to feel like this all matters somehow." Josh stood up and looked away as if it was time for him to move on. "And me? What is my 'god?' I think that it's about helping others. I feel alive and important when I do stuff to help people who are hurting. To me, that's really cool. If I had my way, no one would know about what I did [for the suicidal girl]. Not because I got beat up and isolated, but because it would have been purer if only *I* knew what I had done. Then I could lie in bed at night and say, "Josh, what you did was really cool. The world is different, a bit better because of you. To me, that's what life is about, at least for now. I might add more gods as I plunk along, you know?"

After a moment, he nodded to no one, and then stuck out his hand. "Thanks, doc," he said. "I'm sure I'll be seeing you in the future. Now that I'm this, like, *fighting machine* I'll probably get suspended a lot wherever I go." We both laughed, but his eyes were saying goodbye. He shook my hand, turned, and walked slowly back to the school door. At the entrance, he stopped and took in the years of his experiences from one end of the building to the other. Then as a mass of bigger kids came flying through the door, little Josh patiently made his way through the crowd. He walked taller than any of them.

～

Josh was right about being different. He could speak with adolescent eloquence about things that adults have a hard time discussing, things that most kids find impossible to express. But he was also wrong about being different. His quest for meaning hides inside of all kids, not just kids like Josh who are labeled "different" and are gifted with the ability to articulate complex thoughts and feelings. All kids are searching through their everyday struggles, sometimes fueling the fires of rebellion and risk-taking, sometimes compelling them to stick to the straight and narrow, and periodically haunting their dreams when they are forced to confront the meaning of their own lives.

If there is any good that can come from the inexplicable tragedy of the death of a child, it might be that other kids are forced to face these awesome questions, if only for a minute. And what might our world be like if all kids, like Josh, fought to answer their own questions about the meaning of life, about what truly has significance?

8

MISTRESS MARIJUANA

Dante's Story

Marijuana is a secret scourge of contemporary adolescence, an ill whose true destructive impact is little understood. The rise in its potency and the fall in its age of first use have combined to produce a drug phenomenon that flies below our cultural radar screens. We now know that young teen brains are vulnerable, evolving, neurological works in progress that are powerfully impacted by "soft" drugs that most people don't think of as being powerful—"soft" drugs such as marijuana, a substance that addicts more kids than all other drugs combined.

Many knowledgeable people disagree with that statement, saying that cannabis can't really addict someone like, say, heroin or alcohol. Further, they argue that those drug treatment data are skewed by the fact that many kids are forced into rehabs by courts that enforce ridiculous laws that label "harmless" drugs like weed as being dangerous. Those folks are right, but they're also terribly wrong. Weed won't produce the overwhelming cravings of heroin, and it won't kill you fast like alcohol. But it can kill you slowly—by taking your soul, one tiny, unnoticeable piece at a time, until it owns you.

Ask Dante. At 15, he was the fiercest pro-marijuana debater I've ever met. A true "weed-warrior," he worked long and hard to try to legalize "God's herb." He might as well have been attempting to legalize a cancer. His ultimate battle for his soul made him a hero to me. But his fight began long before he ever met his mistress named marijuana.

~

"OUR SON IS A MANIAC," the phone yelled in my ear. "HE'S CRAZY. NO MATTER HOW NICE WE ARE TO HIM, HE'S LOUD AND INSULT-ING AND OBNOXIOUS, AND THE POLICE TELL US THAT THERE'S NOTHING THEY CAN DO, AND THAT WE HAVE TO PUT UP WITH HIS CRAP—WE CAN'T EVEN THROW HIM OUT! ALL HE DOES IS YELL AND SCREAM AND CURSE. SOMEONE NEEDS TO PUT HIM IN HIS GODDAMN PLACE." I was holding the phone away from my ear, waiting for the parent's yelling and cursing to stop, so I could ask about the son's, but the pause was long in coming. When Mom finally took a breath, I learned some things about Dante. He was 15, he was very smart, and he was very angry. Interestingly, he was more than willing to see a psychologist—he was *daring* his parents to come in with him, since, according to Dante, the shrink would say that *they* were the insane ones in the family. "Isn't that a laugh?" Mom snorted sarcastically. "*He's* punching holes in the walls, and *we're* the crazy ones. Isn't that nuts? As if my husband and I are the problem. What do you think about *that*, Doctor?"

What I felt was discomfort with this woman wanting me to take sides and immediately vilify her son. What I said was, "Perhaps it would be best if we all sat down to talk." What I thought was that this might be one of those cases I wished went elsewhere. In our first meeting, Dante promised that it would be.

"This has got to be *the most* insane family you will ever meet, Dr. Bradley. Isn't that right, *Penelope*?" he said very sarcastically to his mother. She rolled her eyes like a petulant little girl. "My *name* is *Penny,* but that's to my *friends,* NOT to you, Dante. I'm 'Mom' or 'Mother' to you, get it?" "You're a 'mother' all right, *Penelope*," Dante snickered, "you're absolutely right about that." She turned to me for protection. "See what I have to put up with? Tell him that this is not right." Then she turned to her husband, "Grow some backbone, for God's sake, John. Be a man! Make him stop!" she whined. John looked like someone was sticking needles in his eyes. "Look, Dante," he began slowly, "I'm tired of you getting your mother upset like this and . . ." "DON'T EVEN GO THERE, *JOHN*," Dante interrupted. "You hate her even more than me, don't you? *JUST TELL THE F'NG TRUTH FOR ONCE IN YOUR LIFE!* TELL ALL OF US THE *WHOLE* TRUTH!"

In the pause that followed, everyone looked at everyone else, apparently waiting for some terrible news. Lost in this small room was Stephie, Dante's quiet, shy, 6-year-old sister. She was sitting alone in a corner, sadly smiling and playing with a doll she had brought, trying to shut out all of the insanity swirling around her. She looked as if she'd had plenty of practice at this. As if on cue, the rest of the family simultaneously started to yell over each other to me, insisting that I should hear them alone. I cut them off. "I think that's enough," I said. "These are not issues to be discussed in front of a small child." I found myself getting angry, watching Stephie play with her doll, quietly creating soft, protective conversation, inventing loving words that I guessed she rarely heard at home. "Does anyone in this family care anything about anybody else but themselves?" I blurted out. While I was looking to the parents for a response, Dante showed me who was really willing to get honest. "That's absolutely right," he said. "I do this crazy stuff in front of Steph, and she's the only decent person in this family." He dropped his voice and leaned towards his sister. "I'm sorry, Steph," he said. She looked up only an instant at Dante, smiled, and then slipped back inside of her safety bubble.

Dante shook his head. "God, look at what we do to her." But his small sane thought was quickly lost in a yelling exchange between his parents, who were each insisting that they alone were the most injured party, the one to whom everyone else owed an apology. Even Dante seemed too disgusted by this display to join in. Rarely do therapists decide that teens are better off being treated without their parents, but this family was rare. After two months of fruitless family work, I suggested that perhaps I should work exclusively with Dante for a bit. Amazing to me, he agreed.

In our first solo session, Dante told me that he had recently found the cure for his rage, which he only cared about controlling for his sister's sake. "Weed is, like, magic. My anger goes right away. It just disappears." He sat back and pictured a terrible scene. "You've heard my parents *'communicate,'* right? Well, that's what it is every night in my house. Almost every freakin' night, that's like our lullaby song as we go to sleep. My parents screaming and crying—they, like compete to see who can get crazier. Anyway, it used to bother me, but now, after my homework is done, I just slip on my headphones and smoke weed. It's beautiful, man. All that insane stuff inside of me, it just leaves." He took a very deep breath, just as he might if he were smoking. "All my life I've had this, like, sad/mad feeling, right here," he said, pointing to his chest. "Seriously, I thought I had a heart problem or something. And all my life I've been a prick—to everyone—even to my kindergarten teacher. I can remember being horrible even to her, and she always tried to be nice to me. She was, you know, overweight? I used to call her fat-ass—*and I was, like, four!"*

He looked at me, amazed at himself, and at his life-long fury. Then he bent down to fuss with his skateboarder sneakers. "Boarding used to be the only time I ever felt good. I'd let it all out there, in the park. I was good, you know?" He sat up straight and smiled, watching himself fly all over those half pipes." "Are you still good?" I asked, fearing that I'd get the answer I got. "Nah," he laughed, "that's all 'back in the day' now. I'm gettin' old for that. Now, I've got *'mother marijuana'."* He slumped back and smiled a sickeningly sweet, frightening smile.

Over the next several months, Dante began that slow, imperceptible, relentless slide into drug dependence that I've watched a hundred other kids make. What made him unique was his honesty—at first. He was an incredibly smart, incredibly straight-up kid who would fiercely attack anything you said that he thought was dumb, yet he did this with no malice. When I warned him about what science shows that weed can do to things like schoolwork, he laughed at me. "Doc, I thought you were smarter than that. You've been reading all of the government's weed propaganda, man. They don't want the truth about weed told. That science stuff is all bogus. I know lots of kids like me who get straight A's and smoke up. Hey, I swear on my weed pipe, my most precious possession in the world, that if my grades ever go to B's, well, to below B's, I'll quit weed, OK? But don't get smug 'cause you ain't ever gonna' see that day!"

As arrogant as he seemed with authority figures, he'd only disrespect those who were hypocritical or controlling. With blazing eyes, he would argue loudly with you on some point, and you'd emerge with his respect and admiration if you stuck to your point without belittling his. And he would fairly consider what others said, something I had not seen his parents do.

Our marijuana debates were exactly like that. He'd done extensive, if often dubious "research" about cannabis, research that he felt proved it was God's "righteous" gift to the Earth. In one session he espoused its biochemical properties, which he claimed "balanced" all of mankind's mental and moral problems, to include war. "People won't fight when they're high, you know. That's how the Vietnam war was ended. When the troops were all smoking up, they wouldn't fight. End of war. Same with me. You remember—I used to be a bad-ass at school, fighting *all* the time. When's the last time I got into a fight?" he challenged. "I don't hardly even fight with my parents anymore, right?" He was right. In fact, his parents had sent me a note congratulating me on making things so much "better" in their home. But things weren't better, they were quieter.

"Are you saying that fighting or arguing is always bad?" I asked. He thought without answering. "Which Dante is genuine?" I continued, "The sober one who used to fight with his folks, or the high one who smiles and says, 'whatever' to the insane stuff he sees at home. Which one is the 'righteous' Dante?" He countered well. "Dr. B., you keep ragging on me to use that medicine that the psychiatrist gave me. If I took it, which would be the 'righteous' Dante then?" I sat forward to underscore my words. "You know better than that. For you, weed is a much '*better*' drug than the antidepressant. Marijuana turns you into some other person and makes your problems all magically disappear—for, what, an evening? The med does not make you high, and it does not make your problems go away. All it does is give you more choices to do the things you say you want to do to *solve* your problems, like homework, or chores, or remembering to call your girlfriend when you promised. You know, all those 'stupid' things that you used to do?"

He smiled that sickening weed smile that lately he wore more and more. "Oh. That reminds me. I guess I forgot to tell you," he said. "Sherrie [his long-term girlfriend] dumped me a few weeks ago . . . maybe like a month ago. She found this new geek guy, Mr. Straight-edge. Mr. Dudley F'ng-Do-Right. She says that she still cares about me and wants to be friends and all, but she couldn't stand my . . . you know . . ." "Marijuana habit?" I offered. He suddenly looked very annoyed, as if the "business" of therapy had gone very personal on him. "Whatever!" he snapped. "Yeah, 'whatever,'" I snapped back, "your new favorite word. Hey! *Mr. Whatever,* whatever happened to the Dante who was always upfront? You know, that guy who said that the day he started lying about his life on weed was the day he would admit that maybe it was a problem? You went with her for, what, a year? You were in heavy love with her—your 'soul-mate' and all. What's up, Dante?"

His anger evaporated into sadness. He looked hard at the floor trying not to cry. "She . . . she sent me a note in the mail asking how I was, since I won't talk to her online anymore. She mentioned her boyfriend's name. I wrote back saying, 'Thanks for telling me Dudley's name. Now I'll have it for my suicide note." He looked up and tried to smile at his terrible joke. But there was nothing funny in that room.

"There's another new word," I said, "Suicide. Has that been on your mind of late?" His eyes went back to my carpet. "Maybe . . . I don't know . . . nah," he shook his head, "I could never do that. It's just that, like, life sucks for me now. School is gone. The work is just too stupid to believe. They're threatening to flunk me for the year if I'm late or absent anymore. You know about my house. And now I've lost Sherrie." His voice became soft, almost reverent when he spoke about her. "You know, Doc, I never even touched her, aside from kissing her. All those girls I've been with, you know, got with—they don't mean anything. I never wanted to do that with Sherrie. She was . . . special."

After a sad minute, he shrugged. "Anyway, I've got a new girl-friend now—a better one," he sneered, "And this one never dumps you—she's always there whenever you want her, and she never says no. *Mistress marijuana*. She makes everything cool." The weed smile was back, but it wasn't looking smug anymore. Dante looked so fragile that I didn't want to pile on, but I had to. It was time to try and smash that smile of denial.

"OK," I said, "Let's recap Dante's adolescence here:

"Age 15: In *real* love with a bright, pretty, talented, and drug-free girl.

"Age 17: Girlfriend dumps him—over his *drug habit*.

"Age 15: Holds a decent job at the supermarket, gets promoted, makes good money, actually *saves* some.

"Age 17: Fired for lateness, and broke; has stolen from his parents to buy weed.

"Age 15: Straight A's, National Honor Society, national poetry award; swears to quit weed if grades ever fall below B's.

"Age 17: D's and F's, suspensions for lateness, may fail the year, and keeps blaming the poor grades on the teachers. Oh, and yes, Dante seems to have forgotten all about his oath to quit weed if his grades dropped. But, then again, he did swear his oath on a weed pipe, didn't he?

"Last but not least, the final factor. Age 15: Pretty much drug-free. Age 17: Pretty much smokin'-up all the time. Now, tell me again, son, about the *'government's weed propaganda.'* Tell it to me like you did that first time when you were smoking once a week. You were *very* convincing back then. Or tell it to me like that second time when you were, like, *totally* in control of your 4-times-a-week habit. But you were only *fairly* convincing then.

"Hey, why not try tellin' me like that third time, when you just sounded *dumb*. You were doing dailies by then, no?" After a moment, I hit him again. "I'm listening, man. I'm listening—but I ain't hearin' *nothin'*."

I was scared that I'd overplayed my hand. I wished very much that he would rise up and get in my face like he used to. But he just sat, defeated, for a long, long time. Then he sank that once fiercely proud, never-yielding head into his hands, and mumbled. "Last week at school, some kid I don't even know came up and asked me a question about which type of weed is a better buy. I kind of felt proud, like I was an authority on something 'cause I know all about that stuff now. So I told him the answer. He said, "Thanks man," and he took off. As he ran down the hall, I remembered that I didn't even know him, and I yelled, 'Hey, man, why'd you ask *me* that question?' He turned around and laughed and said, 'DUDE! Everybody knows what a stoner [marijuana addict] you are! You're, like, my hero! Thanks again, man.'"

Dante's eyes filled up with tears of amazement and pain, blurred by the debris from the crashing walls of his denial. "He wasn't even puttin' me down, or nothin'," he said, "he was just tellin' it like it is, you know?" "Yes," I said softly, "I do know. But, Dante, do *you* know?" He said nothing until the end of the session. As he got up to leave, he turned, and said, "I do know. I don't know if I can ever stop."

As our eyes locked I saw that the old fire was completely gone from his eyes. That was a terrible sight. Sure enough, later that week Dante called me because he knew that he was going to kill himself if he didn't. He said he could not stop using, and that he could no longer live this way. He agreed to go to the hospital.

His road to recovery [stopping his use of marijuana] was long and bumpy. For another year he fought hard, but his "mistress marijuana" would not let him go. He had lost the ability to tolerate stress. Whenever he was faced with doing a tough exam or term paper, listening to his crazy parents scream, or even talk with a girl, he'd get so stressed out that his craving for weed would return with a vengeance, *even though he hadn't felt the urge to smoke in weeks*. It was truly as if the weed had sucked the life force out of him. He could not find his old fire.

As his 18th birthday approached, Dante sat down to say good-bye. "I've got to leave, Doc. It's my only bet. I can't see myself sober here. I'm moving to California. I can go to school there for free after I live there a while." As he saw me waiting to talk him out of this, he answered my unspoken concerns. "I know, I know," he said, "there's no 'magic in moving,' and I'll be 'packing my problems,' [sayings from his recovery program] but, you know, I've got this weird voice inside of me that says I should do this. Aren't I supposed to be listening to my own voice now?" he asked, turning my own words against me. I hated to admit it, but he was right. For better or worse, it was time for Dante to take charge of himself, to guess what his next best step might be, and to take it. This was his time to make life choices and accept whatever consequences they brought. He knew that, win or lose, that kind of living would help him become stronger, and to stay sober. He also knew that staying at home, he didn't have a prayer.

Eight months later I received my first note from Dante. It read, "Hey Doc! Greetings from California. Man, they got drugs here I don't think you even know about. But guess what? I've only used weed 3 times in 8 months, and NONE of the other crap. You have no idea how therapeutic it is to have to support yourself. I can't believe how expensive stuff is in the world. Do you know how much toilet paper costs? I never did until now. I can painfully quote you the prices of stuff like cereal, milk, toothpaste, Brillo pads— Brillo costs a *fortune*—macaroni and cheese, and even toilet paper. Weed suddenly seems real expensive when I see what I have to give up to buy it. And I was giving up a lot more than Brillo. I was giving up me. It's like you said: Addiction is defined by the price you pay for it. I am feeling good being sober, mostly. Making it on my own out here feels clean, like I can make my world what I want it to be, if I work hard enough . . ."

Dante went on to say that he had enrolled in a community college, was loving it, and was getting A's even though he was working full time to support himself. Pretty amazing stuff for a kid who did no homework for a year. He was even starting to jog to lose some of the "weed weight" he had gained from the years of inactivity and junk food cravings. "I'll be home for the holidays," he wrote, "I have no idea why, but I feel like that's something I owe to my family, such as it is. Weird, no? Anyway, I'll see you then if it's OK with you. Don't know when I'll get access to a computer again, but I'll write when I can."

He was as good as his word, showing up at my office almost 18 months to the day that he left, sporting a 12-month-sober badge from his recovery program. "Being home and being sober feels really strange," he said. "It's like visiting some old prison full of really bad memories that you get afraid of, that you think might get you to start using again. I can see how incredibly crazy my parents were, and still are, but, you know, I didn't have to turn to a drug." As my eyes went wide with exaggerated amazement, he broke into a huge smile. "Yeah, yeah," he smirked, "OK, OK. The word is *drug*. Happy now, *Dr. Know-It-All?*"

I was happy. For his word, yes, but more for his eyes. They showed a fire—small now, but with a clear, steady flame. He was finally fighting again, and it was wonderful to see.

∾

Addiction is well defined by the price we pay to use. If we binge only once a year and ultimately lose our family because of it, then continued use proves that we must really, really love our drug. Or really, really, need it.

Kids like Dante lose so much from the "soft" drug of marijuana that it is amazing how laid-back we've become about it. In one sense, alcohol or heroin abuse is easier to deal with since their impact is usually visible and dramatic like a heart attack. Marijuana abuse is a subtle, wasting virus that drains the life energy out of kids so slowly and imperceptibly that the victim and those who love her get lulled into a stupor of denial. Like a cold-hearted woman, "mistress marijuana" takes everything she can, but not too quickly, so as not to rouse suspicion.

Dante, perhaps, had better reasons than most to use drugs. He did not have the benefit of loving, nagging parents to fight with him about his weed use. His folks, like too many adults, conspire with the weed to take our children. So many of the arrogant, in-your-face-kids become so nice when they're high that many of us parents, teachers, and therapists start to fall into that same stupor of denial by thinking that quiet, smiling teenagers are somehow automatically OK. We forget that teenagers by definition are supposed to be arrogant and in-your-face at times. For this is nature's way for all kids.

Dante's arrogance was much more. He was the smoke detector for his family, a screaming safety device making life unbearable for all around him, trying to get someone to address the real problems in his home. When that did not happen, the marijuana finally destroyed his battery, draining the life energy from this fiery young man, causing the parents to congratulate the shrink.

But Dante's fire would not go out completely. He kept a tiny spark hidden away somewhere, a small, heroic ember that he took with him in his flight for sanity. He found a safe place away from the storms, and fanned that spark into a wonderful healing fire to warm others. Today he is a therapist who specializes in working with drug-involved teenagers, a fiery counselor who hates all drugs, particularly marijuana, the drug he now calls "The Evil Mistress."

9

THE AGE OF MIRACLES

Cheety's Story

"The road to therapy hell," my mentor had to frequently remind me, "is paved with arrogance disguised as the best of intentions." As a brilliant young psychologist, I learned to hate that quote. As a humbled old one, I learn continually about its brilliance.

Unfortunately, arrogance is not something limited to therapists. Indeed, our most defining characteristic as human beings might be our arrogance—our insane, war-inspiring belief that, like Lucy in Charles Schultz' Peanuts comics, we all know what's best for everyone. The problem, of course, is what to do when someone's definition of what's best for everyone conflicts with everyone else's.

Many believe that an awareness of human diversity and an acceptance of uniqueness might be an answer to that conflict, but others see diversity as a dirty word, and view acceptance as defeat. Boy, can I relate. I shudder when forced to think of my earlier days as a righteous Lucy, the 5-cent doctor who knew what was best for everyone. Diversity and acceptance were great by me, as long as they concerned things of which I approved.

Cheety helped to open my arrogant eyes. And whenever I hear a harp, she still does, even decades later.

∾

The soft glimmers of winter's daylight were fast abandoning the huge empty passageways of the girls' Catholic high school. I enjoyed that time of day in that great old building. That's when the halls, well over a hundred years old, would feel lovingly haunted by the soft echoes of all the feet, voices, and dreams that once ran and stumbled, laughed and cried, triumphed and failed. It was at those special moments that the creaky, drafty, and dingy edifice felt like a tired, care-worn grandmother, smiling gently as she thought of nourishing the spirits of her charges, and never complaining about her thousand aches and pains; taking her life's joy from the bright, smiling faces, all full of tomorrow's promise.

As I stood alone in the hall savoring those thoughts, I suddenly realized that the background music to my musing was not coming from my mind. It was drifting softly, eerily down the steps from an area called the tower, an old room used only for storage of older, unused musical instruments. For a ghost, I thought, she sure plays a beautiful harp. I softly walked up the worn stairs, hoping to finally catch a glimpse of one of the spirits I was sure roamed those halls.

My ghost thought that I was her ghost. She leapt up from her seat with a sharp gasp and wide, frightened eyes. "I'm . . . sorry," we both stammered at the same time, but her words were richly tinted with a thick accent, a wonderfully warm coloring that matched her beautifully dark mahogany face. As I approached and tried to explain that she was not in any trouble, she backed into her music stand which fell and knocked a set of cymbals to the floor with an incredible crash. "Oh, my God!" she exclaimed, waving her arms as if trying to catch the raucous noise as it echoed up and down the stair well. "Oh, my God" she repeated. Then, just as upset, she rapped herself in the head saying, "I am so sorry. I know that I am not supposed to say 'Oh, my *God*,' that it is an affront to Christians here. The Sisters have chastised me many times, but in my native language, we say a similar thing all of the time and I . . . and I . . . ." Then, she just stood and began to cry.

"'*Chastised?*'" I repeated to myself, "*Who is this kid?*" I saw by her nametag that she was a 9th grader, meaning that she had only been in the school a few months. Oddly, I had never seen her, and her unusual features surely would have struck me. I tried to glean her name from her tag, but I gave up after getting to the 13th letter of only her first name. "Please," I said, "please, calm down. It's OK. I'm the one who should get detention for sneaking up on you like that. How about if we make a deal: I won't turn you in if you don't turn me in?"

Her crying slowed a bit, but she was still upset. "I . . . I also do not know," she confessed, sniffling, "if . . . if I have the permission to use this [the harp]. Sister Regina said that if I could tune it, then I could play it, but I do not think that she thought I could tune it— or play it. A harp is a most difficult instrument to tune, but I know how. So I thought that perhaps . . ." Then she reached out and stroked that ancient harp with a love that a girl might have for her old dog. "*IT-IS-FINE*," I said in a soft but exaggerated voice, "*IT-IS-OK. I PROMISE.* My name's Mike. I wish I was smart enough to pronounce yours, but I can't. I'm an American, you know—we're lousy at that stuff."

Her tear-streaked face suddenly broke into the prettiest smile you could imagine. "I told everyone here to use my, eh, um . . . nickname, which is Cheeting. I have learned since that it was an unfortunate choice of nicknames. So the kids, they now call me Cheety."

That awkward meeting began a friendship that lasted through Cheety's first two years at school. Whenever she could, she would work with our counseling staff doing whatever needed to be done. She was an inexhaustible ball of energy, one that had to be spoken with very carefully. Once, a counselor named Rene who was going home looked around our large, messy area and casually complained, "This place is disgusting. We should all just take a day and clean it up." The next morning, we walked into an immaculate room, with three beautiful posters of Matisse artwork on the walls and flowers on the tables. We were stunned, all staring at each other, wondering who had lost their mind and stayed hours to clean and remodel, when everyone started to nod and say, "Cheety!"

"Michael," Rene whispered sadly to me, "do you know that her family has *no* money? But don't bother trying to pay her back. She won't accept it." Rene was right. That morning began a "cat and mouse" game where the staff would sneak some treat, or a few dollars, or a badly needed new pair of shoes into Cheety's bag or locker. Then we'd all act amazed and innocent when she'd confront us. "It must be the Saints doing miracles," Rene would lie boldfaced, "they often do that for special students. You can't refuse a miracle, you know. That's a terrible sin." Cheety would pretend that she was angry and then always break into a huge grin. "Well," she'd say, "I would not want ever to offend a saint."

But she would always strike back. Without fail, one of our "miracles" would be followed by someone else's. Flowers, or some wonderfully exotic dish of food would magically appear in our room. After one such counter-strike, Cheety left the center almost swaggering, and calling over her shoulder, "It would appear that you were correct, Rene—the age of miracles is upon us again." Rene stood and shook her head in amazement. "Have you *ever*," she asked me, "*ever* heard a teenager use the phrase, '*the age of miracles*'?"

In fact, Cheety was extremely bright, likely bordering on genius, or perhaps beyond. The teachers were in awe of this girl, reporting that she flew through their materials, self-teaching so far in advance that they had nothing to give to her after half of a semester. "You've got to get her the special courses she needs," they'd say. But all of our letters to Cheety's parents requesting permission to test her intelligence went unacknowledged, and they had no phone. When asked about this, Cheety would shrug her shoulders and look at the floor. She was far too moral to lie to us.

Her favorite thing of all was to treat herself to sitting in the college catalogue area and reading the brochures. This she would do endlessly, devouring every page, picture, and word as if they were sacred. She loved to ask us over and over what it was like "going to university," listening with rapt attention to our stories of all that our colleges had to offer, things that *we ourselves* never really appreciated until telling them to this small girl. "Damn," another counselor said after spending an hour talking college with Cheety. "She makes me feel like an educational heathen, like I have no idea how special it was to have been able to go to college. And I pretty much hated it. She's right—now that I think about it, it really *was* special, and I pretty much wasted it." For Cheety, we joked, college was the city of Oz. And we thought that we were her yellow brick road. I never dreamed that I would end up being that ". . . little man behind the curtain."

Towards the end of her second year, I was summoned to the principal's office. There was Cheety's father, sitting and fuming. Sister Bernice (the principal) shot me her "Look what you've done to me this time" face. "Cheety's father is very upset," she said. "He wishes to make it clear that . . ." "MISTER BRADLEY," Dad interrupted, "I do *not wish* that you should ever talk with my daughter— you or any of the counselors." "But," I tried to explain, "we're not *counseling* Cheety, she just works . . ." "I REPEAT," he almost yelled, "You are NOT to talk to *my* daughter about anything, especially about going to college." "I'm sorry sir," I apologized, "I meant no disrespect. But Cheety might be the smartest girl in this entire school. She's incredible. All of her teachers have said so. She has a great chance get a full scholarship to any of the best . . ." "WILL YOU NOT LISTEN TO ME!?" he demanded. "We, in this country, we are strangers. Things are most difficult for us. I have five children, and sending my daughter to this school is a great strain for me. I must work *two* full-time jobs to feed my family and send her to this school. This is a great privilege for her. This I do out of love for her. But it is my job to protect my family in the best way I know how, or we will all perish. My daughter is our firstborn girl. She must help to care for the other children, and then she is to marry someone of my choosing. This is our way. She *cannot* go to college. You are meddling in things that are none of your concern, that you can never understand. I *forbid* this. Am I understood?"

It felt like Cheety's entire life was resting in whatever words I could find at that moment. Like Dorothy's little man behind the curtain, I found none. And before I could, the principal rose suddenly, looked at me firmly, and shook Dad's hand saying, "You have our word. Cheety will have no contact with the counselors, and I will instruct the teachers that they are not to discuss college with her without your permission. Is that satisfactory to you?"

As we watched Dad leave, Sister Bernice turned to me to cut off my anticipated protests: "If we argue with him," she said, "he'll pull her out of school entirely and keep her home. So what would *your* choice be for her?"

The next year felt so sad to everyone in the counseling center. Feminism was sweeping the nation and one of the brightest, most talented, and energetic girls in our school was pretty much enslaved, no longer allowed to even chat with us. We'd pass in the halls and she would smile and wave her hand ever so slightly, looking around uneasily as if she might get "chastised." Often, late in the afternoon, I'd hear that haunting harp playing high in the tower, but I could only stand below and catch the sad, falling notes, like tears falling from heaven.

Whenever Cheety's name came up, the staff spoke often of rebellion, of just disobeying orders and doing . . . *what?* There seemed to be no good option short of a miracle. One of the nuns who worked with us suggested praying to the patron saint of that school, who happened to be female. One of the counselors, who was Jewish, sighed and said, "Go for it, Sister. It couldn't 'hoit,' right?"

On the first day of Cheety's last year with us, Rene rushed into the counseling center with stunning news. "Sister," she yelled, "maybe you got your miracle." Then she stood for a moment, frowned, and added, "or maybe not. Maybe Cheety has to go back to Kansas." Over the summer, Rene explained, Cheety's father had been arrested and deported on some immigration, extradition, or perhaps even criminal charge. The details were not clear, but the fact was that Dad was gone. We were caught up in ten simultaneous conversations. Was Cheety going to go back to her native country? Would Dad let his family stay here? If he did, would that change things for Cheety's future? Where was Cheety's mom? Would she let Cheety go to college?

In the midst of this chaos, in walked the real Wizard of Oz, Sister Bernice. She told what she could: Yes, Cheety's dad was gone, and likely was not coming back. Yes, Cheety's family would be staying here, at least for the school year. No, she couldn't afford the tuition for her senior year. And, best of all, yes, a donor had been found to provide a tuition scholarship for Cheety's last year. That's when Sister Bernice, was officially dubbed "The Wizard." With The Wizard's blessing, it was decided that she and I would visit Cheety's home to see if it was possible for Dorothy to finally get her shot at Oz. With the best of intentions, I "forgot" to ask Cheety what she wanted. I suspected that she would object, not wanting to upset her parents.

Her home was on a street that had more boarded-up houses than it had trash. And it was awash in trash. Rusting cars, useless tires, and ratty furniture littered her street. The Wizard and I sat in the car, staring. "Incredible," she said, "just incredible. Let's go."

Cheety's mom opened the door carefully, holding a baby and peering from behind two chains bolting the door. She looked suspiciously at me, but smiled broadly when she saw Sister Bernice's habit and greeted us warmly. We had entered into a Third World hut. Plaster was falling from leaks in more places than it wasn't. Windows that had been broken were nailed over with boards, and out back, two dogs were snarling and barking ferociously. We were led into what was likely the best room in the house, the one with the most ceiling plaster, and we were seated to a tea service. Cheety was still at orchestra practice at school. Her other three younger siblings sat absolutely motionless and silent. I noticed that this was the cleanest squalor I had ever seen. This horror of a house was spotless.

Mom had asked a relative to act as a translator, since her English was very shaky. After passing some small talk back and forth, and sipping some wonderful tea, Sister Bernice got down to business. Cheety, she said, was brilliant and talented, and it would be a great thing for the family if she went to college, for then she could get a good job and help provide for the family, and help her siblings get through college and get great jobs, as well, for they were surely also talented.

I sat back, amazed at The Wizard. She was simply fabulous. She added that, of course, Dad would have to approve, and that might be difficult because even good men can be so stubborn and sometimes not see what is best for their families, even though they are good people. Here, Sister Bernice and Mom paused, nodded, and

smiled at me, the only male in the crowd. But, The Wizard continued, a loving mother knows when to speak up to her husband to
help him become wiser.

Then she sat back and said nothing. Mom sat for the longest
time saying nothing, as well. Then she poured more tea and, in
English, said, "I will think." The Wizard took Mom's hands in her
own and said, "And I will pray." We thanked Mom for her hospital-
ity, and The Wizard asked for the recipe for the cookies that Mom
had set out. As we got in the car, I was sure that Sister Bernice had
hit a home run, and I told her so. "Mr. Bradley," she said, "there is
a saying about the counting of chickens." I shut up.

But a home run she hit indeed! Mom sent in a written note
asking that we do all we could to get her daughter into college.
Cheety was getting her shot at Oz.

We had a small party welcoming her back to the center, and
laying out our plans to start the scholarship chase. Cheety was
ecstatic to see everyone, and we couldn't have been any happier
ourselves. But I noticed that whenever we talked of college,
Cheety's wonderful smile would dim just a bit, like a candle flicker-
ing in a breeze. I think everyone saw the same thing but no one
wanted to acknowledge it, afraid of making some unseen gathering storm more real. One that might blow out a candle.

As winter broke into spring, this bunch of counselors couldn't
pretend anymore. Cheety, the queen of deadlines, the first student
who finished everything, was not turning in her college or scholarship applications. Then she stopped showing up at the counseling
center for her shifts. Even the harp music had vanished. The staff
was getting the same shrugs and floor stares when they cornered her
in the halls to ask what was up. I just knew that this was about Dad.

Late one Friday, after almost everyone had left, I heard the harp
again. I stood at the bottom of the stairwell trying to decide if The
Wizard should handle this one. But this had to be the perfect setting to talk, in exactly the same place as we had first met, three-
and-a-half years and a lifetime later. It was now or never.

I walked up the steps and promptly startled another frightened
9th grader, but it was only Cheety's shadow, not her ghost from

years prior. This was her *student*. "Cheety is teaching me to play [the harp]," this girl said happily. "She comes in early every day to show me. She wants me to take her place in the orchestra next year. The harp is so cool—hardly anyone knows how to play it anymore, and Cheety doesn't want this to, you know, like, die out here at school. It means a lot to her. She made me promise to teach other kids, so that this, you know, keeps going on."

I walked slowly back down the steps. This just wasn't right. I decided that somehow I needed to confront Cheety's father. I wrote to her mom asking how I could help convince her father to let Cheety go. Mom's written response stunned me. It said that her husband had given his blessing for her to go to college, that it was *Cheety* who decided not to go, *against the advice of her parents*. I immediately sent a note to get Cheety out of class but the teacher wrote back saying that she did not want to come, that Cheety would explain tomorrow. The teacher signed her note with five questions marks, as if to ask, "What the heck is going on?"

The next day, there was a letter for me taped to the counseling center door. As I read, I could hear Cheety's voice saying her words in that polite, humble, dark mahogany accent:

Dear Friend,

In a month, I will be leaving this school that I have come to love so very much, and I cannot bear the thought of saying goodbye to everyone who has helped me so much. Please excuse my cowardice, but my heart would break to say these words directly.

I am a coward in another way, too. Sister Bernice asked me to tell you earlier what I had decided, but I could not. She understood why I decided what I did, but she said that since you and the other counselors are young, that you might be disappointed. I did not want to see that.

I, alone, have decided to stay with my family and not go to university next year. My mother and my father have encouraged me to go, but I must stay. I know that my father was angry at you, but please understand that he is a good man who loves his family. He is in great difficulty now, and he can no longer send the money for us.

Please picture the house where my family lives. Please think of how my mother, brother, and sisters must live. My father was correct when he first forbade me to go to university. It is my duty to help as I can. Sister Bernice has found a good job for me that might allow us to move to a better place. Besides, how could my mind flourish at university when my heart can think of nothing but my poor family, struggling alone to survive? Such a thing cannot be. Please understand. One day I know that I will honor all of you and go to university. That is my dream, and I will make it real.

I am also ashamed to see all of you because I have no gift that is worthy of all of the things that everyone has given to me here over the past four years. All that I have to give to this school is the music of the harp. I have arranged that this shall stay when I am gone. So please tell everyone to think of me whenever they hear the harp. That must be Cheety's gift.

Finally, please ask everyone to try not to talk with me. These things are most difficult, and this is my way of saying goodbye. I must stay strong like a woman and not weep like a girl. If you see me, it would greatly honor me if you would just wave without speaking. When I smile, you should know that you will all live on in my heart.

Your friend forever,
Cheety

As each counselor read that letter, most watched their own tears splash over the stains that mine had left. We just stared at each other and wondered how much our meddling had added to Cheety's terrible struggles, overwhelming her with conflicts not of her choosing. Not taking the time to learn who she truly was, and instead, pushing her to be who we wanted her to be—or perhaps needed her to be. So much so, that in the end, she could not even face us.

Our arrogance was costly, for she was a hero to all of us, and we never got the chance to tell her that directly. And we never got to thank her properly for her gifts, the first and greatest of which was to help a bunch of well-intentioned counselors become wiser, to understand that there is so much that we do not understand, and to always remember to set out a chair for our ignorance whenever we prepare to meddle in the life of another.

Her second gift was wonderful, as well. For the rest of my tenure at that school, the music of the harp lived on, and, I've been told, still plays today. And whenever the soft glimmers of a winter's sun start to surrender to the evening's gloom, I often close my eyes and listen for the haunting music of a harp, strummed softly and lovingly, deep in the bosom of a tired old school, that smiles.

Whenever I start to make those arrogant judgments we all make about kids based upon the way they talk or look or where they live, Cheety's face softly smiles over their shoulders at me. Without a word she humbles me, reminding me about the terrible dangers of adult arrogance. Her struggle taught me that no builder has ever been able to construct things like character, compassion, or wisdom in a neighborhood, no matter how rich. And that no neighborhood can kill the character, compassion, or wisdom of a person, no matter how poor—or young. She taught me how those treasures only live deep inside of hearts, hidden away from judgmental eyes, even from those that want to help.

Cheety offered another gift, a prescient one that she must have intended for us all, here and now, so many years later. In this age of terrorism, I become terrified when I hear people saying that it's "us versus them," and advocating religious and cultural hatred and fury against wonderful people like Cheety because perhaps her crazy neighbor wants to kill me. I shake my head, wondering how things might be for me if I were held accountable by America for every crazy thing that some nut from Philadelphia does. I'm afraid that we have our share of "extremists" here, as I suspect your community might, as well, no matter where in this world you live. Some dress a lot better than others. Most kill without ever touching a weapon.

I have no idea where Cheety is today. But, having known her, I believe that she would want her story told, particularly in these times, as her gift of adolescent wisdom to us. She would want people to know that "the age of miracles" can return if we so choose. Because the best miracles are those of our own making. A pair of needed shoes, a plate of comforting food, the soothing music of a harp—these are the miracles of human kindness and compassion, the miracles of healing and understanding—brave and profound godsends that our world so desperately needs. Priceless treasures carried lovingly in the huge heart of a small teenager named Cheety.

10

SHATTERED TRUST, BROKEN WINGS

Nancy's Story

The most common form of sexual abuse of children is so rampant in our world that its commonness seems to have diluted our grasp of its horrific, long-term damage to the souls of the victims. Most of us have no idea how terribly often this nightmare occurs for kids, and many of us choose to disbelieve the research that points to "loving" family members as the most frequent perpetrators. We just can't stomach the picture of fathers doing this to daughters, so we pretend the numbers away. Even when we are forced to see it, much as we do with injured soldiers, we are moved and supportive when the wounds are fresh, but once the victims are "rescued," we start to grow weary, intolerant, and even disbelieving of their unending pain. Victims are often told to "get over it," as if the wounded enjoy their torment. In these ways, our own needs for emotional defense and denial can actually prolong the assault of the abusers, often for decades, and sometimes for life.

I was once at a large, posh dinner where the subject of sexual abuse of females came up. The speaker, a female, scoffed at the statistics which suggest that at least 10–30% of American girls can expect to be sexually abused, with the majority of these attacks coming from family members. She was dismissive of ". . . these hysterical women who make such a big deal out of small things like being groped or fondled by some kook." Her solution was to tell girls to ". . . do what I do with creeps. I just lay them out. They never mess twice with me." When I noted that the majority of victims are young children who are not assaulted once by strangers, but repeatedly by trusted adult family members and family friends, she was indignant with denial. "That's a load of feminist crap, portraying women as always being victims, a sick myth whipped up by men-haters for their own political gain. Do you really think that happens in the real world more than once in a blue moon?"

I glanced at the 40-year-old woman to my right. I knew that as a child she had been abused by her father. For a moment, it looked like she was going to speak, but then she dropped her eyes into the silence of pain and shame. As she had done for decades, she sat and silently suffered the cut of ignorance yet one more time.

For several years, my 18-year-old client Nancy was not upset by those kinds of comments, but she should have been. Her brain had protected her with a neurological shield of denial, an armor that her mind had cast around memories of sexual abuse so that no one, including Nancy, could get at them. Her defenses stood well for years, until a day that a sword of truth cut through them, to wound her, and to set her free.

"I don't know exactly what I'm doing here [in my office]. If you want to know what I think, I think that the doctors have no idea what's going on with me, and they dumped me off on you. This whole idea is ridiculous. I'm having *seizures* for God's sake, I'm not having, you know, *issues*. And what exactly is a psychic . . . psycho . . . gen-etic seizure anyway? Does that mean they think I'm *pretending* to have seizures? What the hell is *that* about? I, like, enjoy losing my driver's license? Oh. Okay. Sure. I *want* to ruin my life."

Nancy was a ball of angry energy. I guessed, rightly, that she was an athlete. Short, unattended hair topped her stocky, muscular body, which, like the rest of her, showed no signs of attention. Her legs boasted the scars of hundreds of soccer battles, and her knee showed the red stitching of a recent surgical repair. This was no girly-girl. She hopped all over the couch as she ranted about her diagnosis, stabbing at the file of medical reports she had tossed on the table as she made her points. "I don't get, like, *depressed*—I get *not there*. I zonk out where I can't move or hear or speak for like 10 minutes. Then I can hear what's going on but I still can't speak or move for a while. Then I can move my eyes, but that's it for, like, another 10 minutes. Then, I get this killer headache and I'm nauseous—and they're saying this is all *imaginary*? They're the ones with the *issues*. My *brain* is the problem. I've got epilepsy or something but they can't find it. Nothing personal, but I need a brain doctor, not a shrink." Her voice was very sure, but her eyes flickered with just a glimmer of doubt. It made me wonder whether a part of her knew something that another part of her did not.

"Nancy," I opened softly, "Psychogenic seizures are not imaginary . . ." With a roll of her eyes, she interrupted to clarify her earlier mispronunciation, which she booted again—perhaps purposefully? "Generic, genetic, what*ever.*" "Right," I agreed, "whatever we call them, Nancy, the important thing is that they are not imaginary. They are terribly real malfunctions of your brain, as real and as scary as epileptic seizures. Your 'brain doctors' aren't saying that these are not real, just that they can't treat them as they would epilepsy. That's why they sent you here. I do that work."

Nancy picked at her knee scar, but seemed calmer, perhaps satisfied to hear that someone thought that her seizures were as real as her torn ligament. "So then, why do I need a shrink?" "Because, I answered, "your brain apparently has a kind of circuit breaker that it flips causing seizures that shut you down to keep you from doing something. Something like remembering a bad thing, or thinking a bad thought, or feeling a bad feeling. That's the stuff that shrinks deal with. We have to try to figure out what's tripping your circuit breaker." For a second her calmness vanished, and her eyes shot to the window, as if looking for an escape route. As I noted that behavior, I had no idea that I'd write that same note a hundred times.

For two months, therapy with Nancy dragged on with little gain and lots of loss. She was having seizures and shutting down now more than ever, sometimes 3 or 4 times a day. She insisted that nothing traumatic had ever happened to her, and she angrily clung to her belief that the medical doctors were missing the "real" explanation for her seizures, a belief supported by her soccer-coach father who was dismissive of psychotherapy. But she kept coming back.

In retaking her history for perhaps the fourth time, she casually changed one small detail that provided the break we needed: Her first seizure had *not* occurred after a soccer match as she had been saying, but the day before during a school assembly. The topic was sexual abuse of children. A speaker had been describing her experience of being molested by her father when Nancy had her first seizure. When she saw me suddenly look up, she cut me off. "Don't waste your time. Nothing like that ever happened to me. My dad is, like, the sweetest, nicest father. It's ridiculous to think for one minute that he'd . . . AAARRRGGGHHH!" she yelled. "You guys (doctors) are ALL NUTS. You're not *listening* to me. I can FEEL that something is wrong in my brain. Just like in my knee. WHY WON'T YOU TRUST *ME*?" "I do trust you, Nancy . . ." I answered, "Can *you* trust *me*?" She turned her head and, without moving, escaped through the window once again.

The following week, she didn't show up for her appointment. A week after that, I got a call from a hospital attending physician. Nancy had a seizure while (illegally) driving, and suffered relatively minor injuries when her car ran up an embankment. "She asked that I call you instead of calling you herself," the doc said, "but she wouldn't tell me anything to tell you. Does this make any sense to you?" "I don't know, maybe," I answered. "Please just tell her that I'll look for her at our usual time."

Nancy was right on time for that next session, sporting two new sets of stitches over a bruised face. "Some kids do purple hair," she quipped, "I do face." Without waiting for a laugh, she pressed on immediately as if she had something to say either now or never.

But she could not look at me, so she talked to the table. "It wasn't my father," she said flatly. "It was my uncle—his brother. I was . . ." and then she had a seizure. Her head suddenly drooped awkwardly, and her body froze its endless fidgeting. Her eyes were open, but staring unblinkingly, her mouth agape. For ten minutes she moved absolutely nothing. Suddenly her eyes blinked furiously, catching up for lost time. She looked at me. I could see her calling to me through her eyes, but she couldn't make a sound. "It's all right," I soothed, "You'll be fine. Just relax." As I spoke, I realized how dumb those words must have sounded to her. She had been through this a hundred times and knew what to expect. And "Just relax?" I hoped that she hadn't heard that. Her eyes told me that she had. They were yelling at me.

Like a failed computer restarting, she slowly reclaimed her physical self, part by part. Finally, she hung her splitting head in her hands, tried not to vomit, and mumbled, "Just *relax*?" But she was too exhausted to be angry or even to make fun of me.

"When I told you before that I wasn't, you know [abused], I wasn't lying to you," she said softly, wincing as if each word was stabbing her brain, "These memories started to come back real slow to me when I started coming here, like bits and pieces at different times, of what he would do when he babysat me." She frowned at her own words. "'Babysat me? Wow, that's a strange way to describe what he did. Anyway, I didn't tell you because, I don't know . . . I guess I just didn't—or don't—want to think this really happened. Or that this might actually be causing these things [the seizures]. When I was lying in the hospital bed, the doctors were, once again, telling me that they could find nothing wrong in my brain, and that's when it kind of all came back to me, like in one piece." Here she looked up at me. "So, now we know, then, I'm cured, right? Now what?"

The "what" would become 6 months of agonizing work. In a "three steps forward, two steps back" mode, Nancy courageously fought to recall, and then speak the memories of her abuse and all of the associated feelings of guilt and shame. But the seizures stalked her every effort, shutting her down with each new memory or re-experiencing of old pain, fear, and horror. Her bright eyes, once alert and full of life, seemed to go dark. This maddeningly slow pace led her to occasionally quit therapy and instead try alternative treatments and psychiatric medications, but nothing seemed to help very much. The harder we pushed at her memories, the more her brain would produce new symptoms, new torments to keep the old ones locked away. Often she'd awaken at night, screaming and drenched in sweat, running from monsters barely hidden behind veils of secrecy in her mind, to find her terrified parents standing helplessly by her bed.

"No," she would say firmly when I asked her about confronting her abuser. "I'm never confronting him, or telling them [her family]. It will do no good, and just tear the family apart. Everyone would just side with him. He's, like, everybody's favorite person. He would turn everyone against me, maybe even my parents. No one would ever believe me, and they'd think I was a sicko for saying that. I couldn't stand the way everyone would look at me."

A few weeks later, she proved how wrong I was when I suggested that some people would probably believe her. "You are so wrong," she said. "I did tell once. I remember now. I told my grandmom [her father and uncle's mother]. I guess it was about three months after, you know, *it* started to happen." She still could not use the specific words referencing the abuses without almost always having a seizure. Nancy looked straight at me, but spoke in a strange, detached voice as if mimicking words she could hear in her head. "Mom-mom said that was a horrible, horrible thing to say about my uncle, that he *loves* me. He would *never* do anything like that. She told me to never, *ever* repeat that to anyone or they'd all think that I was a horrible girl, and that I know about the dirty things I imagine. She took me to church the next day and made me go to confession to tell the priest. I went in, but I didn't tell him. I figured that if Mom-mom wasn't on my side, no one would be. We were, like, really close, you know—up to then. After that, she—she never looked at me the same. He stopped doing it after I told her, so I guess she did say something to him, but from then on she always had this—look, like I smelled bad or something. Since then it seems like lots of people have that look . . ." She paused, dropped her eyes, and shrugged, ". . . even you, sometimes."

"Nancy," I said, "I don't think that you smell bad. I think that your uncle smelled bad, and you think that it kind of rubbed off on you, and now *you* think that *you* have a smell that you can't wash off, you know?" She nodded. We had no idea how ironic that metaphor would prove to be.

Two more months of frustrating therapy followed. Nancy was building her nerve to attend a family gathering where she would probably be forced to see her uncle, which she had managed to avoid for years. The morning after that event, she called for an immediate appointment. She sat down and cut straight to the chase. "He . . . he *walked right up to me like nothing ever happened,*" she said incredulously. "How could he do that? How could anyone ever do that? I just froze. I actually couldn't move. Then he . . . he . . ." I was sure Nancy was going to have a seizure, but this time she didn't. For the first time in talking about her attacker, she was not frightened or ashamed. She was mad. "He *hugged* me. He *HUGGED me.* And when he did, I remembered . . . I remembered his . . . *smell.* It was like I went back in time, and he was on me again. I ran out of the room." As she sat and stared out the window, I waited for tears that never came. She was done with running away. "I have to do something." Her words had escaped her before she could reel them in, but she decided that she didn't care. She held her head up, scared but resolute. "I'll let you know next week what I decide to do. I don't want you to tell me to do anything. Okay?"

Nancy cancelled her next appointment without an explanation. I was sure that she had backed out of confronting her uncle, and felt too embarrassed to see me after that. But I had forgotten how tough she really was. One of the amazing things about kids who get abused is the tremendous hidden strength they build, a secret steely tenacity that they themselves don't see, something they must construct to keep from going insane. Once they learn to tap into that resolve, there is little they cannot do in life. Nancy had found her resolve and she showed up for her next session. She was not quitting this time.

"I wrote a letter," she said, "and sent it to him today. Here's a copy for you. I'd like you to read it." "I'd rather hear you read it," I said, "if you don't mind." She twisted up her face in mock protest of being told what to do, but then smiled when she realized that this was her moment, and that reading the letter would be a sign of that. She picked up the folded letter and slowly opened the best gift she would ever receive, one that she had given to herself. As she read, she softly cradled a small smiley-faced toy in her suddenly strong arms, reading to it as if talking to the sad little girl she used to be, letting the small Nancy know how the big Nancy had finally stood up for her.

"This letter has no 'Dear Uncle' part. I tried to write that five different ways and none worked. How can I call you 'Dear Uncle'? I have not forgotten what you did to me. It was wrong, and you made my life a living hell for a long, long time. You did two things that were very bad. The first was raping me." Without pausing, she widened her eyes and nodded here, silently acknowledging that now she was able to use the abuse words with hardly any sign of a seizure. I could almost hear the rusty chains that had imprisoned her brain for so long finally falling away.

"For any man to do that to any little girl or anyone is unforgivable. Why would you want to do that to a 12-year-old girl? You made me feel so dirty and ashamed that I thought I could never be as good as other girls. I thought they all knew about me." She stopped reciting her letter and shared a different thought. "So *that's* why I play soccer like a madwoman." She shook her head and laughed, and then continued reading.

"It would be bad enough if you were a stranger to me. But you were not. And that's the second bad thing, which is worse than the first." In all of the frustrating, painful, and sometimes agonizing time we had spent together, *I never once saw Nancy cry.* Now, for the first time, her eyes slowly rimmed with tears.

"You were my uncle, my father's brother. I trusted you, and looked up to you. When I was small I always felt safe around my uncles, like they were there to protect me. I used to love to

fall asleep at Mom-mom's while the uncles and Dad would sit on the lawn and talk. I could hear you from my window. I used to pretend that I was a princess and you were my guards and so nothing bad could ever, ever happen to me. Then you hurt me. You took all of that away. Now I don't feel safe anywhere, with anyone. If my own uncle, my father's brother, can rape me, then who can I trust? I even stopped hugging Dad back then, because I felt too dirty to hug him. This is some of what you took away from me, things that I can never get back.

"I should go to the police and report you, but I am not going to, at least for now. I want to keep this between you and me. I don't want my parents to get hurt more by what you did. But if I ever think that you might do this to anyone else, I will tell everyone. Don't ever try to hug me again. And stay away from me anytime you see me.

"I signed it **'Nancy'**. Then I added a P.S. It says, 'I think you owe me an apology.' That's pretty dumb, isn't it? Asking an uncle who rapes me for an apology? Sounds ridiculous, doesn't it? Shouldn't I be, like, suing him or trying to ruin his life or something?" "Does it sound ridiculous to you?" I asked. She was already shaking her head before I finished. "No, it sounds like something I've wanted for a long, long time. I don't think I'd feel better putting him in jail. I just want him to say that what he did was wrong, and that it really did happen. And guess what? I don't care if that sounds ridiculous to anyone else. It sounds right to me."

After a few moments I asked how she felt. "Like I can't breathe," she said. "Not scared like before, just, I don't know . . . just real alert, or something, like I'm waiting for something to happen, but I don't know what. I'm not sorry I sent the letter, though. It feels like it's the first thing I've done right in a long time, like I finally stood up for me. But . . . what will he do?" I could only shrug. And hope.

The following week Nancy walked in, sat down, and for the first time in almost a year, she smiled a huge, easy smile. She looked like an entirely different young woman. She was beaming. Very quietly and slowly she said, "You have no idea how wonderful I feel." Then she very carefully said . . . nothing. She looked like a kid sitting alone very early on a Christmas morning, savoring the tree and presents from the stairs, not wanting to lose that precious moment by moving any closer. Finally, she took a breath and exhaled deeply, as if she had just survived a terrible battle. "It's over. It's . . . all . . . over. And it's okay. *I'm* okay." She paused and smiled broadly again, playfully making her eyes bulge as if daring me to make her talk—a very funny, very mean joke referencing her months of staring in stony silence out of my office window. But this time her old, dead eyes were new and gleaming, fairly bursting with some wonderful news. I picked up the smiley-face toy and threw it at her. "No more Mr. Nice Guy," I said. "Give!" For a moment, she cradled "Smiley" as she had so many times before, but then put him down as she spoke. It made me think that the small Nancy had finally begun to heal.

"The day he got the letter, he showed up at my door when no one else was home. I didn't let him come into the house, but it wasn't because I was scared of him like before," she said. "It was more like, you know, he sort of *smells* bad, like he's this horrible memory that I don't want around anymore. I didn't want him to be in my space." She sat forward and stared through me as if watching some incredible scene replay. "*But I wasn't scared of him. It's like he suddenly shrank down from being a scary giant to being this pathetic, old man.* He had my letter in his hand. He couldn't look me in the eyes at all, but I could have looked at his. He just said, 'I got your letter. I'm sorry.' We just stood there quiet for a few minutes, and then he said 'I'm sorry' again, and then he left."

Nancy sat and closed her eyes, breathing deeply and slowly as if she had never breathed clean air before in her life. "You know, I didn't say a word when he apologized. There are no words. It felt . . . it feels . . . *free*. Like I could just . . . *fly* if I wanted to." We sat silent for a long time. Then she got up and said, "Well, time's up. I have to get to work. I'll see you next week." Somehow I knew that she was not coming back. As I followed her to the door, she stopped, sighed, and spoke without turning to me. Very softly she said, "Thank you." "You're welcome," I answered, "but, you do know that *you* made this happen, right?" "Yes," she nodded, "I know . . . *I know.*"

And then she flew away.

◇

When Sigmund Freud wrote of his belief that grotesque numbers of children are sexually abused, he was ostracized and essentially exiled from the medical community, which was enraged by the denial needs of male guilt and complicity. That century-old evil of denial is alive and well today, still condemning kids like Nancy to lives of crippling despair. The terrible irony is that the worst damage of sexual abuse occurs from the silence, the not telling that over time grows the initial horror of assault into an agony deserved, an invisible and inviolate proof of total worthlessness. The lucky and few children who seek and get immediate help have far fewer scars.

So when we are tempted to tell survivors to "get over it" or to dismiss the horrifying tales of molested grandchildren, let's do two things: First, let's walk in their shoes a while, and slip on their gowns of shame—those dark, monstrous suits of iron that slowly grind down the wearers until they can barely walk. Then, let's resolve to be people to whom children can tell the unimaginable. Let's be adults who are caring enough to hear their cries, loving enough to embrace their pain, and courageous enough to confront terrible things in our world.

Then, and only then, can these wounded children heal and fly again, like Nancy, and perhaps some of them will never have to know the terrible pain of wings shattered by silence.

11

THE ANGER MIRROR

Angie's Story

The research proving that fear-based parenting methods don't work well (humiliation, derisive yelling, hitting) is about as questionable as that which holds that smoking cigarettes causes cancer. Yet most Americans cling to the belief that hurting kids is a good way to keep them from becoming bad people. Dads, in particular, often subscribe to these methods since most of us were raised by fathers who hit, and many of us grew up to love and respect these fathers. This "I-know-a-guy-who . . ." thinking is much like the smoker who refutes decades of research by citing one example of someone they know who smoked a lot and never got sick.

When I ask these hitting dads what they loved and respected about their own hitting fathers, they usually say things like, "He worked two jobs to get us through school, took care of the widow's kids down the street, coached all the sports, never had a decent car or coat in his life—he just gave it all away." "That's wonderful," I reply, "but you just told me about the man's values and character. You never mentioned the hitting. You forgave the hitting because of your father's values."

This aligns with studies that show that using fear is, at best, a waste of parenting time. When the connections of love and respect between a child and a parent are strong, the occasional use of fear is a non-factor, neither hurting nor improving the relationship. But at worst, controlling children with hurtful hands or words creates terrible, unseen damage to those critical, loving connections with parents that kids need to eventually control themselves. Fear-based parenting does provide a temporary illusion of effectiveness because when kids are small, they can be controlled with fear, to a point. But hitting small kids can work like a long-term credit card for rage, accumulating "charges" of secret anger over many years with compounded interest. Then one day, the small, scared child becomes a large, scary adolescent who presents a huge "balance due" bill of rage to her parents. Here is the story of one such bill collector.

Nothing bothered Angie. She was way too tough to let anyone get to her, least of all me, a "waste" psychologist. As *we* sat, and *I* talked about all that was going wrong in her 14-year-old life, she reacted just as her dad had predicted: with shrugs, eye-rolls, and sighs of profound boredom. He seemed to be correct in saying that "she cares about nothing except being a bitch." Certainly that's what her school records suggested. As I picked up her school file to review it with her, she popped her gum for the hundredth time, pulled threads from her tattered sweats, twirled her disheveled hair, and stared up at the ceiling. "Wow," I admired, "you must have set the school record for demerits. Let's see: 'disrespect, cursing, refusal to do work, fighting, destruction of school property.' Is there any rule you didn't get to break yet?" Angie kept her head tilted toward the ceiling, but dropped her eyes to stare at me while popping a huge gum bubble: BANG! "Man," I said, "if gum could kill . . ." Judging by her wide grin, she liked that thought a lot.

As she smiled, she suddenly looked like a soft young girl even though in her mind she was loading .45-caliber bubble gum. Still smiling, she pointed her finger at me like a pistol, squeezing the "trigger" along with another loud gum pop. BANG! I raised my hands in surrender. "I'm not armed," I pleaded, "don't shoot. I surrender!" Still she stared without speaking, but now with a softer, smiling face. Her gunfire felt engaging, not dangerous, and a thought suddenly escaped me in words: "Is there someone else you would like to shoot?"

Her smile disappeared as fast as her bubble. "YES," was about all she would say for the rest of that first session.

The next day, Mom and Dad walked in as if they had just walked out of some flashy magazine. Both were beautifully dressed with very expensive casual clothes. At first glance, each looked very polished. She was perfectly thin, and he was perfectly buff. It wasn't until they got close that you could see the fear in Mom's eyes. And the fury in Dad's. "My husband is not very big on therapy," Mom apologized, "Please excuse his not being very pleasant. He and Angie had a huge fight last night, and she said some terrible things . . ." She paused and looked carefully at Martin's feet, not daring to meet his eyes before continuing in a soft voice, "Well, I guess they both did." I was fascinated to see Martin sitting exactly where Angie had the day before, rolling his eyes, sighing, and staring at the ceiling. I imagined him blowing gum bubbles. But he talked a whole lot more than his daughter.

"That's right," he snorted at his wife. "I did tell her that I was sending her away somewhere, that she was insane." He looked at his wife. "OK, I said that she was f'ng insane, all right? And I'll be straight with you, too, Doctor. I've read parts of your books, and I think it's liberal, touchy-feely types like you that have screwed up these kids today. What Angie needs is NOT this therapy crap. She needs the belt, just like she needed it for her whole life. You want to know what's wrong with her? She's a selfish, self-centered bitch who cares only about Angie, and doing whatever the hell she wants. But thanks to people like you, I can't discipline my own child anymore. That's why she's so out of control." Six months earlier, Martin had the displeasure of meeting child protection social workers after the school reported seeing belt buckle bruises on Angie. She had refused to rat out her dad.

It would have been very easy to dislike this guy, but I couldn't help liking him. He was certainly harsh and threatening, even brutal sometimes. And yet there was much more to this father, just as there was to the daughter. As he lectured me about the "good-old-days" of disciplining children with weapons, I could hear his fear and love for his girl hiding under his scary words. He was mostly acting upon what he believed was truly best for Angie when he would rage and hurt her. I pictured poor Angie at only 14 years of age trying to sort out this terrible paradox of a man who seemed to love her so much in so terrible a way.

He seemed to have sensed that I liked him. "Look," he continued in a much quieter voice, "I'm the one—," he sighed and glanced at his wife, "I mean, *we're* the ones who have to decide what's best for our kid. You and your liberal social workers are not going to be around to clean up the wreckage when she gets arrested, or pregnant, or addicted because I can't discipline her anymore. My dad used the belt on me and I know, Dr. Bradley, *I know,* that if he hadn't, I'd be in jail or dead today. There's not a doubt about that in my mind, or in the minds of anyone who knew me back in the day. I was crazy back then. I fought everybody—cops, teachers, other kids. I was in a bad gang, very violent. Today I have my own very successful business, and I provide a great life for my family because of the discipline my father gave me."

Mom didn't miss a beat. This time she looked right at him. "And you also won't talk to your father anymore." She turned to me. "Doctor Bradley, Martin hasn't spoken with his father since he was twenty. He hates him." Dad suddenly looked deflated—sad, quiet, and confused. You could see the honest conflict in his eyes, the terrifying complexity of trying to decide what's best for one's child. But he could not allow that confusion into his words. Or into his heart. Much like his daughter had, he said pretty much nothing for the rest of that session. As he was leaving, he turned to face me. "*Angie,*" he said, "is the problem here, right?" I wasn't sure what he meant. "Martin, are you asking me or telling me?" He searched my eyes as he answered. "I'm telling you," he said. But his eyes seemed to be asking me.

Martin refused to return to therapy after this session, but Angie kept coming. I had no idea why. One of the few sentences she uttered was to insist that her dad attend with her, but she continued coming even though he wouldn't. Her behavior at school and at home got worse and worse, so much so that Angie's 19-year-old sister Amelia asked to attend a session with her. The verbal violence at home was scaring Amelia. She had been gifted with everything that Angie was not. Amelia was athletic, compliant, verbal, and very smart. But her gifts were also her blindness.

"Angie," she pleaded, "I really, really, do not get this. Dad is NOT so hard to live with. Look, I just do mostly what he says and he's great to me. He gives me, like, more money than I can use, and a car, and I get to go pretty much where and when I want just because I don't get in his face over stupid crap like you do. He stopped hitting me when I was, what, eight or seven? I just figured it out. Why can't you?"

The "Un-Amelia" just sat and stared. "Angie," I asked, "Is it OK if I share with Amelia what I told you in our last session?" Angie twirled her hair and shrugged. It was so sad to see how paralyzing it was for her to become vulnerable enough to say what she really thought, or really wanted. This girl had terrible, unseen scars. "Is that a yes?" I asked softly. After ten seconds that felt like ten minutes, she slowly nodded. "Here's hoping," I silently said to myself.

"Amelia," I said, "all her life, your sister has wrestled with something called Oppositional Defiance Disorder or ODD. We think that some kids are born with this. It's like her brain is wired to shout 'NO!' almost every time someone tells or even asks her to do something. She does this automatically, without even thinking about whether she should or even might want to do what she's asked." Amelia nodded wide-eyed and turned to stare at Angie as if years of crazy fighting suddenly made sense. Angie actually looked back into her sister's eyes for almost ten seconds. This was good.

"Now here's the bad part of ODD. If someone like your dad takes it personally and goes nuts on a kid like Angie when she yells NO!, then the ODD kid will go nuts right back. Screaming at and beating an ODD kid to control her is like trying to put out a fire with gasoline. Sure, if you terrify the ODD kid enough, she'll back down sometimes, particularly when she's young. That part confuses parents who think that using rage works to raise these kids well. But when Ms. ODD gets to be 13 or so, all hell breaks loose. She backs down much less, and she seems to get a lot more nuts."

I turned to Angie and asked, "Do you want me to tell your sister why these kids get more nuts?" She gave me that same old shrug. *But for the first time since I had met her, her eyes were filling up. She was getting this!*

"You see, Amelia, all through her childhood, Ms. ODD has been saving up all of the pain, the shame, the humiliation, the terrible hurt of having her own father, someone she loves so much and depends upon and looks up to, use a weapon to . . ." I shut up as huge tears swelled silently out of Angie's eyes and splashed down onto her lap. As if reading my thoughts, her stunned sister reached out to hold Angie's hand. Angie immediately pulled her own hand away, but then after a moment, allowed Amelia to stroke her hair softly, like a parent might. I pushed on.

"The worst part for Angie might be the confusion, Amelia." I waited for some protest from Angie for inserting "Ms. ODD" for Angie's name in my story. There was none. "That's when she feels hatred for her father for beating her, and yet at the same time loves him because she can feel love coming from him at other times. It's sort of impossible to hate and love at the same time, so it makes Angie feel really nuts inside. That just adds to the worst part of having a parent beat you. When we're small, we can't understand why a parent would ever hurt us like that. So we decide that *we must deserve the beatings, that we're really bad, really worthless creatures.* So acting crazy all the time makes sense, you know? Why be good if we're so messed up that our own father would hurt us like that? Why be nice if . . ." Angie's sudden sob was like a half-scream, the sound one would make if a scabbed bandage were suddenly ripped off. "Angie," I apologized, "I'm so sorry. I pushed way too far. I should not have . . ." Weeping softly, she waved me off, shaking her head. "I'm not weak," she protested. "I can do this. It just feels good to cry—I think. It feels like letting something go."

The sudden, profound wisdom in this 14-year-old girl silenced me. After she cried a while, I asked, "Angie, I know you refused 10 times before, but *now*, can you maybe see yourself saying this stuff to your dad?" She didn't hesitate a second. "I want to, but I don't know. Maybe I can, but he won't come here, remember? He says that I'm the insane one, that I'm the one who needs help." "Leave that part to me," said Amelia. "I'll get him here." "How?" I asked. She chuckled. "By asking him what he's afraid of. He never backs down from a challenge. It's, like, a trick I use whenever I have to. I only use it when it's really important." She smiled and stroked her sister's hair once more. Angie's face looked very relieved to hear her "perfect" sister matter-of-factly state that the old man was a little nuts sometimes and had to be managed with strategies. Angie looked at Amelia as if she was seeing her for the first time. Amelia reached out again for Angie's hand. This time, Angie did not pull away.

The minutes before the next session felt like the minutes before a big football game. I stared out my window and wondered. Would Martin come in? Could Angie confront him? If she did, how would he react? Just then I almost laughed as I saw Martin coming up the office walk with Angie and his wife in front, and with Amelia bringing up the rear like a principal herding a group of acting-out students. Dad looked like he was ready for a football game.

Amelia and Martin sparred for twenty nasty minutes, with Dad looking very uncomfortable at hearing his "perfect" daughter suddenly tell him unvarnished truths, as if he were being attacked from the rear. Mom sat stone still, her eyes wide with fear. Angie looked like she wanted to disappear into the couch. "And another thing," Amelia said, almost with her chin stuck out. "What gives you the right to yell and scream because someone else yells and screams? Aren't you supposed to show your kids the right thing, to . . . ?"

"STOP!" Angie cried out, startling everyone in the room. "ENOUGH! Look, Amelia, thanks, but I have to do this, OK?" Amelia took a deep breath, started to say something, and then stopped. She got up, walked to the door, and suddenly spun around to give Angie a hard hug. Amelia looked like she was saying good-bye to someone she might not see again. Then she left.

Mom and Dad looked at me. I shrugged my shoulders to say I was not going to say much in this meeting. This was their family, not mine. Angie looked like she was deciding between running away or throwing up. She decided to throw up. "Dad, Amelia was yelling at you for *me*. She's been telling you stuff that I need to tell you, that I've needed to tell you, like, forever. But I've been too scared. I'm still too scared." I waited to see if she was saying that as an ending comment, or if she had finally found her courage.

She turned to face her father, and he squared up his shoulders, waiting for the assault. "Dad," she said with a shaky voice, "Do you remember what it was like for you when your dad used to beat you, and scream at you?" The simple elegance of her question stunned me. Dad's eyes went wide. This was not what he expected, or wanted. He would have preferred an assault. "That's beside the point," he growled. "I was out of control, and I needed a strong hand to keep me from going over the edge. The point here is about your . . ." "ANSWER MY DAMN QUESTION!" Angie yelled. "For once, *just once*, can *you* answer *my* question?"

Dad deflated suddenly just like the first time I had met him. "That was different, Angie. My father did not love me . . ." We all waited for Martin to say ". . . like I love you" but those words never came. Angie looked crushed when Dad did not finish his sentence. I was sure that this was the end, that she could not possibly have any strength left in her. I was wrong. Like in some Rocky movie, she reached down and found the will to keep going. Her voice was shaking and hesitating even more, but she kept going. "What—was that—like, Dad? How—how did it feel to think that your own father really, you know, hated you, was so disgusted with you that he would hurt you like that?" Dad looked at me with a look of furious pleading. I shrugged again and then stuck it to him: "Martin, *do* you remember those feelings?" "This is bull," he answered. "This is not going to . . ." He paused again. Then he put his strong, chiseled face into his huge, powerful hands and came as close to crying as he probably had in twenty years.

No one knew what to say. We all sat in silence as Dad buried his face, as if in deep pain. Or shame. Without exposing his face, he spoke very quietly. "Angie, I—I do remember those feelings. I remember them the most after every time I snap out on you."

Angie's voice stopped shaking. "THEN HOW CAN YOU DO THIS TO . . ." Martin quietly cut Angie off. "The lousy truth is that when I snap out, I hate you for making me feel all of that crap again, for bringing it all back." Angie was sputtering mad. "Please hear me out, Angie. I don't know if I can ever say this to you again." He never moved his hands as he spoke. "When I snap out on you, it's like you become me, that worthless kid who deserved to be hurt so bad, and I become my insane father. That picture is so awful that I just put it out of my head and tell myself that you are just like me, that you need to be whipped to keep you from going crazy like I did." Finally he dropped his hands from his face, but couldn't lift his head. "Does that make any sense to you, Anje?" Calling her "Anje" must have meant something important to the two of them.

She shook her head. "No, it makes absolutely no sense to me," she said. Dad buried his face again. "But," Angie continued, "somehow, what you said," here she exhaled as if she had been holding her breath for an hour, "somehow, that makes me feel a whole lot better." After another minute, she found her gold. "I guess I don't feel so worthless anymore, like maybe this really is not all my fault." And then she made the greatest leap of all. "Dad, it's, like, OK. We can be OK, you know?" She looked as if she wanted to reach out and help Dad uncover his face. Her arm started to move towards him, but it stopped. I wondered if he had seen that.

Angie looked at me and shrugged. Her eyes said that she knew it would take time before she would be able to lovingly touch her father, just as it was hard for her to be touched by her own sister. But she also knew that the day would come when she would help him uncover his face, the soft, confused, and loving one that he kept hidden so well behind those hard, hard hands. And then, their hearts would touch as well.

∼

While most of us parents do hit and scream at our kids, most of us wish that we didn't. We seem to intuitively know that fear only teaches what not to do, instead of what to do.

That's a terrible waste of critical parenting time. It is ironic that we use these methods because we are afraid that our kids will become bad people who hurt others. We are driven by fear to create fear to fight fear. As Rocket J. Squirrel said to Bullwinkle, "That trick never works."

The immense power of parents to positively influence their children is diminished ten-fold when we diminish our children. That power is enhanced ten-fold when we find the grace and strength of character to be patient, calm, and tolerant, especially in the face of provocation. Only then do our children see us as truly powerful. They feel fear as the tool of the terrorist. They feel love as the weapon of the wise.

12

PRISONS WITHOUT BARS

Ronald's Story

Forced education of adolescents is so ingrained in our world that most of us have little sense of what an incredibly complex, difficult, and overwhelming challenge it can be for those kids who struggle with school. Understanding how teens learn, and why many can't, is only now beginning to be studied in depth. Most of us assume that if kids really wanted to do well in school, then, well, they just would. This simplistic view is a distorted memory of the "good old days" when kids weren't allowed all of these "excuses" not to learn, excuses such as learning disabilities and attention disorders. The contemporary facts are that those disabilities are real and are occurring in much higher numbers now for reasons that we don't understand. Learning-challenged kids have always existed, but only recently have we attempted to force them all to stay in school until the 12th grade. These students used to leave elementary school and go to work in the factories or fields, able to make their way into self-sufficient adulthood without a formal education.

The factories and fields of the 1950's have virtually vanished, and the young, hardworking laborer of yesteryear often becomes the young, hardworking gangster of today. For a learning-challenged kid, there are desperately few other options. Ironically, the gangster and the worker can share a high level of motivation to try to succeed, whether in a factory in the 50's or on the streets in the new millennium. The differences between these kids are not as great as many imagine, and the similarities can be very compelling. Perhaps the greatest similarity is the terrible, grinding, and demoralizing pain they both endured while trying to succeed in schools that couldn't begin to address their learning problems.

Today we can address many of those needs. But first we must understand the terrible pain of those learning-challenged kids for whom school is prison. A prison, some would say, worse than the kind with guards. At least that's what Ronald believed. And Ronald knew both kinds of prisons very well.

The group sat and stared as the huge kid and the bigger guard went nose to nose. As a skinny, young psychologist newly working in a prison for adolescents, this situation was a bit out of my skill area. I was locked in a room for a therapy meeting with a group of ten mostly black kids with one mouthy, racist, white guard there to keep order. At the moment, he wasn't doing that job very well. As the guard suddenly grabbed for his walkie-talkie, the big kid started swinging at him. The fight raged for a good 30 seconds that seemed like 30 minutes until the big kid finally knocked the guard down convincingly. He smashed the walkie-talkie, turned, and slowly started towards me. I was frozen with fear. A voice behind me quietly but firmly said, "Enough, Jamaal. It's done. Dude ain't hurt you." I was the dude in question. The big kid just kept coming, and the voice behind me morphed into a 16-year-old black teenager who stepped in front of this scared, white psychologist, shielding me from a big, angry, black kid who had been taking racist crap from a white guard for a long time.

"Out my way, Ronald," Jamaal said, panting, sweating, and bleeding from his fight. "This be *my* day. Been waitin' a long time for this. You know what I'm sayin'." He towered over Ronald, but seemed reluctant to push past him. "It's done, bro'," Ronald said, locking his eyes on the big kid's. "You backed your word. We're done here." They stared at each other without blinking, but Ronald's gaze was stronger. He had these bright, blazing eyes that spoke of confidence even in such a scary scene. Jamaal finally blinked, waved disgustedly at me and snickered, "Yeah, he ain't even worth it."

Suddenly a thundering wave of guards with clubs charged into the room and started to knock all of the kids down to the floor and handcuff them. I rushed up to the guard who was taking down Ronald to explain that he had saved me. With eyes wide with fury, the guard screamed, *"SHUT THE **** UP OR YOU'LL GET THE SAME!"* Ronald was lying on the floor in handcuffs, with a mouth bleeding badly from the "takedown." He looked like a farm animal about to be slaughtered. He gazed up at me with eyes that I will never forget.

About a month later, I was finally allowed to see Ronald. In the middle of thanking him for possibly saving my life, he interrupted me. "Wasn't about you," he said. "Was about Jamaal. If he'd hit you, he'd have killed you. Don't want no more brothers doing life at Graterford (a terrible adult prison)." But as he denied caring anything about me, he looked away.

That began a series of weekly meetings between Ronald and me that would last for five months, until his release from the juvenile prison. I grew to very much admire this young man who had highly developed ideas of morality and purpose despite having a record of numerous but minor run-ins with the police, all as a result of his gang membership. His parents seemed like decent people who, ". . . only hassle me over my bad grades and being in the gang. My dad, he gets most upset about the grades. He says that school is my only ticket out of where we live. He's a baker. He works real hard from, like, 4 in the morning to 7 or 8 at night. He had to go to work when he was 12 years old because his family was poor. He can't understand why I wouldn't try at school. But now, I see that he's right. This time I'm gonna do great."

Ronald seemed to like our talks, and he slowly opened up a bit. He even eventually admitted that he had rescued me from Jamaal because it "was the right thing to do," (although he then added that he was also motivated by cleanliness since "white boys splatter somethin' awful when Jamaal hits them.") Mostly, he spoke about his impending release, about what he would do when he got out. His plan was to get great grades at high school, and win a college scholarship to become a teacher. Then he would teach in the worst schools he could find where there were kids like him, to keep them out of prisons and gangs. He often spoke passionately about going back to "real" school (versus the prison school, which he said was a joke) to "get my life, and never, ever work the prisons, as a guard or an inmate." But the closer he got to his release, the more agitated he became, even surly at times, trying to pick verbal fights with me. He even got a formal warning from the staff that if he didn't shape up, he might get his stay in lock-up extended. Whenever I asked him what was up, he'd just wave me off and shut down.

In time I'd learn that he knew that he was leaving a very bad prison to go back to a worse one. Where the bars are not on your windows, but on your mind. A place where you can suffer terribly from beatings and scars that no one ever sees.

Two months after being released, Ronald appeared for his first mandated counseling session, after having been threatened with jail for skipping the four prior meetings. I hardly recognized him. Gone were his relaxed smile, his edgy humor, and his confident manner. In their place were an angry scowl, one-word answers, and the gangster hunch. Worst of all, those blazing, bright eyes had gone dim. He was a walking ball of anger.

After an hour of getting nowhere, I handed him a cartoon that one of his friends from prison had drawn and recently sent to me. The artist had been in the room on the day of that fight when I first met Ronald. The drawing showed me as this muscular, he-man figure intimidating Jamaal and protecting a scared, crying Ronald. Playing on the then-popular *TERMINATOR* movies, it was entitled *THE SHRINK-INATOR*. Ronald looked at it without laughing for a long time. Finally, he smiled a sad, tired smile, like he remembered something he could be proud of from about a hundred years ago. "OK, Ronald," I said, "What's going on?"

"Nothin'," he said, as he tossed the cartoon on the table, "absolutely nothin'. Probation, man. That's what's going on. Can't see my friends, can't hang out, can't do nothin'. *Jail* was better than this." He shook his head disgustedly and looked away, but he was upset by a lot more than restrictions. "How's school going?" I asked. Suddenly this tough kid's eyes slowly filled up, his breathing got heavy, and his voice became thick with pain. "It's not goin'," he said. "I . . . can't make it happen. My dad, he was, like, so proud when I got out of prison 'cause I had this paper that said I did great in that dumb-ass prison school. He was so happy, and I was, like, 'yeah, I get it now. I'm gonna go tear up real school and get into college and be a teacher and . . ." Ronald's voice went higher and higher until he couldn't finish his sentence.

"Ronald, I know that dream was really important to . . ." His cracking voice cut me off. *"You know what the math teacher said to me today? He said that I was an IDIOT, and that I ain't even trying or else I must be on drugs. Well, I ain't no idiot, I don't do no damn drugs, and I am trying, but . . .* it's no good. I try. I try as hard as I can, but my brain, man, my brain it, like, keeps changing channels on me. I sit there in class, you know, and I keep saying, *'Concentrate, Ronald. Concentrate, Ronald. F'NG CONCENTRATE, YOU F'NG LOSER!!!'* I bite my cheeks inside my mouth so hard that I bleed. I do that to try and keep focused, but nothing works for long."

He picked up the cartoon again. "Maybe you don't know," he said, "but this kid, James, he's back in [the prison]. He couldn't stay away from the gang. I didn't talk to him before he got sent back, but his mom says he thinks that the gang is the only way to get by, you know? The gang's got big plans . . . I hear things, you know? They're goin' big time, do some real money, take care of their own." "And are you re-enlisting?" I asked. He acted as if he hadn't heard me. He held the cartoon up to me and tried to flash that old, wonderful smile. *"Doc B: The SHRINK-INATOR!"* he bellowed. But his smile was as fleeting as his hopes. "James is right. Ain't nothin' else out there. My father, you know, as lousy as his job is, I couldn't even do that. There ain't no jobs. His bakery is probably goin' to close. They keep cutting his salary, and he's got to keep takin' it 'cause he's got nowhere else to go. *And I can't even do as bad as him? Because I can't do school?"*

He thought some more. "Do you know what it's like to be bad at school? It's like being disrespected on the street, but, like, *all the time—and you can never fight back.* You never win—you never get respect. For 6 hours a day, 5 days a week, from when you can remember until when you finally quit. I can't sleep lots of nights knowing I got to go to school tomorrow. Everybody looks at you like you're some fool, like you're stupid, like you're some crack-head loser who don't even care about himself or his family. And after a while, *that's what you become*, you know? You get two problems: one, you can't get your brain to do the work, and you feel like crap. And two, you can't even get yourself to try to do homework anymore 'cause all you can think is . . . *what's the point?* How will I ever be somebody, get a life, take care of my family?" His eyes filled again. "My little sister, you know, she's telling everybody how I'm gonna be a teacher and all. She calls me 'teach.' "

He turned angrily on me. "You're always telling us to be strong, to avoid the gangs, and do the right thing, like it's sooo easy. Tell the truth, man: If you was me, would you keep flunking at school, or would you join the gang so you could take care of your family, have some respect? Maybe you die quick there, like you say, but maybe that's better than dying real slow like my father?"

I let him sit and think for a while. Then I answered his question. "Well, you've seen first-hand what a success I could have been as a tough guy." He tried hard not to laugh, but the cartoon caught his eye again, and he finally grinned and nodded. "Yeah, if you was me, you'd be dead, all right." He paused and shook his head. "But, man, if *I* had been *you* . . ." He didn't finish his thought. "What if you still can be me," I asked, "Do you have it in you to take a shot, to try again?" He didn't answer. But he didn't say no.

After a lot of begging, Ronald finally agreed to be evaluated for learning problems. His testing came back saying that he had a severe memory learning disability and attention-deficit disorder. This meant that, first, it was impossible for him to pay attention to anything for more than five minutes, and, second, that whatever he did learn in that five minutes was terribly difficult for him to remember later. Yet the testing showed that *he was very bright.* As I read his report, I almost cried. School could not have been much more difficult or painful for him. I pictured this bright, courageous, young man dragging himself to school every day for ten years, only to be beaten down day after day, year after year. Too smart not to know where he was headed, and too disabled to do anything about it. And too nice for too many years to attract the attention of teachers by misbehaving. For if he had, they might have looked more closely at him and discovered that he was disabled, not dumb; undiagnosed, not unmotivated.

In our next meeting, I read the report line by line to Ronald, expecting to have to explain it word for word. But, once again, he amazed me. He mostly understood exactly what this complex document was saying. In fact, as we plowed through the paragraphs, he leaned closer and closer as if huge mysteries were unfolding before him. When we finished, he sat back, dazed and wide-eyed, thinking of what might have been had this report been written 10 years earlier. "Damn," was all he said. "Yes," I agreed, "Damn."

Ronald was a hero to me three times over: first, by standing up to Jamaal; second, by forcing himself to attend school under such terrible circumstances; and third, by enduring what was yet to come—the treatment of his disabilities.

The psychiatrist placed him on a series of medications to try to help him focus, and the cures seemed to be worse than the complaints. The first filled him with rage and sadness. The second exhausted him. There was almost no third because he was so angry and distrustful of the experts that he badly wanted to quit the whole process. Just *trying* was so scary for him. The thought of exposing himself, of becoming vulnerable to another round of crushing failure at school seemed too much to ask. "You are *serious*?" he growled. "You are actually asking me to try another pill? Do you not remember that the first pill made me nuts, like I was mad at the world? And that second one, oh, that one was great. Man, I was a zombie. I was so tired, my eyes wouldn't blink. Now I'm supposed to put more poison in my body, so maybe this time I just die? You tell me why I should go through anymore of this crap?"

"Because," I said. "I think that you're worth it. Do you?"

The third try was the magic. After five weeks, Ronald talked like a 16-year-old jigsaw puzzle that had finally found its lost pieces. "My brain, like, it *works* now," he reported. "I never knew how much it wasn't working until this past week. Man, I can *sit and listen and remember what a teacher says.*" He sat and savored that thought. "Is this what it was always like for all the other kids since kindergarten?" "Mostly," I answered. Ronald closed his eyes and shook his head. "Damn," he said, "Damn."

If life was fair I could report that Ronald made an immediate academic turnaround. But it's not, and I can't. Just trying to do school was still very frightening for him since the ravages of a decade of undiagnosed learning challenges had left him with a shattered sense of confidence that took years to heal to any degree. This is how learning problems create a second maddening set of motivation and behavior problems. And Ronald's decade of missed learning skills was so damaging that average classes were like grueling marathon events for him, even with medication and tutoring. Reading in particular is one of those tasks best learned at early ages, and terribly difficult to master in later years.

Yet, the unfairness of life can sometimes have an upside. With Ronald, those agonizing gang and schoolwork struggles became a hardening process for him, one in which he learned that he was far tougher than he ever knew, both on the street and in the classroom. When I told him that I admired his street toughness, he told me that he admired my school "toughness." He wanted to learn how to do in school what he could do so well on the street: be challenged, get knocked down, and then rise back up and go toe-to-toe until he eventually prevailed.

And prevail he did. Ronald fought and fought until he eventually earned his high school diploma in "a real school," not in the "dumb-ass prison school." He displayed that piece of paper with a fierce pride, the way he once flew the colors of his gang. Perhaps most impressive of all, he managed to finesse himself out of that gang, a task that requires an incredible amount of skill and courage. Picture telling Don Corleone (of "The Godfather") that you're sick of being in his mob, and you get the idea—except that Ronald and his family also had to then try to live on the same block as the gangsters. These are truly elaborate skills of negotiation that an ambassador to the United Nations might envy.

His challenges had been like an ocean tide that had relentlessly eroded Ronald's sense of worth and competence, inch by inch, day by day, for more than ten years. But, like a tide, that current finally reversed and began to restore this hero. Now every week he seemed to blossom more and more into a confident, optimistic, and peaceful young man. Even his clothes and language were changing, becoming more sedate, as if he had so much less to prove. *He was smiling.*

In his last note to me, he said that he was joining the military where he hoped to pull the money together to take a shot at college—"at a real teachers' college."

When I wonder where Ronald is, and I worry if he ever found his dream, I remember all of his incredible heroics in the face of those overwhelming odds. And then I think about tides. I smile and nod my head. And I say, "Damn."

Ronald's life struggle was more dramatic than that of most kids with learning challenges, but the agony of a classroom is the same for all such children. His path to prison shows just how devastating these undiagnosed problems can be. The fact is that most kids in juvenile prisons have severe learning challenges that go undetected for too many years until the damage is just too great.

Think for a moment: Imagine yourself being forced to go to some place where controlling teachers put demands upon you that you cannot possibly handle, say, translating Chinese. Imagine that all of the other people in your class seem to be able to understand Chinese, and get lots of smiles and awards from the teachers, while you get lots of sighing and eye rolling. Imagine that the other people, your peers, the ones you hang out with and depend upon for friendship and support, start to laugh and make fun of you, whispering and calling you names. Finally, imagine that this is your lot for 5 days a week, 42 weeks a year, for essentially forever, for as far into the future as you can reasonably see.

How would you be? Who would you be? Would you be righteous enough not to join a street gang?

Please think long and hard about this. And if you meet a Ronald, or a Rona, in a classroom, or in a courtroom, try to have some sense of his pain, of her struggle. Then please remember how you would like to have been treated when Chinese was so painful for you.

And please remember Ronald. Knowing that his story helped create some understanding for hurt kids in this hard world would probably make him close his eyes, smile, and say, "Damn."

13

LIKE A SILENT SCREAM

Nick's Story

Homosexuality is a chasm, a non-negotiable canyon that profoundly separates people from one another. It is an explosive issue that pits the religious against the scientific, the conservative against the liberal, with no apparent middle ground, no livable compromise. The distance between "anathema" and "orientation" seems overwhelming to those listening to the debate.

Nick was overwhelmed by the debate, as well—not by the debate going on outside of him, but by the one inside. He was a breathing debate on sexuality, a walking conflict of irreconcilable values and beliefs. In the time that I knew him, his daily life was often a battleground upon which these two views would fight it out to the bitter end, with only one victor.

In war, it is the innocent bystanders who are the most hurt, and the least responsible. Nick was the innocent bystander who got caught up in a war not of his choosing. He became my hero in patiently suffering through his war with grace, with humor, and with wisdom, all of which he allowed me to share with you in the hope that it might help people who live near canyons think more of building bridges, and less of burning them.

∼

The 15-year-old boy furrowed his brow and pondered my question about something in his life that he would change if he could. Suddenly his face brightened into a beaming smile. "I know one thing. It's my little brother. He's 35—in dog years; that's 5 in people years. He thinks he's a dog. *I'm not kidding.* He runs around the house on all fours, wears a leash and barks all the time, especially if my friends are over. My mom, she lets him eat under the table whenever my dad's not home. My dad makes him sit up at the table like a good puppy." Watching me laugh made this boy smile even more. "Seriously," he added, "I guess I should be glad that he doesn't pee on my leg, or, you know," here he deepened his voice and wagged his head for effect, *"whatever."*

Nick loved making people laugh. What he really loved was helping people feel better, and he was great at doing both. His gifts were a distraction in therapy. He was so funny and so caring that he had a hard time staying focused on himself. He did talk about getting some good-natured teasing at school for the professional modeling he had done, and how the guys always bug him about getting them hooked up with the girl models. Seeing his beautiful blond hair, deep blue eyes, and huge, warm and engaging smile that lit up the room, a line from "The Mary Tyler Moore Show" popped into my head. When Ted Baxter met Mary's gorgeous boyfriend, Ted's wide-eyed, envious greeting was, *"Man, you must have to beat them off with a stick."* When I thoughtlessly shared that scene with Nick, his face kept smiling but his eyes did not. "Oops," I thought. "Sorry," I said, "I have no idea about your sexual orientation or popularity, and neither is any of my business. That was a glimpse of my own nerdy, neglected adolescence. You just met my inner Ted Baxter. I think he's jealous of your looks."

Nick liked my self-disclosure but his mood had suddenly shifted. He tried to be free and funny again, but because of my stupidity, he had gone somewhere else, to a place of uncertainty and fear. We had only been chatting for 15 minutes, and already the brutal politics of sexual orientation had raised its ugly head. We avoided talking about the elephant that was now in the middle of the room for the rest of the session, talking instead about his conflicts with his dad, which was the reason he was sent to see me.

As we concluded, I had to point out the elephant. "Look, Nick," I started, "It's crazy that I have to say what I'm about to say, but it's the way things are. You might need to know that I view sexual orientation as just that, as an orientation, not a choice. I do not see any true sexual orientation as good or bad, right or wrong, normal or abnormal—just whatever it is, it is. OK?"

Nick studied my face carefully before he spoke. "And what if it's *not* OK—*for me*?" he asked. His reckless, careful question bewildered me. He could mean that on so many levels: as inquiry, statement, worry, insight . . . He made me think of French resistance fighters in Nazi-occupied France, terrified to be identified, yet longing to be known for who they were, and for what they believed, principles that could cost them their lives; where every conversation becomes delicate and dangerous, where a turn of a word can completely rewrite someone's future, and perhaps even threaten their existence.

"What do you need to know?" I asked. Nick studied my face some more, and then smiled and stuck out his hand. "I'll call if I decide to come back," he said, "and thanks."

Eight months later, Nick came in for the second time. He opened as he had the last time we met, with that great smile and a funny story. He repeated my question to him. "What's new? Um—I spent the summer on a cross-country trip with my grandfather," he offered. I bit. "Wow," I said, "that sounds interesting." "Well," he said, 'Easy Rider' it wasn't. Actually, it was pretty much the trip from hell. We traveled in his camper-van that has Yosemite Sam [the Warner Brothers cartoon character] mud flaps, the naked girl outline decal, and a bumper sticker that says, 'BACK OFF OR I'LL FLUSH.' He's been a little different since my grandmom died."

This time I just smiled and sat quietly until he began. "I'm not who you think—I think—you know? I'm not who most people think I am. First, I'm Catholic—I mean I'm *really* Catholic. I go to church every week, and I was even going to be a priest for a while. I still consider that at times. I'm, like, the only 16-year-old at Mass. All my friends have quit going. My family doesn't even go now, but I still do. It's like a secret of mine. It's weird, because I don't believe everything that the church says, but it's still real important to me. Kids think I'm this crazy party animal, you know, hooking up with models and stuff, but I'm not like that. I'm actually pretty conservative, at least that's what my social studies teacher says." He shot a look at me. "I'm not what a lot of people think."

He got up and started to take books off my shelves and peruse them as he spoke, seeming to actually read chapter titles and headings as he conversed. He was the first client I ever saw do that. "But all of that might change shortly." He turned and suddenly sat back down in front of me, like someone who finally decided to do a cliff dive. "One of the gay kids at school says that he's going to 'out' me if I don't do it myself."

There it was. He just laid it out there and stared at me. "Well," he asked, "no reactions?" "About a hundred," I answered, "but what are yours?" He smiled that great smile, but this time with very sad, tired eyes. "I had to leave my last school, in 9th grade, because rumors started about me then, that I, like, raped someone. I got threatened a lot and beaten up once—pretty bad, actually. It's weird. That school was a pretty tough school with a few gangs, but I did OK until the gay rumors started flying. The cops were involved and everything."

Nick exhaled sharply. "You want to hear something funny? Of all the people involved in that mess—you know, the principal, the counselors, the police chief, the mediators—they brought in these, like, aging hippies from a place called 'The Peace Center' to talk to everyone—of all those people, it was a *cop* who made the most sense. He listened to everybody talk, and then before he left, he took me aside and said, 'Look, kid, I don't give a rat's ass if you're gay or bi [bisexual] or whatever, but there are kids in this school who might kill you just because they think you are. Get the hell out. But I never said that, OK?'"

Nick stopped again to search for my reaction, and then just kept plunging on. "I shouldn't have to say this, but, like you said before, it's the way things are: No, I didn't 'rape' anyone, and I never would. I've never had sex, and I don't want to until I'm really in love—maybe married. I believe that sex should be about love and commitment. Being gay does NOT mean that you sleep around, *rii-*

igghht?!" he said probingly. When I nodded, he sat back, a little relieved. "Well, that's not what the world thinks. To the world, gay equals sex-crazed-maniac, someone who preys on little kids and tries to *convert* them." His eyes went wide with amazement. "*Convert* them? *Convert* them? This ain't like Jews for Jesus. Being gay isn't a *choice*. Who would *choose* to be gay, at least in America? How stupid can people be? The other night on TV this guy was yelling about the 'immoral' people who 'choose the gay lifestyle'? *What the hell is that? Do people really think that being gay is like moving to California, that you just like it better there or something? Did blacks move to Mississippi in the 1930s and CHOOSE to be black because it was, like, so cool?*"

Nick hated being angry, so he took breaths to calm down. Then he looked ashamed. "You know, I think I get so mad at that right-wing, whacko stuff because . . . because part of me *believes* that, or at least did believe that—I don't know." He went back to my book-shelves, but just talked to the texts. "After I saw you last, I went to see this shrink who says he can change gays into straights. There are a lot of them [conversion therapists], or at least they have a big website." He held a book without opening it. "Do you think that's possible?" he asked. "Do you?" I deflected. "*Not anymore!*" he retorted immediately. "I went for six months. The guy was religious. He said that he and God would cure me. He was real shocked when he found out that I'm real religious, too, probably more than he is. I think that upset him."

He sat back down holding the unopened book. "It wasn't a waste, though. It helped me sort out stuff. Like knowing that I can be a moral person *and* be gay. Like knowing that I can't try to be what others want me to be because I make them uncomfortable—a lot of stuff. That shrink, he didn't like me, and he couldn't 'fix' me, but he taught me a lot without knowing it. He actually did 'fix' me. He helped me see that I am gay, that it's not a disease, and it's not a choice—it is what it is."

Nick's smile romped across his face again. "I should write him a note telling him what a *wonderful* service he's providing for the gay community. Because if he stopped doing the work he does, there'd probably be a lot less gay people in the world." This time I had to laugh. "And now," he laughed back with his eyes, "we return to my *new* shrink, who, when asked what I should do about getting 'outted' at school, will say, '*Well, Nicholas, what do YOU think you should do?*' You know, Dr. Bradley," he wagged, "at least the other shrink gave me lots of advice. *PERHAPS* you should consider actually *TALKING* to your patients?"

My laughter was cut short when I saw the decades-old book that he was holding. It was *The Manufacture of Madness* by Thomas Szasz (Harper & Row, 1970). It contains an extensive historical review of the terrible and brutal persecutions of homosexuals, along with a powerful and prophetic section chastising the psychiatric community for (at that time) almost unanimously declaring homosexuality to be a treatable disease. A disease, as Szasz argued, defined not by a dysfunction, but by a *difference*, something we humans do not tolerate very well.

In the next few sessions, as Nick tackled other issues related to his sexual crisis, another elephant slowly crept into the room, until we could no longer ignore it. Mom, he believed, almost certainly knew that he was gay. She had done everything but say it, nervously but quietly allowing Nick his own space and time to decide who he was. He felt confident in her love, assured that, no matter what, their relationship would survive. She, he predicted, would prefer that he were heterosexual, given that it's a much easier life. But, Nick added, she would prefer lots of things for him that she could accept would never be. Dad was the elephant. When I suggested that there was no way to get him out of the room without first getting him in, Nick agreed.

For some reason, Nicholas decided to tell Dad on the night before our session that he was "pretty sure" he was gay. Dad was still smoldering from the horrific explosion that followed when the family walked in. In true form, Nick opened up the meeting. But there was no smile this time.

"Dr. Bradley," he commanded, "please tell my father the medical view of homosexuality. My father says that doctors know that it's a perversion. And *please* don't answer my question with a question."

"Well," I started, "I can't speak for all doctors, but I can tell you that both the American Psychiatric Association and the American Psychological Association have said that it's not a disease, and that . . ." Dad went for my throat. "Right," he said, with as much sarcasm as he could muster, "and neither is having sex with your daughter, your friend's wife, or little kids, right? Nothing's wrong if it's what you feel like doing, right? 'Cause there is no more right or wrong anymore, according to people like you." He angrily sat forward and jabbed his finger at me like a knife. "*It's doctors like you who made my son . . .*" "STOP IT!" Nick yelled, jumping to his feet, "OH, SURE. DOCTORS CAN MAKE KIDS GAY, RIGHT? MAYBE THAT'S BECAUSE THEY'RE ALL A BUNCH OF FAGS, RIGHT? ISN'T THAT WHAT YOU SAID? ISN'T THAT WHAT YOU ALWAYS SAY ABOUT ANYONE YOU DON'T LIKE?"

I watched Nick closely now. He was always so controlled, so good at handling people, that I wondered if he would revert back to his verbal skills to avoid this conflict, or stay real. I could almost hear him asking himself the same question. He decided to do both.

"Dad," he said softly and pleadingly, "do you know or care at all about what I've been through, what I'm going through? Have you ever asked yourself what my life has been like? Right now, do you know what's happening? Remember when I got beat up at my old school? Do you know why *that* happened? Because of the, quote, *normal* kids who want to maybe kill me because I'm different. Even the cops pretty much told me to get out, that there was no way to protect me from the crazies—you know, those kids who are not per-verts like *me*. Dad, it's not like standing up to a bully. When you're a 'fag' they're allowed to gang up on you, and they still look cool.

"Well, all that might happen again, and do you want to know why? Because *another* crazy kid, one who happens to be gay, is threatening to tell everyone at my *new* school that I'm gay. I'm, like, surrounded by insane people, who are so different sexually, but have something even bigger in common: *They're jerks and they can ruin my life.* And I haven't even touched on how weird everyone else in the world is to you, if they think that you're gay."

Nick exhaled a long, loud breath, and sat back down. "And since I'm on this confessing roll, here's the rest." He looked up timidly at his father. Dad was frozen in his seat. "Do you have any idea what it's like to hear you tell 'fag' jokes? And please don't tell me that you never suspected that I was gay. I've tried to tell you a thousand times, but you never wanted to hear that. Remember when I carried a handbag all last summer? *I don't even like to carry one, but I was, like, 'Hello? Are you getting this, Dad? Don't you want to ask me some-thing?'*" Dad started to stir but I held up my hand to ask him to let his son finish. "Look," Nick said, "I know—I know. I really didn't *want* you to ask, but *I did at the same time.* I might have even denied it—I probably *would* have denied it, but, like, I wanted to know that you . . ." His voice became barely audible. ". . . that you . . . cared. I *needed* to know—I *need* to know. Because, I feel like I can handle the crazies, you know, whatever their orientation, if . . . if I've got my family in my corner."

He turned towards his mother. "Somehow, I just know, Mom, that you're there no matter what. But, Dad, when I see that look in your eyes, you know, of disgust or whatever, it makes me want to scream. It's like I'm always screaming, just . . . silently. So no one ever hears."

Mom's soft weeping was the only noise in that room for the longest time. Finally, Dad tried to say something, but his voice had disappeared with his rage. He choked on a word or two, and then stood up and walked to his son. Nick stared at the floor, his perfect face now beet-red and puffy. Dad cleared his throat, but finding no words, reached out his weathered hand and tenderly held his son's face. Nick's eyes, still aimed at the floor, filled and overflowed as he finally placed his own hand over his father's. For a moment, they said ten-thousand things that no one could hear. Then Dad slowly turned and walked out, overwhelmed by his emotions. But he left closer to his son than either could have ever imagined.

∾

Nick was lucky in spite of his enormous challenge. He finally found his lost father and was able to draw on Dad's formidable strength to survive his eventual "outing" at school. The father's gift to his son was priceless.

Dad was luckier in spite of his enormous rage. He finally found his lost son along with the best parts of himself, the loving, caring parts that enabled his eventual reconnection with his family, and with himself. The son's gift to his father was even greater.

Their continuing journey back to each other was not a quick or easy one, and they had some big bumps along the way, but they shared a characteristic much more significant than their sexual orientation—courage.

In that book that Nick held, the brave author wrote:

Words have lives of their own. However much sociologists insist that the word "deviant" does not diminish the worth of the person or group so characterized, the implication of inferiority adheres to the word . . . They describe homosexuals as deviants, but never Olympic champions or Nobel Prize winners . . . For this reason I repudiate the tacit assumption that because such persons differ, or are alleged to differ, from the majority, they are ipso facto sick, bad, stupid, or wrong, whereas the majority are healthy, good, wise, or right . . . Majorities usually characterize persons or groups as "deviant" in order to set them apart as inferior beings and to justify their social control, oppression, persecution, or even complete destruction.

Long ago, Dr. Szasz challenged us canyon-edge dwellers to find the courage to rise above our secret and deadly hatred of all things different, and to embrace the humanity, sometimes hidden, in all people, be they the persecutors or the persecuted. For when we build bridges, we get to walk away from ourselves, look back, and see things we could never see from only our side of the canyon. We can see ourselves as others do. Then, and only then, can we understand . . . and truly love.

14

A FATHER IN THE EYES OF THE SON

Mark's Story

Most fathers and sons go through a painful cycle where, almost overnight, Dad's major league throwing arm suddenly becomes pee-wee league, and his eight-foot height shrinks to four.

And where, almost overnight, jovial, easy-going fathers suddenly become drill sergeants, barking insults and orders at amazed and hurt "recruits," large, little boys who suddenly awaken in boot camp, not remembering having ever been drafted, wondering what the heck happened to their loving dads.

In the proper dose, this cycle is a very normal and very important "breaking-away" chapter in the process of growing up, part of nature's plan to help children to separate and become adults. But sometimes that cycle spins too fast and too hard, taking on an energy of its own which can blow apart a close family and even threaten the bonds of love that connect children with their parents, those invisible safety lines that make all the difference.

Mark and his father were caught in a breaking-away cycle that whirled into a tornado that threatened to break their loving grasp on each other. But there are some things that even tornados cannot destroy.

$\sim$

Dad looked like a good man, with a calm, open, but very strong face. I guessed that his were waters that ran slowly and deeply. He apologized for his greasy hands and clothing, the products, he said, of his work as a mechanic. He had the smell of old motor oil about him, a grounded, honest scent that I had long forgotten, and another thing for which he apologized. "I just came from the shop," he explained, "they make us work into the evenings now. That's the only time lots of people have to get their cars fixed these days." He was not complaining or asking for sympathy, just stating a fact of his life. I asked him to please not worry, that I actually liked that smell, and that I missed my teenage days of messing with motors. Dad looked sad. "My son, he says he hates that smell, and he hates working on cars. I do a little side work at my home, but Mark won't come near the garage. He's a little ashamed, I think, of what I do for a living. I've managed to keep him in a good prep school, but most of the other kids come from professional families, and I think that I sort of embarrass him. He goes to other kids' houses and he tells me that most times they're mini-mansions. He never invites kids back to our home. It's nice and all but it's no mini-mansion. But those are tough things when you're 14, you know?"

Dad's eyes were clear and direct, fully aware of the "professional" distinctions between him and the other parents at school, but also knowing who he was and being comfortable with that. "But Mark's tougher than most, which is why I'm here. He was recently caught smoking marijuana on his school trip, and his teachers are worried that he just seems angry all the time.

"He seems nothing but angry to me, too, now. I worry that I'm doing everything wrong with him, making him mad, no matter what I say. I think maybe I'm too hard on him." Dad rubbed pointlessly at some stains on his hands. "It's been rough since his mom died 4 years ago. She died just after giving birth to Katelynn, my daughter." He looked straight into my eyes. "My wife, she was our anchor, you know?" He shook his head in loving admiration. "She . . . she always seemed to know just what to do, what to say to make things OK. I never realized how good she was at *so many things* until . . ." He sighed, ran his hand through his uncombed hair, and sat back, giving up on his indelible stains. For a moment, his eyes glistened with his unspoken words of missing her so terribly much, tears that he made no attempt to hide.

"My wife's mom has been great, you know, filling in. She's there most of the time. She and Mark used to be very close, but even she says that he's changed. We're real worried that this all means that he's into drugs. I guess the best way to describe this is to say that I feel like . . . *like I've lost him.*"

Dad's eyes began to glisten again. "We used to hug every night before bedtime. Even after he was too old to tuck in, we'd still hug real hard. We used to all hug together with Emily, my wife, before she died, and me and Mark kept doing it even after she was gone, except we'd hug harder then—like we were trying to feel her still there, you know? Mark never minded how I smelled then, and I smelled like oil lots of times. But sometime last year, he . . . he said he was sort of allergic to that smell, and so we stopped hugging. I really miss that, you know? Do you think that's part of why I get so tough with him now?"

"I don't know," I shrugged, "but next week I'll chat with Mark and then we can all talk together. Maybe you guys could ask each other those questions." Dad shook his head. "Maybe, but I don't think so. I'm useless to Mark. I don't think he thinks I've got anything worthwhile to say."

The following week, an angry, sullen Mark slunk into my office and sat down with a disgusted sigh. "Let's just get this bullshit over with so I can get back out with my friends, OK?" he sneered. "OK," I said, "I'll do my best, but . . ." "Yeah," he interrupted, "you do your best." I tried again. "What I was trying to say was that . . ." He interrupted again with a smirk. "*I* don't give a shit what *you* were trying to say."

I sat back and watched him a moment. He was having fun. "Wow . . ." I said. "Wow, *what?*" he angrily interrupted for a third time. "Wow," I clarified, "as in, 'wow, you're really good at this.'" "Good at *what?*" he demanded, "What the hell are you talking about?" "Mark," I said, "you're really good at blowing up counseling sessions." He looked sideways at me. "No," I continued, "I'm not being sarcastic. I really mean that. Your dad told me about the two shrinks you went to before who said that they couldn't help. Now I think I know what happened. Shrinks are supposed to be great at getting people to talk, and you just, what, get them so pissed off that they all quit?" He smirked. "Well, that's what I mean. At 14, you are able to control highly educated experts who are supposed to be smarter than you. That's pretty impressive."

He smiled like a Mafia assassin hearing his criminal record read aloud in court. "Can I ask you a question?" I said. "You don't have to answer it if you don't want to, but I was curious about something." "Sure," he sneered, but with less venom, "you can ask." "OK," I answered, "here it is. How do you *feel* when you get the adults all pissed off and upset?" He smiled like the Cheshire cat. "I don't know," he mused, "like . . . satisfied, I guess." "Like they deserve it?" I asked. "Yeah, yeah—like they *deserve* it," he nodded. "OK," I said, "now can I ask you another . . ." *"Just ask your questions,"* he interrupted again, *"you don't need to keep asking my permission."* "Good—thanks," I said.

"So then, adults *deserve* to be hurt?" He nodded slowly, perhaps sensing a trap of insight, but still wanting to see where this was going. "OK," I said, "now this next question is a little tricky, so do I still have your . . ." "Just *ask* for God's sake," he huffed.

"Mark," I asked slowly, "what have *your* adults—done to you—to deserve to be hurt like that?"

His eyes flew open. The last thing he expected was to feel something. "Well," he said, "how the hell would you feel if your parents dumped you, you know, like, one becomes a prick after the other one dies having a baby for god's sake—*who does that? Nobody dies having a baby. What . . ."*

He froze and stared at me like he was suddenly panicked that he might not survive the rush of thoughts and emotions that he had kept dammed up. He slowly stood as if to keep his head above water, and then realized that he was standing up and didn't know why. "I'm . . . leaving," he said, perhaps as a way to explain being on his feet. But he spoke without his sneer. "I hope you come back," I said. "And thanks for letting me ask you those questions, Mark. That was a very tough thing for you to do. That took guts."

He did come back the next week, but only on the condition that his father would be in the room with him. Dad looked exhausted, having worked well into the evening in a sweltering shop. As they sat down, I noticed Mark's shirt, which read, *"It's really funny how you think that I'm listening."* Pointing to it, I laughed loudly. Mark gave an easy smile, as if saying, *"Thanks for not taking yourself too seriously,"* but an embarrassed father tried to apologize. "I told him not to wear that shirt, that it was insulting, but he wouldn't come without it. He's like this all the time, just aggravating and insulting for no reason. He's not part of our family anymore. He does very few chores, his grades are dropping and he . . . he's, like, just *not there* anymore."

"Why would I *want* to be there?" Mark asked incredulously. The sneer was back. "All you ever do is tell me what a screw-up I am. I can't do *anything* right. Dr. Bradley," he said turning to me, "did you know that there is actually a *correct way* to put lids on trash cans, and that I'm too stupid to know it? You see, it's, like, *REALLY* complex. There are these scientifically engineered indentations that . . ."

"STOP IT!" Dad yelled. "I was only trying to keep the lids from blowing away if it storms. Why do you have to be so *sarcastic* all the time?" Mark was ready with a killer sneer and a voice that mocked and mimicked his father's: *"Why do you have to be so STUPID all the time?"*

Dad looked up at the ceiling as if praying for the strength not to strangle his child. "What are you feeling?" I asked Dad. "I FEEL LIKE I'M GOING TO KILL HIM!" he answered. "Because?" I asked. *"Because he makes me so mad!"* "Because?" I asked again. Dad searched my eyes looking for his answers. As his anger slowly drained from his face, he retraced his emotional steps back through all of those screens we use to conceal the sources of our rage; the secrets that we carefully cloak with anger to reveal ourselves the least to the people we love the most.

"Because?" he searched, "because . . . because . . ." Mark couldn't tolerate the tension of intimacy. He had to blow it up. "Because," he interrupted Dad with a sneer, "you're too *stupid* to even know what you think—which is that I'm a worthless piece of crap!"

Dad turned to Mark, and half reached out to him, finally seeing Mark's rage for what it was—a shield, just like his own. He paused, trying to hold onto his new realizations which were slipping through his grease-stained hands faster than he could tag them.

"I . . . think . . . I'm not sure . . . but, Mark, it's something like, well, first, I'm *scared*. I'm real scared of you not being OK." Mark tried to angrily interrupt again, but Dad finally had his number. "Please, son, *please*—can you give me just two minutes to say what I feel?" The guerilla fighter part of Mark quit the field of battle. He sat back defeated.

"Son, I worry like crazy about what will happen to you when I'm not around. I worry that you will be sad and scared because you can't do things like fix your car, or change an electrical outlet, or get a job that you actually like, or . . ." Dad's voice became small and reverent, ". . . or find a good wife, a wonderful woman like your mom who will love you forever. I stay awake at nights worrying about those things, and a million more. Then I get up in the morning and I start to pick you apart, you know, telling you all the things that I need you to do better so I won't worry about you—or for you."

He paused and waited for Mark's counterattack. There was none, so he continued. "You know, I keep wondering about how things changed between us, and losing Mom was a big part of it, at least for me. I just now realized another reason that I pick you apart: I'm trying to do as good a job as your mother would have. I feel like I can't live up to her standards. That's funny, isn't it? I pick on you because I think I'm not good enough. That's another thing, you know. I think that you're, well, ashamed of me, like I'm not someone you can look up to anymore."

Mark looked sick to his stomach. He stared at the floor, and then said, "Do you really want the truth about that?" Dad nodded yes and braced himself. Mark's eyes looked like he was climbing aboard some crazy theme park ride with no idea of where it might take him. He looked at me as if for guidance, but this ride had to be his choice.

"Well, OK," Mark said, "If you really want the truth, I am ashamed, a little, of where we live and how we live . . . I guess I am embarrassed that you're just a loser mechanic." He looked up to plead his case. "You've got to understand—all the kids at school, their fathers weren't rich when they were young just like you weren't, but they became, like, lawyers and bond traders and executives. That's what I want to do. They worked their way up so their kids could have everything they want—nice cars and summer houses at the beach and trips to Europe and stuff. Dad, you should see their houses, they're . . ." Mark's voice trailed off awkwardly, sinking like the spirits of his father. Mark was embarrassed at hearing his own cruelty and smallness. Dad was crushed.

"I'm . . . sorry, son," he said, pushing hard at the grease that would forever stain his hands. "I, well . . . I just do the best I can, you know? It's hard . . ." As I watched those two sitting there, 12 inches and 12 miles apart, I imagined or felt the presence of another in that room, someone yelling at me to say something smart. It was someone who would have found a way to connect her husband and her son, if only she could be heard. But Mark got up and stormed out, muttering, *I knew it, I knew that this was a stupid idea . . .*"

As Dad got up to leave, I instinctively reached out to hold his arm for a moment, just as one father to another. "It's OK," he said. "Maybe Mark's right. Maybe I should have done better. Maybe I did let everybody down. I . . . I don't know anymore." And then he left.

After seeing himself as a "loser" in the eyes of his son, the father was now losing himself.

The following week, as I prepped for their next session, I was haunted by my memory of Dad's sad eyes as he left my office. Like a novice therapist, I planned a series of strategies to try to repair the damage. And, like a novice therapist, I was about to be once again reminded of how little impact shrinks really have in the course of a life, and how we therapists are at our best when we do the least. Mark walked in solo to re-teach me these things. He looked strangely older.

"I asked my dad not to come in right away with me tonight. I need to talk alone for a bit." He rubbed his hands together just like his dad often did. Mark's grease stains were invisible to me, but he saw them clearly. "I'm, like, a little bastard, you know? I'm, like, so critical of my father all of a sudden. Everything about him makes me nuts. I go off whenever he criticizes me, but I'm putting him down, like, 24/7. His clothes, his music, his job, his dumb little house that he's so proud of . . ." Mark sighed, trying to release some of his disapproval of Dad. Then he got to the worst of it, the worst part for him.

"I don't have kids to my house for another reason. I am embarrassed of the house and the garage [where his dad works on cars] but I'm more embarrassed by the yard. You see, my mom, she was this, like, crazy gardener lady." Mark smiled softly. "She loved planting things and weeding and all that. The yard was so nice that people would walk by just to see it—*total strangers* would do that. Anyway, after she died, the yard went to hell. It's all mud and weeds now, except for one corner. My dad, he . . . he has this, like, I don't know, little *shrine* area where he keeps one of each of the flowers and plants that she loved. That's all he has the time to do."

Mark paused and then stunned me by repeating his father's words almost exactly. "She always seemed to know just what to do to make things OK. I never realized how good she was at stuff until . . ." Mark's voice faltered here as well, but then he courageously pushed on to show the scar that he shared with his father, ". . . until she was gone. That's when you see the hole that people leave—when they're gone, you know. Kind of like our yard. When they're there, you just take them for granted.

"I was sitting out there thinking the other night, and it hit me, that maybe I'm, like, hating my dad because he can't fill in the hole that she left, you know? He can only remember her with his silly shrine. The yard and that hole, they're just way too big. Nobody can fix that up." Mark's eyes glistened just as his father's had. "Then, when I went back inside, something big happened—well, not big like important, but . . ."

He sat forward, a suddenly very earnest and thoughtful young man. "My dad worked crazy late. He didn't get home until, like, 10:30, so he didn't get to see my baby sister before she went to bed. He always goes in first thing to see her every night when he gets home late, even if she's asleep. I never thought about that before. Anyway, he didn't see me, but I saw him walk in all tired and hungry and crummy and all, and he went right up to her bedroom and kneeled down and talked to her real soft, so she wouldn't wake up. This time I snuck up to the door to try to hear what it is that he says to her every night."

Mark's eyes finally overflowed with tears of admiration for his "loser" father. He spoke now with a cracking voice. "My dad, he tells her how much he loves her, and how proud he is of her, and how he'll always be there for her, no matter what. Then he says that . . . that mommy loves her too, even though she's in heaven now, but that mommy is now an angel who lives inside of her heart, and that she's there to listen whenever Katelynn needs her."

Mark paused to control himself. "Can you believe that?" he said, shaking his head. "And *I* call *him* a 'loser mechanic,' right?" After a few moments, I asked Mark if he had told his father any of this. He said no, that he was too ashamed of himself. I asked if we could bring Dad in. Again, Mark shook his head no. "I don't think he'll ever want to talk to me again after what I said to him—*I* wouldn't want to talk to me." "Perhaps," I said, "but you're not a dad. Trust me on this one—let's bring him in."

Dad sat 12 inches from his son, just as he had before being wounded by him. He looked at Mark, then at me, and then back at Mark quizzically. "Am I supposed to talk?" he asked. Mark sat silent for a long time. "Well," I finally said, "I had thought that . . ." Mark interrupted me for the final time.

"Dad, I've got a million things to say to you and I don't know where to begin. The first is that I'm sorry that I act like such a little sh . . . , um, like such a spoiled brat. The second is that when I said that awful stuff to you, I never finished thinking that stuff through."

Mark turned to face his father, but his shame would only let him hold his dad's eyes about half the time. "You know those kids I'm so jealous of? Well, most of them come from busted families. Those parents didn't lose someone like you did, they just dumped somebody because they got mad or cheated or whatever. And, guess what? It's almost always the dads who do the cheating and dumping. You loved mom like crazy. You never quit even when things were really hard. Mom told me about those days when you guys had, like, no money. And those houses I want? Well, a lot of the time the moms are, like, screaming at us for messing up their perfect rooms, like their freakin' white carpets are more important to them than their kids are, you know? You, like, *you give it all away*, you know? You're all about your family."

Mark stopped to take a deep breath to compose himself again. Dad sat stone still. "I always call you stupid," Mark said. "*I'm* the stupid one. I never realized which stuff is important. It's not about the cars and houses and money and all. It's about, like, coming home all tired and crummy and still loving and worrying about your family, even about punks like me who put you down. You're not a loser, Dad—you're the biggest winner I know." Mark's voice got so tight that he could only squeak out his next words. *"I hope I can be, like, half as successful as you one day."*

After a minute, Mark finally lifted his eyes to his dad's and said, "That's all I have to say, I think. There are a million other things but I can't think of any right now. I think my brain is fried." Dad looked at me. "Are hugs allowed?" he asked. "I don't know," I answered. "Hey Mark," I asked, "Are hugs allowed?"

The father and the son hugged and cried, so hard and so long that the shrink finally got up and quietly left the office. He had to make room for the mom.

~

Therapy is sometimes a process of simply clearing away the debris that clutters the bridge between people who love each other, removing the rubbish of anger, fear, and resentment that accrues from the stress of life. Nowhere is this more true than in dealing with fathers and sons who get trapped in the common and vicious cycling of mutual criticism, judgment, and resentment, a fiery circle that creates so much smoke that the light of love begins to dim, and soon, everyone loses their way.

Mark became a hero by way of the gifts he gives to the rest of us with his story. His gift to sons is letting them know that the breaking away from their fathers is normal and healthy and that, in its proper dose, it leads us eventually back to see the wisdom and love that can reside within some very dumb clothes worn far too often, and amidst some very corny jokes, repeated too many times.

Mark's gift to fathers is reminding us to say much more to our sons about our concern and love for them, and to say much less about our criticisms of them. Like Mark, we must remember what is important, and then live, not preach, those things in order to teach our sons. For, in the end, it is not the chores or sports or grades that make the future man, or that distinguish the "winner" from the "loser," it is the heart and the heart alone that defines the worth of the future man—the person who, for the briefest of moments, is our son. Let us use our moments wisely.

Finally, Mark is a hero to me for the amazing efforts he made to push himself so hard and so fast to confront his own pain, showing a steel that most adults would envy. It makes you wonder where that kind of strength comes from, but, come to think of it, I did meet his dad.

And perhaps, even his mom.

15

THE CONCRETE ROSE

Alena's Story

The sparkling, brand-new high school rose up like an act of defiance against the bleak poverty of its neighborhood. It was the first day of school for both this beautiful facility and for its beautiful 9th grader named Alena. The building's beauty was a superficial one that meant little, a shallow smile that would dim quickly in its hard world. Alena's was a beauty hidden deep inside of her, harder to discern, but made of stronger stuff that could somehow flourish in this, the most barren of gardens.

~

Murphy's law of new school openings was running rampant—everything that could go wrong, did, often with a flourish. The human chaos and confusion in the halls seemed to infect the structure. In our little corner of that world, water poured from the ceiling into wastebaskets strategically placed around the counseling center suite. Staff members yelled and slammed down phones that wouldn't work, and threw carpets, coats, and even themselves over computers and file cabinets that were getting drenched. One office lock refused to cooperate with its key as water started to run fast from under its door. The staff gathered to vote on whether the glass should be broken to try to get in.

As we professionals unprofessionally argued, pleaded, and cursed, Josie, the director, shushed the group and pointed to an oddly dressed, chunky African-American girl standing in the entry of our suite. "Our first customer!" Josie announced, trying to remind us of our responsibilities. "I'm sorry," said the girl, "I see that things are messed up here, too, but I don't know what to do. There's a girl in the bathroom, and I think . . . well, I know that she's cut her wrist, and she won't come out of her stall, and I went to the nurse's office but no one's there, and I think that we should, like, help her now. She's not bleeding a whole lot but I don't know . . ."

Josie and I took off running with this girl leading the way. "WHICH BATHROOM?" Josie yelled over the hall noise. "THE ONE RIGHT OVER YOUR OFFICE," the girl answered, "THE ONE WITH THE OVERFLOWING TOILETS." "PERFECT!" yelled Josie as we ran, *"JUST FREAKIN' PERFECT!"* *"Well,"* the girl observed maturely, *"things could be worse. She's alive, and she was talking to me about why she did it. That's a good thing, isn't it?"* Josie looked quizzically at our young guide, then at her obscured nametag: "WHAT'S YOUR NAME?" she puffed as we ran the steps. "ALENA," the girl answered. "WELL, ALENA," Josie yelled, "IT LOOKS LIKE YOU ARE OUR FIRST PEER COUNSELOR. WANT THE JOB? IT PAYS ABSOLUTELY NOTHING." Alena grinned broadly. "YES!" she shouted, "IS THIS WHAT YOU GUYS GET TO DO ALL DAY?"

By week's end, that crisis and four others had passed (with no fatalities) and Alena had pretty much moved into the counseling center. At only thirteen, she seemed to fit perfectly with the staff, which almost instantly saw her more as a younger "social-worker-counselor-type" peer than as a student. She had an extremely conservative look for a student at that school. Unlike most other girls whose provocative clothes made one think about the advantages of school uniforms, Alena dressed in the somewhat worn but very high-quality clothing of a successful, middle-aged professional. A look, Josie used to half-joke, that ". . . perhaps some of the paid staff might wish to emulate." Alena explained that her parents were strict Baptists, very overprotective but very loving parents who would never allow her to dress like the other kids.

Over that first year of school, we grew very curious about Alena's parents who, we all agreed, had done a phenomenal job of raising this incredible young woman in what we knew to be a very poor, and very tough, neighborhood. Alena explained how their faith anchored her family, how they attended church several times a week, and how her parents were on every committee. Whatever their secret was, it certainly showed. Alena was a school workhorse, volunteering for every task that arose, working early mornings, nights and even weekends. We worried that kids in her peer counseling groups might ride her about her conservative style of dress, and her enthusiastic style of participating. But they also seemed to see her as someone much older than her years, and she had developed a reputation as the "go-to girl" in the school, the one that everyone could trust with problems before allowing the adults in. Alena became our "color bridge" to the student body, helping particularly the Anglo staff to gain relationships with the non-white kids, many of whom came from terrible places where adults were often crazy, scary predators or addicts, and whites were people simply not to be trusted at all.

Her only flaw was her strangely poor grades. Verbally she seemed very bright, and she had shown unusual, highly creative problem-solving skills. For example, it was her idea for the counseling staff to eat lunch with the students to help reduce the stigma of kids coming (or being sent) to the counseling center. Sitting at her desk, she would seem to study ferociously, attacking her work with a passion that never showed in her grades, but she refused any help. The only day that she would never appear in the counseling center would be the Fridays on which report cards came out. We had learned that by the following Monday, she would mysteriously not be able to recall her grades. We also learned not to embarrass her by asking. But we knew that they were not good.

Finally, towards the end of her second year, she was in danger of failing the 10th grade, and we had to confront her. She panicked at the idea of us contacting her parents, since they would be so ashamed of her grades. Her father, she had often told us, was a very proud man who valued education above all else. He had put himself through night school to get his 2-year degree from community college. Her mother, she bragged admiringly, was a nurse who went back to school to get her degree even with four young kids. She begged us not to call them, finally agreeing instead to get some minor testing done.

As the psychologist on staff, that job fell to me. After 20 minutes of testing, Alena was in tears. "Please, *PLEASE*," she begged, "*you can't tell anyone about this. Aren't you supposed to keep my information secret?*" she asked, "*like I have to when I'm talking with a student? Don't I get the same consideration?*" she sobbed, "*don't I rate that?*" I sat and stared helplessly, with twenty questions flooding my brain. How had she gotten this far in school? How could her highly educated parents not have known? What could I say to make her feel better? What could I say to explain this to her parents?

Alena could not read. I told her that I would have to talk this over with the others and that I'd let her know what the next step would be.

The following week, her desk at the counseling center was empty. Suzanne, the loud, feared, and fearless attendance officer known by the kids as "The Suzanne," told us that Alena had been out of school all week and her parents had not called in to say that she would be absent. She was shocked at how out-of-character this was since she knew Alena and worked with her to help get other truant kids back into school. A mechanical voice had answered Suzanne's repeated calls to the home, saying that Alena's number was not in service.

"It's home visit time," she said. I asked to go along, hoping that I could convince Alena and her parents that illiteracy was not a mortal sin, and that with some effort I was sure that we all could help her. I suggested to Suzanne that since Alena's parents both worked long hours, perhaps we should go in the evening or on a weekend. "The Suzanne," a 20-year veteran of the "missing kid wars," stared through me like she was just now understanding a two-year mystery that she should have picked up on a long time ago. "I doubt that will be necessary," she said.

Alena's address was a vacant lot on a street where the empty spaces were the best features. Suzanne never even slowed down, as if she had known what we were going to find, and she just headed for the neighboring high school. That one was a terribly run-down, bug-infested, hell-hole that had the well-deserved reputation as being the most dangerous school in the city. There we found an

angry attendance officer who was very annoyed that we were ruining his day by inquiring about a student's address. "What's the f—
—ng point?" he snarled, caring little about who overheard him.
"One less f——ng cockroach to worry about, right?" "The Suzanne"
apparently had this guy's number. "Why don't you and I go down-
town [to the school board] and see how they feel about you losing
one of your 'f'ng cockroaches'?"

Thirty minutes later, we stood at the curb of Alena's real
address and looked around carefully, getting stares from scary
people that told us that we should consider getting right back in the
car. Comparatively speaking, Alena's fake address was a much
better place than her real one. "Just stay *with* me here," Suzanne
murmured through gritted teeth, trying to shore up my nerve. We
walked up to Alena's half-open front door, and called into the
house. No one answered, although we could see people lying on a
sofa, and on the floor, either sleeping or passed out, or likely some
of both. "Strict Baptists?" I asked Suzanne, but she apparently had
not heard that part of Alena's story.

A man with bulging neck veins on a skeletal face walked oddly
up to us. "F'y'all lookin' fo' Alena, she work at the [grocery store].
Y'all better leave this place, you know what I'm sayin?"

We finally found Alena at the store, stocking canned goods.
Suzanne headed for the manager's office to check in, and I stood
alone with Alena. Still holding her cans, her arms dropped to her
sides, and her head sank very low as if she had been caught commit-
ting some terrible crime. We said nothing for a minute, and then,
staring at her shoes, she quietly asked, "Have you . . . were you . . .
at my . . . you know, *house*?" She said the word "house" timidly, as if
hoping against hope that she might maintain at least a shred of her
fantasy of dignity. I nodded softly. She sagged against the wall as if
the last decent thing in her world had just been taken from her. All
she ever had was one pretty lie, and now even that was gone. Huge
tears rolled out her sad, sad eyes. She tried to wipe them but found
cans of beans in both hands and seemed too overwhelmed to figure
out what to do. This strong, smart, energetic girl was suddenly as
helpless and hopeless as her shattered home and broken family.

"That ain't my home. My sister and me, we got to live there, but that ain't no kinda' home," she sniffled, "We ain't got no home." She was now speaking street dialect I had never heard her use, as if she wasn't sure who to be right now.

"I didn't mean no harm, didn't mean no disrespect," she explained. "I just wanted to go to a better school, you know? Have you ever seen my old school?" I nodded. "Would you go there?" she asked. Without waiting for an answer she went on, confessing to her various crimes. And she was absolutely guilty of many things such as wanting to go to a school that she might survive; wanting to learn how to read; and, the worst offense of all, wanting a shot at a decent life. "I went to the Goodwill [thrift shops] and got these clothes, you know, that make me look smart, and, you know, not like some crack head. I dressed up to look like I was my own mother when I registered and all, and I forged the papers that I needed. And it nearly worked, too, until you, you know, tested me. And," she said, feeling compelled to tell it all, "I'm 16, not fifteen like I said. I got left back one year." She paused, put down her cans, and wiped her eyes and nose. "So do we call the cops now? Am I going to get arrested? "

"The Suzanne" had quietly walked up behind us, and had heard most of Alena's confession. The fearsome attendance officer gently put her arm around Alena and said, "Girl, that's about the *dumbest* thing you *ever* said. *NO, you do NOT get arrested, as long as you get YOUR behind back in OUR school by 7:45 A.M. on Monday.* That's when we're all going to sit down and figure out how we're going to get you reading, and if you want, maybe living in a better place. But I *will* get you arrested faster than you can say 'canned beans' if you are not there. *AM I UNDERSTOOD?*"

Alena just stared at the floor for a moment, and then she threw herself into Suzanne's arms, crying, and saying, "*Thank you—thank you, so much—thank you!*"

I stood there, watching Alena share tears of joy as if she had just won the lottery. And all because some hard-nosed and soft-hearted attendance officer was bending some rules to try to give a struggling, decent, hard-working young woman the very thing that she was supposed to have been given, the thing that so many entitled kids throw away like a piece of trash: *a basic education.* It suddenly hit me that I, a highly educated professional, had no idea of the worth of that until I watched a very poor, very moral girl lie, cheat and steal to try to get what she was owed from a world that tried even harder to crush her. This was a lesson I vowed I would never forget.

Apparently, I was not the only person standing in the canned goods aisle who never forgot. I'm not able to swear to this, but I think I actually saw *tears* in the eyes of "The Suzanne," the most feared woman in our school. And now, the one most loved by a drug-orphaned child who had finally found her way home.

~

A team was assembled that got Alena placed in a foster home, diagnosed her learning challenges, and set about fixing them. Her foster parents were good people who eventually also took in Alena's younger sister Jasmine, a very troubled, truant girl who unfortunately did not share Alena's amazing resistance to the toxicity of poverty. Jasmine dropped out and became pregnant. At age 13.

Jasmine's is, tragically, the more common American story. As of this writing, the world's wealthiest nation has the highest school drop-out rate of any industrialized country in the world. Nationally, only 66% of our kids graduate from 12th grade. Only half of our children of color ever walk down a graduation aisle. In urban and rural areas, the numbers are absolutely staggering. In New York City, for example, only 18% of all kids earn the degree needed to be only eligible for college. That figure drops to 9% for black kids.

The long list of bad things that happen to good people who drop out is frightening. Some people ask if high school diplomas mean anything anymore, if they are even worth pursuing. The fact is that they mean everything. Dropouts earn ten-thousand fewer dollars every year, a devastating deficit in lower income ranges, causing them to suffer poverty at twice the rate of graduates. They also find themselves in prison and on drugs much more often.

The short list of fixable things that lead to dropping out is infuriating. The majority of dropouts are kids who, like Alena, never got the special help they need to learn. Yes, you could argue that it is the job of the parents to oversee their kids' education, and to support schoolwork at home. But the brutal fact remains that the state of American parenting is such that complaining about this won't make it so. Unless we are prepared to legislatively mandate parent training and legally-enforced supervision for all parents, our only other shot at saving these kids happens at school. And we have found that intervening early and powerfully with kids who struggle with school can make an amazing difference.

Are such programs expensive? Yes. They cost a lot. But it costs much more not to have these programs. The accountants tell us that funding these programs costs just one-tenth of what it costs not to provide such assistance. That second figure is truly astronomical. For that tally includes the tariffs of lost taxes, squandered productivity, welfare assistance, subsidized medical fees, drug treatment programs, homeless shelters, criminal activity, court costs, and incarceration.

Of course, those are only the losses we can count with dollars. But how do we place a price on the more important human losses, the pointless suffering, the needless degradation of a human spirit? Like a loser investor, America continues to find trillions for causes that return nothing or worse, while whining about the "high" costs of education, fees that return every dollar many times over. It is absurd and shameful. And it is our shame to bear.

Alena's secret was terribly shameful for her, but incredibly heroic to us. She was, as her social worker put it, ". . . a superhero from another planet . . ." She had pretty much raised herself and a sister in a ramshackle house with drug-using parents whose best quality was that ". . . they were usually too high to beat her very much . . ." Alena clearly merits hero status. But is she really so unique?

My friends who work with the least heroic teens you might imagine would say no, that she's not so different from other teens. They believe that inside every teen is a hidden Alena, a "superhero" who wants to succeed. They have known many, many terribly troubled kids who masquerade as gangster/ loser "Clark Kents" while sullenly waiting for a chance to change into their hero clothes, a chance that very rarely comes. Giving them that chance is admittedly time consuming, difficult, and expensive work. But what are the options?

After her crisis, Alena was a spirit reborn. She attacked her learning challenges with a ferocity that made even "The Suzanne" proud, and became a student mentor for younger kids facing challenges such as her own. Like a beloved football coach she would hound, plead, yell, and, most of all, teach her toughness by example. I can name six other kids whose life courses were profoundly changed by Alena. I suspect that there are many more.

She was admitted to a special community college program for learning-challenged students, and academically held her own there. Even after graduating from our school, she continued to visit us often, much as a child returns to visit her family. Although the homecomings became fewer and fewer over the years, just like with a loving family, we felt no lessening in the love between us all.

Today that beautiful brand-new school has lots of dents and dings, like any once-new home that loved the children that lived within. Over the years, its young, radiant, perfect face became lined with creases just as with a young mother as she fights to raise her children in this bewildering world. In that strange way, Alena's school grew to resemble her middle-aged foster mother. But, between you and me, I find a lined, worry-worn face much more attractive and interesting. For there, in those lines that women hate so much, you'll find the character, the caring, and the love that sets free the spirits of heroes like Alena.

16

EXPOSING A SECRET WAR

Rosa's Story

No matter how long you work with teenagers, it seems that you never come close to having "seen it all," particularly with that strange and powerful adolescent code of morality which seems as arbitrary, convoluted, and contradictory as that of some ancient bandit gang—and every bit as passionate. Yet if you are ever lucky enough to have a kid guide you through that code as she relates her odyssey, you will return to your own moral home a wiser person, someone less reluctant to judge anyone.

This story tells of two female heroes of mine who broke laws, did drugs, and lied, all for the best of reasons: They were trying to survive a hostile world that has defined them as sexual objects, semi-humans with less worth than males, and ultimately and tragically, with less worth to themselves.

To most in the world, Bobbie and Rosa were "troubled teens"—adolescents who stole, had sex, and smoked marijuana. To me, they were more like resistance fighters, striking back in the only ways they could against an invisible fascist force, one that had occupied their world, methodically crushing any passive attempts at freedom they dared to make.

∼

The staff at the alternative high school couldn't make up their minds whether the student counseling groups should be sexually mixed or segregated. Finally, they decided to try both, where each week the girls and boys would meet together and then separately. As a consultant, asked to help the school to evaluate their group programs, I was to attend all three weekly meetings and help them decide which model worked best.

The groups had been meeting for over a month when I joined them. Thanks to the new popularity of TV "reality" shows, everyone in the mixed group enthusiastically agreed to be videotaped. We planned to play those tapes for the segregated groups to view and discuss, and we taped those segregated meetings, as well. The idea was to see if and how kids acted differently when they were around the opposite sex.

The first time the girls watched a co-ed tape, they were fascinated to the point of obsession, but not with what was being said. They were furiously critiquing each other's appearance (never the boys) and usually in cutting, derogatory ways that caused such an uproar that I started to get worried. When the shy and quiet Rosa appeared on the screen, one of the viewers viciously announced that Rosa had "the perfect crack-slut look, and Rosa should know." Rosa collapsed in tears, and another girl named Bobbie jumped up to go nose-to nose with the vicious kid. As the staff cleared the room, I asked if I could chat with Rosa, who just sat and sobbed like a girl lost and alone in the world. Bobbie asked if she could stay, too. When I asked if that was what Rosa wanted, she nodded yes.

I sat and let her cry for a while. Bobbie just sat next to her, staying close without touching, saying nothing, just wisely lending her presence. They looked like bookends. Rosa was short, dark and Hispanic, with shy eyes and long hair that had been meticulously woven into a series of elaborate hair wraps. Bobbie was Anglo and tall, her shorter blonde hair perfectly combed, with eyes that were sharp and direct. Rosa's clothes were definitely not from the top-end mall shops that had provided Bobbie's. They shared a slight chubbiness and a strong bond of compassion.

"I hate it here," Rosa finally said, wiping her nose. "Where I come from, the school is not as nice as this one, but nobody there treats you bad. Not like this." Bobbie chimed in, "Well, at my old school, this is exactly how the girls treated each other. And my old school was brand new and beautiful."

"Rosa," I said carefully, "I know that you hardly know me, but can I ask you a question?" "Can I not answer if I want to?" she asked. "Absolutely," I assured her. "It looked like what that girl said really hurt you." Rosa fell back into sobs, and Bobbie went nose-to-nose with me. "Well, *DUUHH*," she said, wagging her head, "how would *you* feel?" "I'd feel like smacking that other girl hard," I said, "particularly if she had hit a sore spot in me, something that bothered me a lot for some reason. That's what I wanted to ask you about, Rosa." "She doesn't need to tell anybody about anything," Bobbie declared protectively, "You just need to tell [the vicious girl] to shut-up before I shut her up, OK?" Rosa then said that she was OK and just wanted to leave. "If you change your mind," I said, "here's my number." Rosa took my card and held it while looking up to study my face for a bit. Now she was the one evaluating me.

The next week, Bobbie and Rosa were not at school. They had been arrested for shoplifting, and the school was deciding whether they would be allowed back. That afternoon I got a call from Bobbie who said that she and Rosa wanted to see me. "You told her to call if you could help, right?" she said. I could hear the testing in her voice, wondering if that was just another phony adult line.

That night they both came in, traveling hours over terrible bus routes. Bobbie was all business. "We need two things: First, we need you to get us back into that stupid school. If they don't take us back, we've, like, got no place to go." "Wow," I said, "that's a tall order. And what's the second thing? I hope it's easier than the first." It wasn't.

Bobbie started to ask questions about confidentiality, and then stopped mid-sentence, looking at Rosa. Then Rosa took over. "My cousin, she thinks that she might be pregnant, you know? She might want to get an abortion, but she can't get one without her parents being told, you know? And she, my cousin, she's . . . she can't tell her father because he's . . . well, he's got some problems, you know, and . . . well, she just can't. So we were wondering if you could give us that stuff to give her, you know, the morning-after medicine that makes you not be pregnant anymore?"

"Ladies," I said solemnly, "I'm afraid that I'm not a medical kind of doctor—I can't give anybody any medicine. Even if I were a medical doctor, that pill you've heard about wouldn't help your cousin if she's been pregnant a while, even if she could get it somewhere. That's why they call it the morning-after pill. It's really meant for that "morning-after" time, that's all."

They both looked crushed. "Rosa," I said, "Is it OK if I ask you a question?" She nodded. "Your cousin, how long has she been pregnant?" "Maybe 5 weeks," she said. "Is she sure she's pregnant?" I asked. Rosa looked at Bobbie and I saw Bobbie nod ever so slightly, like an attorney advising her client. "No, my cousin, she is not sure. That's what we got caught stealing—a pregnancy test for her. That and some make-up. Makeup is expensive, too. Her family hasn't got any money. And, oh yeah, we took some candy for us. But we're very bad thieves."

"Rosa," I asked, "can your cousin tell the counselor at school that . . ." Bobbie jumped on me impatiently *"We already told you. We don't go to that school anymore."* She shook her head, as if she was accepting defeat. "Let's go, Rosa," she sighed. "He's as useless as the rest of them." Rosa did not get up. Although Bobbie was her voice of anger and defense, she knew that she needed something else. Perhaps Bobbie did, too. She sat back down next to Rosa.

"I . . . I *am* my cousin," she admitted. "I think he already guessed that," she said to Bobbie. "I need to find out if I am pregnant. In my world, for my father, such a thing is not possible. He's told me many times to not come home if I were to do such a thing."

"Rosa," I offered, "perhaps that's just what he said, you know, to try and scare you. But maybe he would take this better than you think? Has he ever . . ." Bobbie was on me like an attack dog again. I felt like I needed my own attorney there. *"Don't you listen? Didn't she already tell you? Don't you know what she means? HER FATHER'S CRAZY! HE, LIKE, SCREAMS AND YELLS OVER DISHES AND GRADES! SO HE'S GOING TO SUDDENLY SAY,* 'Oh, that's OK, sweetheart. I slap you for forgetting the dishes, but I'll understand completely that my pure little girl might be pregnant—that she was *screwing her boyfriend.'"* Bobbie spit out that last phrase. She immediately looked upset with what she had said, and she touched Rosa's arm as if in apology. Rosa just sat and wept as if she knew what was in Bobbie's heart. Then Bobbie leaned forward with a question and a statement. What she said was so profound to me that I wrote every word as soon as I could, like I was copying a manifesto from a freedom fighter.

"Don't you get it?" she asked. *"Do you have any idea, ANY IDEA what it's like for us?"* "I probably don't," I answered honestly. "Can you teach me?" My words sounded corny, even to me, but they were real. Bobbie narrowed her eyes to see if I was being sarcastic, and then went on. *"I* can answer for you," she said, "NO-YOU-DON'T! Want to know why? Because you're a *guy,* that's why." She sat back and took a breath.

"When I was in first grade we used to have these, like, chant contests where we'd yell, 'Girls rule and boys drool.' Well, guess what? We were wrong. The boys rule—everything and everywhere." Bobbie leaned forward again. "Let *me* ask *you* a question: If a boy tells you that he's had sex with three girls last year, what do you think? And if a girl tells you that she's had sex with three boys last year, what would you think?" Having laid her trap, Bobbie sat back and studied me carefully. "Well," I said, "I hate to admit this, but I probably would worry that the girl had some issue and that the boy was pretty normal. And if you want to hear from the ugly side of me, that part might think that the boy was sort of cool, and that that the girl was sort of slutty."

Bobbie sat back up, and took off her body armor. "Thank you," she said quietly and earnestly. "Thanks for not bullshitting." A new Bobbie emerged. "That's exactly right. And do you want to hear something worse? *That's exactly what we'd think! Rosa and me!* That's what you saw on that tape at school. Girls do this stuff to themselves."

Bobbie's voice became very small, but her courage just filled the room. "When boys sleep around, they're, like, heroes. If girls sleep around, they're whores. If a boy has sex with a girl, do you know what words they use? They say 'he *got* her' like she was a target and he was a good shot. If a girl sleeps with a boy, suddenly she's, like . . . vulnerable, you know? Waiting for the news to get out that he 'got' her. And it always does. They never say that she 'got' him.

"It's like a bizarre game. I had a boy . . . he chased me for like, three months." Her eyes went down to the floor. "I had made up my mind that I wasn't going to get hurt again, you know, so I decided that I wouldn't have sex with him until I was sure that he really, really loved me. He put on the best act you'll ever see, and . . . I bought it. The night we had sex was the last night he was ever faithful. He went right into his next game, with the next girl. When I told him that I knew, he just laughed at me, and said that there were a million like me out there."

She exhaled sadly. "I even called the next girl up, you know, to warn her, you know, like 'sister to sister', right? She flipped on me, sayin' I was just jealous and that he REALLY loved HER, and that he had told her how *I* cheated on *him*. So, a boy's lies are automatically worth more than a girl's truth, to both the boys *and* the girls? *WHAT IS THAT?*"

She looked softly at Rosa. "I think the worst is that first time," she said. "When you get conned like that you just feel, like . . . I don't know, like dirty or stupid or . . . I work at [a grocery store] and whenever I find a package of whatever that someone opened and took a bite of, and then threw it on the floor, it makes me remember how I felt when I got . . . when I felt like how I think Rosa feels. The only time that feeling would go away is when I'd smoke weed. That's how I got into weed. You know, the music videos and all, they show everybody having lots of sex all the time and they look real cool. They don't show what it's like the next day for the girl. Or the next year. Kids look at that and think that's how it is, you know? All cool? And it *is* all cool—for the boys. It's crap for us. Rosa, she had sex one time—*one time*—and look at where she is. And her boy? Where is he? He's running around telling everyone how cool he is 'cause he got Rosa pregnant. Of course, he doesn't call her anymore."

Then Rosa stirred. "Last week when that girl got me upset, it wasn't just what she said. It was that tape." Rosa looked at Bobbie with disbelief for herself. "I was *playing* [flirting]," she said. "I think

I'm pregnant, and I got used, and my life is maybe ruined—and I was *playing* with Manny. Right there, on that tape. I couldn't watch me anymore."

Bobbie explained that to all of us. "When a boy is chasing you, right? It's like you're in charge, right? It's like you've got the power. That part is fun, you know? You can make them do whatever you want because they want you. That's what we do all day long. And then, as soon as . . . when, it's over, *they* have all the power and we're nothing.

"*We have no choices. Whatever you do, you lose. If you have sex, you're a whore and kids make fun of you and you feel bad. If you don't, you're a loser who can't keep a boyfriend, and kids make fun of you and you feel bad. So, girls only get to choose which kind of pain they want.*"

Those thoughts hung long in the air. Then Bobbie spoke again. "You know what I think about a lot now? Like, Mary Poppins, and Tinkerbell, and Eloise [the book about the little girl who pretty much ruled a big hotel]. I miss all that. I miss that a lot. Isn't that stupid? All I used to worry about was getting a skinned knee, you know—and not, like, getting my heart ripped out. I never worried what other girls might say about my clothes or whatever. And now . . . it's like something inside of me left . . . and I can never get it back."

No one spoke for the rest of that session, except to agree to meet again. As it got quiet, I heard that it had begun raining outside. We all sat and listened to that soothing, sad sound for a while. When they left, I watched them disappear into the rainy darkness, like hurting, dutiful soldiers heading back to some secret war that no one wants to talk about.

But Bobbie was no slouch rebel. She got the pregnancy test for Rosa, which came back negative. The school allowed them to return, and Bobbie's first mission was to insist that those group tapes be run again for everyone to watch and then discuss, boys and girls, together in one room.

All hell broke loose once again. Kids were shouting and gesturing and the staff sent eye messages to each other many times about clearing the room, but I had asked them to let this roll a bit.

I wanted to see if Bobbie could speak to them as she had to me. And speak she did. She stopped the tape at times to show how the girls were acting stupid and cutesy when the boys were there, but not when they weren't. She showed how the boys took over the co-ed group and *how the girls let them.* She showed the girls gushing over the boys for doing incredibly dumb things, and she showed the girls just tearing each other to shreds. Suddenly, the two "coolest" boys started to laugh and call Bobbie a dyke [lesbian]. In a flash, Rosa leapt up to confront those boys, a sight I never thought I'd see, one so out of the ordinary that it even silenced the group, if only for a minute.

"A DYKE?" SHE YELLED, "A DYKE? ANY GIRL WHO'S IN CHARGE OR WHO DOESN'T THINK YOU ARE, LIKE, GOD'S GIFT IS AUTOMATICALLY A DYKE? I HAVE NO IDEA IF BOBBIE'S GAY OR NOT, AND I DON'T CARE. BUT YOU HAVE A PROBLEM WITH *ANY* GIRL WHO SPEAKS UP, DON'T YOU?"

There was a moment of stunned silence, and then Rosa quietly said, "You know something? You guys are really . . . pathetic." Then she laid out a question to all the girls as she opened her hands. "Why do we act like they are so cool? What is up with *us*?" As she sat back down, all hell broke loose once again, with the loudest voices belonging to the girls.

Thanks to two hurting, heroic teens, their war was no longer a secret one.

∼

Bobbie's Tinkerbell, Mary Poppins, and Eloise were much more than fun childhood story characters. They each were powerful females in their own right, girls and women who made waves, who changed things, and who spoke up. These were imperfect females, not Barbie dolls. These were male equals, not male-haters. These were women who passionately chased after things like truth, courage, and character, and not controlling, contemptuous male approval.

I always meant to see if Bobbie understood any of that, but I never did. She was returned back to her original school and, sadly, I never saw her again.

I did get to see Rosa a few times when she made it back to her first school. She was a very different girl from the one who had left there six months before. She was active in a number of activities and doing well academically. Best of all, now she walked the halls with her head up high, laughing and talking as if she belonged there as much as anyone. It was great to look at her, and to see the best of Bobbie in her, along with Tinkerbell, Mary Poppins, and Eloise.

17

THE SCHNECKEN GUY

Luke's Story

Bullying is perhaps the most denied and devastating epidemic disease of childhood. It is denied by adults who have become blind to its true nature. Most can only see bullying in the physical intimidation of a smaller boy by a larger one. Few see it in its more common and deadly forms, such as when a child's head drops and her worth collapses as the captains choose up the teams, and the winners choose the worthy, while the unworthy are left last, or even worse, left unchosen.

It is devastating in the toll that it takes through its ceaseless, grinding, soul-infecting messages of exclusion, worthlessness, and hopelessness. And these quiet, poisonous exchanges rarely appear on the radar screens of the caretaker adults: the teachers, parents, and playground aides.

Many like to laugh and belittle people who worry about such things. Bullying and teasing, they say, are normal parts of childhood—a toughening, strengthening process of nature. Besides, they argue, fierce competition is good for kids. Coddling them with "everyone-plays" games, they believe, teaches kids to be weak and unrealistic about the real world.

But those are beliefs usually held by adults who once were the captains or worthy kids, children who were lucky enough not to have "won" that mysterious, terrible lottery where you're selected by your peers to be a "loser." I've yet to meet an un-chosen kid who thinks that being bullied or picked last is OK, that these are strengthening processes. They do make kids tough, much like combat hardens its soldiers.

Luke had learned how to be hard. But he knew that hardness is very different from strength. He had yet to learn that compassion is more strengthening than competition—and much more precious.

~

My eye was drawn to a kid of perhaps 17 standing in the rear of the community college auditorium, carefully keeping away from the crowd and the lights as if they might hurt him. As new people walked in the door, he would casually provide more distance between himself and them, retreating further and further into the darkness, maintaining a moat of safety and anonymity.

I was on the stage as part of a panel to address adolescent bullying, a recently popular topic since a local kid who had been bullied stood accused of plotting a school shooting. A fellow panelist, a newspaper columnist, was doing a great job of mocking my words about the complexity of bullying, and what I see as its terrible effects on kids. To rousing rounds of applause, he espoused the virtues of fist fighting as a bullying remedy, and he blamed "politically correct" zero-tolerance policies as being a cause of school shootings.

"Bullying was *never* the concern years ago that it is today," he preached. "You tell these kids that they can't fight and then the only other option they have is to take it until they go nuts with a gun. I got bullied, and my *father*, not shrinks, taught me how to handle it—*with a right hook*. One good shot to the chin was all it took. That bully never tried me again. In fact, he respected me standing up so much that eventually he became a friend. So tell me, Dr. Bradley, exactly what was wrong with my cure?"

"Well, perhaps nothing," I opened as the applause died down. "If that felt right to you, and it worked out well, then maybe that was a good option—*for you*. But not all bullying is . . ." "Y . . . YOU'RE WR . . . WRONG," a voice cried out from the darkness, interrupting me. "AND H . . . HE'S WRONG TOO," it said of the columnist. The boy had left the safety of his moat.

One of the event moderators rushed back to tell the young man that questions were to be held until the end of the meeting, but I wanted to hear this kid's words, since they seem to come so hard to him. "Please," I said, "can we let him finish, maybe give him that microphone?" While the moderator reluctantly walked over to the kid, most of the audience swiveled around and squinted to see the kid in the darkness. One member of the TV crew turned a light on him for the camera. Suddenly illuminated, he looked terrified, and, at first, waved off the microphone that the moderator was trying to give to him. Then, resolutely squinting into the bright light, he grabbed it. With a quavering voice he said, "Y . . . you are b-both . . . wr-wrong." He swallowed hard and exhaled loudly to steady himself. "B-bullying does not get fixed . . . by fighting. If it does, then that's not really bullying. That's . . . something else . . . like a sport. In a sport you get a chance to win. In bullying—well, you don't get any chances to win." He looked like he wanted to say a lot more, but he just stared for a moment, shrugged, and then apologetically offered the microphone back to the moderator.

"Please," I called to him, "please finish your thought. Why do you think that fighting doesn't work . . . and could you tell us your name?" He wouldn't share his name, but he would share his thought. His voice suddenly became very clear, almost impassioned. *"Because,"* he said quietly and firmly, *"because . . . I fought. I fought many times. And it only made things worse. A lot worse."*

The boisterous audience became absolutely silent, as they might if a disfigured, wounded veteran was about to speak of his ordeal, just after they had voted to go to war. There was something about this kid. "That's all I had to say," he murmured as he handed over the microphone. Then he grabbed the moderator's arm, leaned back into the mic and added, "You've got to do something for those kids, OK?—for those kids who get bullied? There's more than you know. It's harder than you know—*and it's a lot different than you all remember."* And then he turned and left, quickly.

I made a mental snapshot of this young man, hoping to find him during the break. He was about average height, but very thin and gaunt, with heavily stooped shoulders. He had sad eyes that seemed to sink into a scruffy beard, one that looked very out of place on such a young face. Later, as I searched the crowd, I recalled thinking that it was a face that somehow looked as if it did not belong. He was gone.

A few days later I was parking on that campus and found that face again. It was reading a book while leaning against a motorcycle underneath a tree in the far, empty corner of the lot. As I pulled my car over towards him, I saw him close his book and start to gather his things without even looking up to see who I was. The closer I got, the faster he pulled his gear together. I rolled down my window and called, "Hey—hello? Is this spot taken? I hate parking where I get dinged by the idiot next to me, you know?" He ignored my joke and straddled his bike, getting ready to start it. "Look," I said, "I'm sorry. I didn't mean to ruin your reading. I'll just park somewhere else."

I was sure that he had no idea who I was since I never saw him look anywhere near me. But he was very good at seeing people without looking directly at them. With his eyes focused only on his gas tank, he said, "You want to talk more about the other night, right?" "Yes," I answered, "if . . . that's OK with you". He stared at the tank without talking for a few moments and then simply said, "OK." I pushed my luck a bit.

"I want to write a story about bullying," I said, "and I'd like to interview you on tape to get your exact words. I'd like to let people know what it's like, what it's *really* like to have gone through that." His eyes did not move. "People like that newspaper guy from the other night?" he asked. "People *exactly* like that newspaper guy," I answered. He smiled very slightly. "Yeah," he said, "OK. But only on voice tape—no video," he added. "And you can't use my name." "Deal," I said, "but what is your name?" "You can call me Luke," he answered.

We arranged to meet at the college later that week. I found Luke sitting alone in a corner of a huge community/coffee room where students gathered in small groups to chat. Warm laughter, soft music, and coffee aromas filled the room, but none seemed to reach into Luke's corner.

"Hey!" I said, "Can I buy you a coffee?" He reached down beside himself and produced a bag containing two coffees and some great-looking small cakes. "I make these," he said, referring to the baked goods. "They're called schnecken. This is the one useful thing I got from my secondary education. Things were so bad for me at high school that they sent me to voc-tech school for a while. I stayed there long enough to learn how to bake. I'm pretty good at it. So what do you want to know?"

He had an unusual style of interacting—of speaking, for sure, but it was more than that. He was like an immigrant still learning a language and a culture—able to communicate, but lacking the word styles and behavior nuances that tell you he's been in the country a while. He was missing those little things that help people feel so much more at ease. He was a foreigner in his own town.

"Anything you'd care to tell me," I said, setting up the recorder. "Good," he answered flatly, "Because you've got a lot to learn." I studied Luke's face for belligerence or stridence that would match his words, but there was none. This was just his way of talking. *"So,"* I asked myself, *"what is it that makes me want to dislike this kid? Why is he someone I would avoid when I was 13?"*

Apparently hearing the unintended harshness of his words, Luke tried to clarify: "I . . . um, look, I didn't mean that you were stupid or anything. It's just that everyone's got this bullying thing wrong. It's a word problem. You guys use words like 'He gets bullied' or 'She gets teased,' but that's not what being bullied is about. There should be another word to describe real bullying.

"Adults might see some kid getting teased and pushed around in school, but they don't get it. They only see it as it would be in their own lives, as a one-time thing, like if they went to the 7–11 to get milk and some jerk pushed them around. They'd go home all hurt and upset and mad, but the next day it would be forgotten. They'd go to their job and be with their families and be happy or whatever. And if it happened every time they went to the 7–11, they'd just go to a different store.

"*Really* being bullied would be like this: They'd be little kids who are *forced* to go back to that *same 7–11*, for *12 hours a day, 7 days a week, 12 months a year.* And people would tell them things like, '*Oh, it will get a lot better when you grow up because adults don't do that stuff. So just put up with this for maybe 10 or 12 years, and then things will be fine.*' Real bullying is *not* just getting beaten up. Real bullying is more like a torture. It follows you home from school to your neighborhood, and from your grade school to your high school.

"It's a label that gets attached to your forehead, telling all the new kids that you meet that you are a loser, and to stay away. Did you know that kids actually spread the word to new schools so that you get bullied there, too? Real bullying is what people might go through if they're in prison or in a war where everyday, when you wake up, *you're trapped there. It's like you're waking up to your nightmare, and you wish you could stay asleep because that's the only place where you feel safe.*"

Luke paused, took a breath, and sipped his coffee with a hand that trembled slightly. He seemed upset with the inside burst of feeling that was now visible outside on his cheeks, as if he was being too emotional—which was probably very dangerous in his youth. But that was the exact risk that I needed him to take. "Luke," I said gently, "what you just said is very helpful, talking about how bullying is in general. But I was also hoping that you'd talk more about yourself, about your *personal* experiences and feelings. That's what might make more people think, you know?"

He sat and swirled the coffee in his cup, watching the ripples and waves as if they were snippets of memories threatening to surge past his defensive dikes. "No," he said quietly, "I can't do that. That's why I walked out the other night [at the seminar]. I can't go back to those feelings." He swept his arm across the college campus before us. "This is my new life. No one knows me here. No one hates me here. I'm studying to be a psychologist. That's why I agreed to talk to you. I'm going to find ways of helping kids like me *before* they get trashed by the bullying.

"You see, it's, like, a *killer circle*. First, a little kid gets picked out to get bullied—God knows why—maybe he pees in his pants or can't play sports or something—and then the *killer circle* starts. The more he gets teased and excluded, the weirder he feels about himself. The weirder he feels, the weirder he acts, the more he gets teased—*GOD*" he suddenly sighed loudly, "*I hate those words—'teased' and 'bullied'—they don't come close to what it is.*"

Luke worked to calm himself, and then answered my question again, sounding even surer. "No," he shook his head, "I can't go back there. I have to move forward in my life and help other people." Then he showed that common, secret motivation that leads so many to become therapists: *the intense wish to fix ourselves without having to face ourselves*: "I'm going to keep my personal side out of my work," he said. "I just have to forget about what happened to me and move on."

"Luke," I asked, "isn't that like picking up where your jerks left off, saying that your feelings have no worth, that you're supposed to just shut up and take it and feel terrible all of your life? Won't that keep your own 'killer circle' going around?"

Luke weighed my words for minutes, but they came up light. "No," he said, "I can't go there. Not now. Maybe another time." He packed up his things, carefully wrapping the remaining schnecken as if they were the best part of himself, and handed them to me. "Sorry," he said, and then he left.

Watching him walk away I realized that he had already explained why an old part of me disliked him: *His "killer circle" had left holes and scars in his ability to easily connect with another human being.* Even after 20 years of working as a psychologist, a small-minded, 6-year-old part of me was repulsed by Luke. I stared down at the schnecken in my hand, thinking that perhaps they were the only part of him that he could share, that he had given me what he thought was his best, since the rest was so worthless and unlovable.

I felt sad, and ashamed. I wanted to run after him and apologize—for everyone.

About seven months later there was a message on my machine. "I don't know if you remember me?" it said, "I'm the schnecken guy from [the college]. Call me if you still want to talk."

We met in the same room as before, but today it was nearly empty. The tall, soaring windows welcomed bursts of sunlight that periodically flooded the room, blasting through breaks in the winter clouds that were moving past. It felt like seasons were changing.

Luke had coffee and determination waiting again. "I decided that there's a reason I should do this. Right now, I'm like a war correspondent who just came home—things are fresh in my memory. I can help people know what it's really like. I'm at the perfect age. I'm old enough to be able to put feelings into words, but I'm still young enough to *really* remember what it was like. I'm afraid that as I get older, life might get better for me, and I'll forget, like everyone else does, just how bad it really was. And that would abandon all of those kids going through this now. I can't do that to them."

In a strangely detached fashion, Luke went into a lot of detail about his specific memories of teasing and bullying which started at about age 6, after he had a wetting incident at school. He recalled having had a few friends periodically, but these were methodically targeted by the bullies and ultimately forced to choose sides, choices where Luke lost every time. He recalled being so incredibly perplexed about why he had been picked as the "loser" that he would furiously study himself in the mirror, trying to find and fix any tiny flaws that might explain his rejection. But it seemed that no matter how hard he tried, things only got worse. Over the years, that fixation would grow into all-consuming attempts for unattainable perfection. His obsessions and compulsions grew like a thousand strangling vines, all from one maddening, unrelenting question: *Why do they hate me?*

Speaking in flat, emotionless words that were wrenching to hear, he chronicled an escalating pattern of brutality. He detailed one of the many days when it took him hours to make what should have been a ten minute walk home from school because the tormentors were all lying in wait for him on each route he had tried. As he spoke I pictured a hunted, terrified creature, desperately trying to find safety from wild packs of killer dogs. I found myself unconsciously wishing that he had taken a stand, and refused to run. That's when he explained what happens when "losers" follow the advice of journalists, or the wishes of psychologists. He told what happens when the hunted take a stand against the hunters.

"One Christmas day they wanted my go-cart. That was the best present I ever got, and they surrounded me and demanded that I give it to them. That day, for some reason, I just refused. I knew that they would beat me, but I didn't care. They tried spitting on me and pulling me out, but I wrapped my fingers so hard around the steering wheel that they couldn't pry them off. One kid had some matches and said that he was going to set me on fire. I really thought that I was going to die, and I still wouldn't budge. The last thing I remember is getting punched a lot, and a kid doing these karate kicks to my head. My parents found me an hour later. They told me that I was unconscious and still in the cart, still gripping that wheel. They said that it was hard for them to pry my fingers loose. I ended up in the hospital.

"When my folks told me about how they found me, I thought that what I did might cause the bullies to back off, you know, showing them that no matter what they did, it wouldn't matter." He shrugged. "It didn't change a thing. Neither did fighting. One of my counselors told me to fight, so I did. Amazingly, I won. I beat one of the cool bullies. I didn't know that I could fight. I thought that I had found my answer. At the end of the fight, I offered to shake hands, and the rest of the kids . . . they ganged up on me, like I had ruined their fun, like I was a boxer who was supposed to lose a boxing match that had been fixed. Like things were not the way they were supposed to be, because . . ."

Luke was becoming increasingly agitated as he spoke. "*This* isn't right," he said, annoyed with himself. "This is *not* what I want people to hear about. See, getting hurt physically—even real bad a few times is *not* what does the damage. I'd take that stuff in a minute compared to the other stuff. For my graduation project [from high school] I did a research paper on bullying, and I interviewed some girls who had been 'teased,' as they call it. What they went through might be worse—and they hardly ever got punched. The really bad part is . . ."

He paused and looked down as if to gather his courage. He looked up at me as if I was the toughest challenge of his 18-year-old life, and he didn't know if he was up to it. I felt as if I represented a world that had tormented and abandoned him, and now wanted *him* to help *us* out. He was willing to do this.

". . . the bad part is not the hurt outside, but the hurt *inside*. I remember all those faces that would laugh, or tease, or not invite me to their parties, or play a game missing one player rather than having me on their side, or just refusing to talk to me. That stuff, the non-physical stuff, that would happen every day. Even when it was quiet, the hatred—*it was still there,* you know, ready to happen in an instant. If I was dumb enough to try and act like I was OK, like I was as good as anyone else, I'd get flattened in a minute—with words and looks and laughter. The beatings and chasings were almost like a weird relief to the quiet bullying, where no one says a word. That was the worst—just living every day knowing that everyone hates you." His head went back down, but there were no tears where tears should have been. It felt like Luke was way past tears, into—"*What?*" I wondered.

Luke now spoke so softly, I had to lean forward to hear him. It seemed he was slowly and agonizingly tearing a scar off of a terrible wound that never had healed. "Then, one day, you . . . you suddenly quit trying," he said. "One day, you just accept the fact that you *are* a loser, and always will be, even though you have no idea why. You suddenly understand that they [the bullies] have the power of life and death over your world—not the dying kind of death, but the *always alone* kind.

"That's the day when you start to really get weird. You become the thing that they said you were: the weirdo-loser-geek-misfit. Everyone becomes your enemy or your potential enemy, because everyone either torments you or eventually turns on you. So you stay alone, and you get worse and worse at being able to talk to people. Oh, yeah, you go to the soccer games that the counselor tells your parents to sign you up for, and you act like you're having a good time, and you lie and tell your parents how you're making lots of friends. You do that because suddenly it's too embarrassing to even tell people who love you that you are a loser."

Luke paused another moment and then winced as if from an intense pain. "I remember the last time I tried to tell my dad the truth. I was, like, 11. He was making me go back to a soccer team that hated me. They had pulled my pants down in front of everyone at the last practice. He said that they were just fooling around, and that kids do that to everybody, and that I needed to learn how to take a joke to get along. I remember looking hard into his eyes and realizing that he was *ashamed* of me, and that he desperately needed me to be normal. That's when I saw how completely alone I was in the world. I had even lost my parents to the bullies.

"That's when I began to pretend that it wasn't happening, and that's when you just get weirder and weirder. I tried to kill myself when I was 12. The hospital said that I was the youngest suicider they had ever seen." Luke looked sideways at me. "Do you know what my first thought was when I woke up? That the kids would find out that I was such a loser that I *couldn't even kill myself right*." He exhaled sharply. "And they did find out," he nodded. I sat quietly as that pain surged and then faded for Luke. "For a long time when I was young, I remember wanting to scream. Not scream curses or even to yell at kids to be nice to me—I just wanted to scream . . . 'Why?' That's all—just—'Why?' 'WHY?'"

A group of laughing, chatting students walked in, shattering the quiet. Another huge volley of brilliant spring sun burst into the room, causing the group to point and cheer for the nearing end of winter. Luke just sat and watched. "And them?" I asked, "Are they still the enemy?" He leaned back and swept some unseen dirt off of his pants. "Those kids have no idea," he said. "They probably watched someone get 'teased' or 'bullied' through school, or maybe some of them did it themselves, and they think like the journalist did—that it's no big deal. That's why it's still so hard for me to talk to them now. It's like there was some war that no one knew about, but I was there, and I got hurt. They don't remember—and I can't forget."

Luke started to gather up his things, even though I had made no sign of wanting to end, as if he had a practice of leaving people before they would desert him. "I've been thinking of getting this tattoo," he said, ". . . a big, ugly one on half of my face. I didn't know why until just now." He turned and looked at the crowd of happy kids, and then turned to me: *"Part of me wants everyone to know that I'm scarred."*

He stood up, signaling that we were through. I packed up my things, and thanked him for his time. Then, looking to lighten the moment, I said, "What? No wonderful schnecken?" Luke smiled the first real smile that I'd seen and pointed towards the empty coffee counter. "You know," he said, "I just had a thought that maybe tomorrow I should bring in a tray and just leave it for the students. Maybe some will like me for that." He shook his head. "So I guess another part of me wants to come home from the war."

A week later as I walked through that room, on the coffee counter sat a large tray of schnecken. Behind it there was a sign:

SCHNECKEN
PRICE: ONE ACT OF KINDNESS FOR A STRANGER
To Starving Students,
Compliments of:
Luke, the Schnecken Guy

I stood there next to some happy students who were eating and raving about the goodies. Nodding my amazed head, I softly said, "Welcome home, Luke." Hearing me, one kid turned and asked, "Huh?" "Oh, nothing," I said.

They wouldn't understand. They probably had forgotten.

Whenever I deal with kids who are being bullied, Luke always pops into my mind as a kind of mentor. Few of them have been bullied as viciously, but all know his intense pain of inexplicable and devastating exclusion and rejection— not just from the jerk kids, but also from the "nice" kids and parents, who, like "nice" psychologists, often feel a strange aversion towards a victim.

He also helps me to confront adults who never knew that pain or who have forgotten it, people who like to ridicule the concept of self-worth in children, distorting what it means, and mocking its life-sustaining importance. Luke reminds me that good self-esteem is not thinking that you're better than everyone else, or that you're entitled to win every game that you play. Love of self is a simple, healing awareness that you are as worthwhile as everyone else, and they are as worthwhile as you. He reminds me that fierce, win/lose competition is wonderful when it occurs on an athletic ball field among those intense kids who enjoy the sport of a game, and not when it occurs on a social battlefield among brutal kids who enjoy the sport of a wounding.

Losing athletic or social contests does not make you a loser, just as winning them does not make you a good person. Competition has little to do with character. Compassion has everything to do with it.

In my last contact with Luke, just before he finished his community college stint, he told me that he had switched his major to business, since he wanted to open a chain of "schnecken houses." I joked that he should be careful, because there were parts of the country where they think that "schnecken" means illegal sexual activity. He stood and laughed, loud and full, for anyone to see. That was a good moment.

Last week I was romping in the community pool with my 7-year-old and her friends, and a shy, downward-looking little boy stood painfully on the edge of the action, wanting so much to join in, but not knowing what to do, perhaps terrified of being told that he wasn't worthy. Without a thought, Sarah tossed him a lifeline. "HEY," she yelled, "HELP US GET MY DAD—HE'S CRAZY!"

"Way to go, Sarah," I thought, "Way to go. That's one for The Schnecken Guy!"

18

THE LIONESS IN
THE LEG TRAP

Becky's Story

I've come to believe that the only certain thing about raising children is the uncertainty. As a parent, I'm often panicked as I watch other parents much better than I am, getting ambushed by crises that no one could have anticipated—no one. Drugs, arrests, pregnancies, even suicides can seem to spring out of the jungle to devastate our children, even those who seem so strong and so wise.

Becky caused me a lot of panic. If I, the psychologist, could never have anticipated what happened to this child, then how can I, the father, protect my own children? The fact is that none of us can, not fully. We just have to look to child-heroes like Becky to learn what wisdom she can offer to help us to help our children avoid the leg traps of adolescence.

$\sim$

I had to laugh when I saw the message from Becky's mother asking for an appointment for Becky. *"Uh-oh, girl,"* I wondered with a smile, *"Who'd you punch this time?"* Now 16 years old, she was a client who made me feel like an old-time neighborhood physician, the doctor who would get to watch children grow up in medical snapshots over the years. But it was not mumps or measles that caused her to be dragged into my office; it was Becky's indomitable spirit.

I pulled her file and flipped through it, noting the complaints that would leave her sulking in my waiting room every few years, almost like clockwork. At age 4 she was refusing to go to her "stupid, boring school with the poo-poo head teacher." At age 6, she was referred by her summer camp for fighting—elective combat, it turned out, during which she simultaneously beat up *two* male campmates who were picking on a 4-year-old, and who were dumb enough to laugh at her repeated warnings to stop. "I warned them. I warned them a bunch of times," she had said, "but they wouldn't listen. They listen now."

She took a hiatus for a few years, but when she turned 10, she actually asked to see me. She found herself locked in a running verbal battle with her Sunday school rabbi, who, she said, was teaching, ". . . a bunch of crap, and he knows it, and he gets real mad when I tell him that, and he tells my parents, and then I get in trouble." She wanted me to tell the rabbi "what was up." She was nice about the disappointing fact that I was a wimp for declining to argue Jewish law with a rabbi. She said that she and I were becoming friends. Becky had once told her mom that one day she was going to marry a man just like her dad and Dr. Bradley, except "somebody more braver."

Age 13 presented a tough 8th grade situation. Becky was so smart that she had been placed in an 11th grade advanced math class where she instantly mastered the material while refusing to do any of the teacher's ". . . ridiculous, pointless homework that he assigns just so he can look like he does a good job—which he doesn't, because he's a moron . . ."

Bright, fearless, artistic, pretty, athletic, Becky was one of those kids loved by almost everyone, and unloved by anyone foolish enough to *tell* her to do something, instead of asking and explaining why. For Becky's most formidable characteristic was her fierce independence, an autonomy on steroids that kept her in the frequent company of disciplinarians, playground aides, and psychologists. A decade earlier, I had learned that the only way to influence her was to treat her with honesty, respect, and caring, and then to engage her through a set of logical questions which she would consider at her own pace, instantaneously disregarding any thoughts that she saw as flawed. If I batted .300 with her, I thought that I was doing great.

At the conclusion of each round of counseling, my closing chat with her very patient, very tired parents was always some version of: *"She's great. I'm so glad that she's not my daughter, but she's great. One day, if you guys survive her childhood, you'll likely see her blossom into an incredible young woman. I have no idea what she'll do, but I believe that she'll do it 110 percent. See you in a few years."*

As I dialed her mom's number for this next round, I got my pen ready to write down the new "presenting problem" in Becky's file. Mom said that Becky would only come in to see me if Mom promised to say nothing about why. I laughed, hearing what I thought was a classic Becky proclamation there. But Mom did not laugh at all, and in a week, neither would I. Because nothing could have amazed me more than the new problem that my disbelieving hand would eventually scrawl. And, just as I had predicted, she would do it at 110 percent.

A week later, I found myself stunned in my own waiting room, facing a girl named Becky whom I did not recognize. Gone were the brilliant, flashing eyes, the well-fleshed, athletic limbs and the in-your-face-cockiness. In their place were dark, sunken eyes, bony arms and legs, and a profound air of defeat. When she saw me, her angry face suddenly broke into a weak smile that seemed to surprise her, as if she had found an old, forgotten friend. And perhaps remembered an old, forgotten piece of herself.

She struggled to find something witty to say, a tradition from our earlier sessions, one that used to be so easy for her. "Same tune, different shit, huh doc?" she said coarsely. The old Becky always avoided profanity, saying that cursing was just too easy a thing to do, that it was just for little kids trying to look cool. We both became a little uncomfortable, likely thinking that same thought. "Oh—yeah," I stammered, "something like that . . . I guess . . ." As I reached out to shake her hand, she froze and shot a panicked look through the window into the parking lot. "Um, my hands are, like, a mess from lunch," she said, "you know, grease burgers—I'll catch you on the flip side, OK?" she said, referencing her withheld hand. "Sure," I said, turning to see a car just outside the window with a young, tee-shirted, shaven-headed male in sunglasses watching our every move. "Is everything—OK?" I asked. "Is that a friend of yours?"

Becky didn't answer. She just got up and walked hesitantly into the office, like something was pulling her back. I turned and looked again out the window. The boy slowly took off his sunglasses and glared. "Sweet-looking guy," I joked. Becky still said nothing as she sank down on the couch, kicked off her shoes, and curled her legs up underneath herself just as she done since she was 4. She closed her eyes and seemed to just drink in the comfort of the room, as if she had been gone for 30 years, not 3.

"Where's Elmo," she finally asked, looking for her favorite office toy. "Sorry," I said, "Elmo ran off with a very sad little girl who loved him very much. She had lost her dad so I thought that it would be OK with you." She nodded, and then said, "I think that I've lost my dad too—and maybe my mom." "Because of the sweet-looking guy?" I probed. *"Don't call him that!"* she said pointedly. "What's his name?" I asked. "You don't need to know his name," she answered, but she spoke as if she were repeating the words of another. "Well, can I call him Smiley?" I joked, realizing two seconds too late that I was acting like her dad, unconsciously caught up in a contest with the scary kid in the car. **"F— YOU!"** she yelled, **"F— YOU! OK?"** She stared out my window, arms angrily crossed—but she didn't leave.

Remembering how she hated indirectness, I cut to the chase. "OK," I said. "I got it. I'm sorry. I was being stupid. I'm doing that insane adult thing where I'm assuming that you are who you were at 13, when you said you would never have a boyfriend. Now, can you tell me what's going on?" She drew a huge breath, held it for the longest time, and then exhaled slowly. Her fury seemed to vanish with her breath. But the overwhelming sadness that remained made the fury look much better.

"He," she nodded towards the parking lot, "He wants me to move in with him. My parents say they'll call the police if I do; actually, that's what my father says. My mother, she's just crying and upset and begging me not to go. Legally, I don't think they can stop me, but

. . . I don't know . . ." When she said nothing for a bit, I asked, "And what does Becky want?" She walked over to my shelf and grabbed a Bullwinkle figure, another old favorite of hers. She sat back down and hugged Bullwinkle hard, unashamed of acting like she was four again, looking like she would go back there if she could.

"What Becky wants doesn't matter. All Becky wants is for everyone to be OK. But Dad's gonna' call the cops if I go, and he [the guy in the car] said he'll . . . well, he didn't say kill, but he said that nobody better get in his way, since he loves me so much." Her eyes flashed up at me. "He's a hunter—he's got guns. But he's not violent, really. He gets mad sometimes and . . . but, he'd never shoot anyone, OK?" "I don't know," I answered, "do you think it's OK?" She peered out the window as if she were seeing him, although his car was around the corner. But for the first time since I had known her, she was telling the "denial lies" of adults who don't want to see the things that they already know.

"He's, like, incredibly loving. He's completely devoted to me. He says that we belong together for the rest of our lives. He says that he goes crazy whenever we're not together. He's, like, sensitive, you know? Oh, he acts all tough and everything but that's just a cover for him. He gets so sad that he cries with me."

"Becky," I maneuvered, "can you tell me about the last time he cried?" She shot up like a rocket: *"My mom talked to you, didn't she—she broke her promise. He was right. He told me that we couldn't trust either of you. WELL, THE COUNSELING DEAL IS OFF!"* As she headed to the door, I said, "Becky, I give you my word that your mother said nothing except to make this appointment. I asked, but she refused, since she had promised you. You know me, Becky. Now ask yourself, would I say that if it weren't true?"

She kicked my door hard, over and over. "***I DON'T KNOW!*** she sobbed, ***"I DON'T KNOW! THAT'S THE PROBLEM! I DON'T KNOW WHO TO TRUST, OR WHAT'S RIGHT OR . . . ."*** The door suddenly flew open, knocking her hard on her head, as "he" rushed in. **"WHAT DID YOU DO TO HER?"** he screamed in my face. **"IF YOU HURT HER I SWEAR TO GOD I'LL . . ."** "Becky-is-not-hurt," I said methodically and firmly, "at least she wasn't until that door hit her. Son, if you think that I hurt her, there's the phone—call 911—*right now*. If you want, I'll dial."

His eyes told it all. They danced around, trying to figure out his best play to keep this girl under his thumb. "Yeah, well—you *better* not have," he warned. "C'mon Becky, I'm gettin' you out of this bullshit place." He put his arm around this sobbing child, and led her out. As they left I could hear his voice trailing off, scolding her: "I *told* you. Now didn't I *tell* you? *What did I tell you*? Didn't I tell you that doctors just mess you up? From now on you'll just listen to me and *do what I tell you to do* 'cause . . ." I didn't want to hear anymore.

I called Mom. She painfully painted the same picture that too many other parents have painted—but the other parents were describing how they watched their kids slowly and imperceptibly slide into drug addictions, not boy addictions. The similarities were incredible.

Becky had met him about six months ago, a cousin to one of the girls that was in a school play with her. Things were fine at first, although Mom worried that he was 19 and he had his own apartment. Becky was still Becky back then, she said—happy, doing way too many activities, trying to keep up with way too many friends, and on the go all the time. Initially, Becky spoke openly to her mom about him, saying that at first she mostly felt sorry for him, since his two prior girlfriends had cheated on him, breaking his heart. Then, very slowly, as water dripping from a faucet can eventually cause a flood, things in the relationship began to change—and so did Becky.

He would call her night and day with emotional crises, things that he desperately needed to talk to her about. But the crises always seemed to occur most whenever Becky had some activity planned. Soon, teachers, coaches, and directors started leaving messages on the home phone asking where Becky was, and why she had missed her commitments. He would appear outside of any activity she attended, waiting for her and insisting that she spend time with him—not with friends, not with family, just him. And, to Mom's knowledge, he never went to even one event of hers.

Conflicts between Becky and her folks started getting more frequent and louder, commonly ending with Becky crying and running out of the house. He always seemed to be there waiting. The teachers, coaches, and directors stopped calling because, one by one, Becky dropped out of her activities. She always had a good reason, or so it seemed, like saying that she was tired of soccer or that she had outgrown drama. But the worried calls of the adults were soon replaced by the worried calls of the kids, friends wondering where she was, asking what hole in the ground she had fallen into.

With tears, Mom said that she finally realized things were out of control when three of Becky's friends came to see Mom, saying that they were scared about the control he had over Becky. He had now forbidden her to see her friends, telling her that they were a bad influence. Out of love for Becky, one of the friends admitted to Mom that she had smoked weed a few times, but that Becky never did, and that Becky used to argue against drugs. He, according to the friend, used that to tell Becky that she could not hang out with "drug users." Now, Mom said, they were living in this precarious situation where there seemed to be no options.

When they would forbid Becky from seeing him, she'd run away. The cops would bring her back, but said there was little else that they could do. They advised counseling, which Becky refused until finally agreeing to see me in exchange for a bribe. She had started smoking cigarettes and always needed money. "It's horrible, isn't it?" Mom sighed, "Cigarettes are the best thing that's happened to her in 6 months. Otherwise, we'd have no control at all."

"Becky wouldn't tell me his name," I said, "Can you?" "It's Michael," she answered, "same as my husband's." It was also the same as my own name.

We set up an appointment for the following week, and we waited and hoped.

Becky was a no-show for three appointments, but she made the fourth, thanks to the power of the Marlboro Man. This time, Michael brought her into the waiting room, hanging all over her, insisting that she sit on his lap. "Perhaps you should both come in . . ." I started to ask. He interrupted with a snicker and said, "Yeah. OK." I continued my sentence, ". . . if it's all right with Becky." Still draped over her, he glared and said, "Yeah, it's *all right* with Becky."

"Well," I said, "there's this rule I have to follow about having people speak for themselves, so, if you don't mind, can I ask *Becky* what *she* wants to do?"

Her eyes locked on mine and flickered as if something had hit her, like someone beginning to wake up. She stood silently for thirty very long seconds, until she finally said, "Yes, I think that I *do* want the two of us to come in." Michael suddenly looked very uncomfortable.

He sat on the couch and patted the seat next to him, an apparent command of where she was to sit. She paused, and then took her decades-old spot, away from him. She kicked off her shoes, and curled her legs up under herself. He stared at her as if she was breaking some sacred law, and then he shifted over, smiling and draping his arm around her. Giving him a small smile, she lifted his arm off her shoulder, and then tried to simply hold his hand. He angrily pulled his hand back.

I didn't want all that was being said to be spoiled with words, so I just sat quietly. It felt like Becky was thinking new, old thoughts. "So," Michael sneered, "this is what they pay you to do? Sit and stare?" "Sometimes," I nodded. "This time is for you guys to talk, not me." Becky looked like she was going to burst. She turned on an astonished Michael. *"What the hell is it with you?"* she snapped. *"Why do you hate everybody I like?"* They stared at each other for a long time without words. It felt as if Michael was reaching for word weapons in suddenly empty holsters. Finding none, he fell back on his ace.

"I . . . I love you . . ." he stammered, "I need you so much . . ." "STOP THAT!" Becky yelled. "Every time I try to say something I'm mad about, you either scream at me or you cry and say how much you need me, that you can't live without me, that you'd kill yourself if I ever left . . ." "I *never* said I'd kill . . ." Michael interrupted. Becky interrupted right back: "DON'T EVEN GO THERE!" she yelled, "DON'T YOU DARE GO THERE! STOP MAKING THINGS UP LIKE A LITTLE BOY! I CAN'T . . ." Becky started to cry. ". . . I can't . . . fix you," she said. Michael tried to put his arm around her, but she stood up. "There's something wrong with you, and I've tried and tried, but nothing's ever enough. Whatever I give to you, you need more and more . . . like I'm heroin or something. I've got nothing left to give and you still need more."

Michael was almost gagging, like he might throw up. "I NEVER ASKED YOU FOR A THING!" HE YELLED, "I GAVE UP EVERYTHING FOR YOU. YOU'RE JUST A LYING, DRUGGIE BITCH LIKE THE REST OF THEM. AND I KNOW YOU SLEEP AROUND ON ME. HAVE YOU TOLD THE DOCTOR ABOUT THAT? HUH? THAT YOU'RE A WHORE?"

His eyes shifted back and forth as if he had vomited out things that he could not believe. Neither could Becky. "You're . . . *really* . . . crazy, aren't you?" she said incredulously. They just looked at each other for a while, and then Becky sat back down, bewildered. She turned to him to say something, but he abruptly exploded out of the room, screaming curses, and slamming my door so hard that my wall clock crashed to the floor. Becky sat frozen for a moment, and then ran after him, begging him to stop and come back. Through the window, I watched her burst into tears as he roared out of the parking lot, throwing fingers to the world. She stood and cried hard, like something was tearing inside of her. Slowly, she walked back in and sat down.

"You know who's more nuts than him?" she said, "Me. If you think that I'm, like, done with Michael, you're wrong. I still love him. I still feel like he needs me, that he won't be OK without me. How can I leave him like that? He's a little boy—he really might kill himself, and then . . . *it would be my fault.*" "So," I asked, "you must give up your life because he tells you that he can't handle his life on his own?"

She looked straight at me, nodded and said, "Yes." "And so," I continued, "the only way you can leave is for him to throw you out, or . . ." "Or . . . for me to die," she said. "No. I haven't tried killing myself, but . . . I thought about it once . . . or twice. But I'd never do it." "Becky," I said, "please stand up." I led her to the wall mirror. "Tell me what you see," I asked. She looked long and hard, as if she had not really looked in a long time. "I see a girl who looks like crap," she said. And then her old wit reappeared. Quoting a famous children's book, she asked me, "Brown bear, brown bear, what do *you* see?"

"Me?" I said, "I see a *dying girl* looking at me—one who's not sleeping or eating or taking care of herself. I see the most courageous, determined, pain-in-the-ass kid I ever knew, a once-proud lioness, now with her foot caught in a trap, gnawing her own leg off because she can't figure a way out. She can't see that guys like Michael are leg traps that suck the life out of girls like her, and then throw them away one day. I see a girl who doesn't know the difference between love and neediness, or the difference between a man and a boy. That's what I see."

She turned towards the door. "I have to think," she said firmly. "I'll call you." Then, slightly embarrassed, she turned and sighed, "but first I need to call home for a ride."

Becky's path was not easy. Guys like Michael are very good at their game. Girls like Becky are very bad at letting go. For another few stormy months, that game raged back and forth until, at last, one day, Becky finally drew her line in the sand and obtained a protection order. Michael had been slapping her around.

In our last session, Becky had given up the denial lies of adults, and had grown back into the truth telling of children. "It's embarrassing to say this," she said, "but I recently learned a lot about the real Michael. His other girlfriends, the ones he says cheated on him? Well, he slapped them around, too. One he beat so badly that she was in the hospital. And, the hardest part, or the part that makes me feel the stupidest? Remember that guy who couldn't live a day without me—remember him? Well, the day after the protection order was served, *he got a new girlfriend.*" For a long time, Becky sat thinking all of the things I had hoped that she might.

Sensing another ending, we chatted about her old times in the office, and laughed together about our memories. Then she paused and said, "I changed my mind about you letting Elmo run off with that other little girl. That's not OK. Elmo was a nice guy. Nice guys are hard to find." "Nice guys," I said, "love women who don't *desperately* need them. And they love women who don't *need to be desperately needed* either. They love women who just like hanging out together—maybe together for the rest of their lives—but as *individual people*, OK on their own."

Her eyes flashed an old familiar light. "You can, like, shut up with the shrink stuff," she smiled, "I get it. I'm not stupid, you know."

Becky was back.

~

Reliable numbers support the astonishing nightmare that one-third of our daughters can expect to be in at least one abusive, controlling relationship before they graduate from high school. The psychic damage is appalling for both the girls who get snared, and for the boys who are allowed to believe that leg traps disguised as love are OK.

So many girls, just like Becky, seem to stumble into these traps without any warning. So many girls, just like Becky, seem so strong and vital that the thought of these daughters getting caught in controlling, abusive relationships never enters the minds of the parents. But such is the way with traps. They're hidden, deadly, and seem to spring out of nowhere to take down even the strongest lionesses. The only defense is to talk with our children, the girls and the boys, about these pitfalls that can be hidden in that enchanting garden called love before they start to wander through. They step a lot smarter that way.

And Becky? In my last update, her mom told me that at age 24, she was dating "a really nice guy" for two years, one who thought that Becky was just terrific as she was—a guy who didn't want to own her. Mom said that like everything else she had done, Becky was into that relationship 110 percent, talking about marriage and houses and children. I guess it can be that way for once-abused women when they finally find their Elmo.

19

THE SHOOTING STAR

Karin's Story

As I prepared to write about adolescent heroes for this book, I found myself shielding this heroine from my editor by leaving her off my list. I thought I was avoiding her tale because it is sad, perhaps too sad for the telling. In truth, I was also hiding it from myself, trying not to relive the dark pain of pointless adolescent tragedy.

But Karin's brave life demands so much more than obscurity. Hers is a story far too heroic to be left untold, and far too valuable not to be shared with others who will be wiser for the hearing. In the end, this sharing was Karin's decision to make.

She wanted you to know about her.

~

The 15-year-old girl caught my eye immediately. She was sitting with a group of teenagers who were snickering and laughing about the film they were watching on teenage alcoholism. Prior to the film starting, she had been clowning along with the best of them. She had a quality that somehow set her apart from the others. It was a sort of energy, a brightness in her face—not a niceness, but more of an intense power not often seen in 15-year-olds. But as the story on the screen progressed, the light around her face began to dim as she slowly withdrew into some other world apart from her friends. The subject of the film was talking about his experiences as an adolescent alcoholic, and she seemed riveted. I ran down my list of names and decided that she was probably the one who had signed in as "Karin—that's with an *i*, not an *e* (*pulleeez*)."

As the boy in the film spoke of his dangerous, alcohol-fueled behaviors, she began to grow distant to the point that another girl began looking curiously at her, apparently wondering why Karin was no longer in the fun. When the boy spoke about having blackouts (alcohol-induced losses of memory) and doing things like running drunk into traffic, her eyes suddenly went wide. At the same time, some in the group started shrieking with laughter after one yelled, "*Hey Karin*! This is all about *you*!" Karin startled as if waking up from a bad dream. Then, one by one, she slowly met every pair of mocking eyes in the group without fear or shame, just with the thousand-yard stare of a gunfighter. And, one by one, the kids stopped laughing and jeering, and sullenly settled down to watch the rest of the film. Karin stared out the window, but still listened to the boy on the screen until the film was over.

As the group got up to leave, I held up my clipboard, pointed to her name, and jokingly asked, "Excuse me, but are you "*Karinwithan'i'notan'e'pulleeez*?" I got the same gunfighter stare. "If this is going to be a lecture," she said flatly, "I'm busy." "Five minutes?" I pleaded. She sat back down without answering. "That was pretty amazing," I said, "the way you silenced those kids in the group. You looked like Clint Eastwood in 'Dirty Harry.' I always tried to pull that look off, but I never got it quite right. Actually, I never even came close. But you—you got it right."

She sat and stared unsmilingly at me for a few seconds and then said, "If you've got something to say to me, just say it, OK?" "OK," I answered, "but is a question allowed?" "Depends," she answered, and then she immediately pushed on without waiting for the question. "Yes, I do drink—a lot. Yes, I get blackouts, and yes, I do dangerous things when I'm like that." Then she sat and studied my face as if waiting for a reaction. "And . . . you do know that can kill you?" I asked. She nodded slowly, still watching my face as if she was looking for something. "Do you *want* to die?" I asked.

She sat and stared without answering for a very long 30 seconds or so. "My last shrink, I wouldn't talk to her. I stared out the window until she finally gave up." Still not answering my question she added, "I have to think about this. By the way, my father knows about my drinking. That's why I wouldn't talk to the last lady [therapist]. It wasn't that she ratted me out—which she did—it was that she made my dad worried and upset. I warned her about that, but she wouldn't listen. My pop, he's not . . . not very, um . . . strong. When he gets upset, then he drinks, too. A lot. There's no point in getting him involved. OK?"

I shook my head sadly. "Not OK," I answered. "Sorry, but I won't con you on this. What you're doing can *kill* you, so I have to be sure that your father fully understands that. I don't have a choice here. It's the law." She smiled a strange half-smile and then flattened me with her insight and awareness—not to put me down, but to let me know who she was.

"You're wrong," she corrected. "You've got lots of choices—you don't *have to* tell him. You could pretend that I never told you so you'd be off the hook with the law thing. Or you could decide that it was more important to get me to talk to you since I might not come back if you don't do what I say. Or . . . you could blackmail me and try and make me promise not to drink anymore or you'll tell my father. Or you could lie to me and then secretly tell him like the last shrink did. It's all about the choices we make—we really don't *have to* do anything, do we?" I humbly nodded. "OK," she said. "Good luck with pa-pa." As she left, she turned around and added, "I won't hold that [my calling her father] against you. If I don't come back, which is likely, it will just be because . . . well, because . . . I decide that there's really no point."

"And if you don't come back," I asked, "would that be something you *have* to do or just a *choice*?" She smiled, sadly but appreciatively, and said, "Peace up." And then she left.

She was right about Dad, but wrong about herself. For in my meeting the next day with her father, Karin amazed me by showing up to sit in on my "ratting-her-out" session. When I got to the bad news part, he promptly flew into a rage, screaming about how unfair this all was to *him*, how *he,* as a single father, should not have to deal with this crap from his daughter, what a "bitch" his daughter was, just like her "bitch" mother who left him stuck with Karin as a baby, and so on, and so on, mostly about himself. With some bemusement, Karin sat quietly and watched as I unsuccessfully attempted to get Dad to talk about Karin's situation.

After my third attempt at refocusing Dad, Karin jumped in, angry at first, but then eventually controlling herself and calming her father. She started as a vicious, angry teenager searching for a parent, and then gradually evolved into the comforting 15-year-old mother of an overwhelmed 43-year-old boy.

She began with *"AIN'T IT INTERESTING, FATHER, HOW THE WHOLE GODDAMN WORLD IS ALL ABOUT YOU?"* and fifteen minutes later she ended with "Look, it's all right, Pop, it's all right. I'm sorry. I know you did the best you could. I know you're just worried about me dying and all. I promise you, I won't hurt myself—*I swear on grammmom's grave.*" Karin reached out and took her father's hand. *"OK? Look at me, Pop—look at me. Are we OK here?"* And like a recently panicked 4-year-old, Karin's father nodded as he stifled his rage and wrung his hands, sucking up all of the comfort and reassurance in the room, leaving none for his daughter.

As he quieted, Karin glanced towards me. I expected to get an "I-told-you-so-you-dummy" look. What I saw instead were the eyes of a 50-year-old in a 15-year-old face, showing understanding and sadness—for *her father,* not for herself. To the 50-year-old Karin, I nodded a silent apology and acknowledgment. Then, to the 15-year-old, I asked, "So where do we go from here?" Dad never even considered that I might be speaking to him, as well. He just let Karin take over, as, apparently, he always did.

"From here," Karin sighed, "I guess that we try to stop drinking." And then with only concern in her voice she added, "Maybe we both should stop, huh, Pop?" Dad's fury reappeared in a flash, a child insulted by an insinuation that he drank too much; a little boy having a childish tantrum that pretty much confirmed the difficult truth. Like a caring, disciplined parent seeing her child overwhelmed by the difficult truth, Karin apologized again to restore her father's dignity, and gently led him out of the room as the session ended. Probably only as a comfort to her father, she said to me, "Let's make another appointment." Then to her father she added, "I'm sorry I made you mad. I think Dr. Bradley can really help me with this. I really do."

I think that was the only lie Karin ever told in front of me. I also think that lying was very hard for her to do. I wondered if she felt like she needed a drink.

The following Monday she did show up for her appointment, but looking awful. Her face was drawn and splotchy, and her eyes looked scared. She waved off my concerns and spoke in her intense, quiet voice. She held a pillow in her lap, but awkwardly, as if she didn't quite know how to hug it, but very much wanted to feel its warmth—like she couldn't connect, or was somehow afraid of connecting.

"It happened again," she said to her pillow. "On Saturday I went out with my friends and I tried not to drink. They don't believe that I get blackouts, you know. They think I just like to pretend that I don't remember what I do when I get drunk, because I do crazy, raunchy things." She paused and looked up. "Do I have to tell you exactly what I do?" Before I could answer, she answered herself, speaking again to her pillow. "I guess that's another one of those choices, huh? OK. Well, I do sick sex things that *I don't do*, and I do crazy risk things that *I don't do*. What I mean is that those are things that are not me, but when I drink, they are me, except that I rarely remember doing them. I hardly ever remember anything after my first drink or two. My friends tell me that I drink until either everything's gone or until I pass out or get, you know, picked up by some guy I don't even know. This past weekend, on Sunday morning, I . . . I, like, woke up in the worst neighborhood with, you know, this older guy . . . I've woken up twice in the hospital after drinking so much that they told me I could have stopped breathing."

Suddenly she jerked her head up to look sharply at me. "Do *you* really believe this? Do you *really* think that I can do . . . stuff like that and not remember it? I need to know this—the *truth*, now— don't bullshit me."

I explained the impact of alcohol on neurologically soft adolescent brains, and its particularly vicious attack on the part of the brain that controls memory. I also noted that many people have virtually no tolerance to the toxic effects of alcohol, people who after only one drink are unable to stop drinking until they pass out. Finally, I explained how some drinkers literally become different people when they drink and do things that shock and disgust their sober selves.

She listened intently, asking many detailed questions, writing down my answers, insisting to know exactly where this information came from so that she could read it for herself. Then after putting down her notebook, she sat sadly, looking almost vulnerable for the first time. "There was something that I hoped you *would* say that you *didn't* say about people who drink, something that happens to me when I drink. Something I don't know if I can tell you."

Then her vulnerable little girl face shifted back to Dirty Harry. "Nothing personal," she said, "but there aren't many adults you can trust, particularly men. Another shrink I went to once—I wouldn't talk to him because he asked way too many questions about sex, like he was getting off on hearing stories or whatever. He skeeved me really bad. You might be a perv, too. When you're a kid, you have to see whoever they tell you and you have no way of knowing until it's too late, right?" I nodded. "That's another tough thing about choices," I said, "some require some risk. I think that's particularly true when we choose to trust someone. I guess you have to decide about me."

She cancelled her next appointment without an explanation, but asked to be seen in three weeks, signing off with her signature phrase, "Peace up." Three weeks later, a Karin I had not yet met showed up for that meeting. Even in the waiting room, you could see a difference. Her face seemed to glow and her eyes looked bright, but softer somehow, with a new kind of intensity. She was smiling. She looked like . . . *hope*.

As she walked into the office, she almost swaggered. She held her head high. Dirty Harry was nowhere to be seen. "One month," she announced. "I've been sober 30 days. Not one drink—not one drop in 30 days. Do you have any idea how hard that is to do? Everybody where I live drinks—all the time. My friends and I started when we were, like, 12, every weekend during school, and then every night in the summer. There's nothing else to do. At the playground, or in the park—that's all that's going on. That and marijuana and pills and some harder stuff once in a while. So the kids who just drink, they're seen as, like, almost Straight-Edge [teens who do no alcohol or drugs].

"All the kids' parents drink, too. Some drink with us. Some get beer for us." She sat and ran a list through her head. "Yeah," she said, "every one of my friends' parents drink a lot. I'd say about . . . half? . . . yeah, at least half get drunk every weekend. You see, that's the part that adults who don't drink don't understand: *Everybody drinks,* at least in my world. There are bars on every corner. Drinking is like no big deal to anyone."

As I started to respond, she cut me off. "I know, I know—booze is, like, a serious drug. Maybe the worst one out there. I looked up those things [the research references] you gave me. Pretty scary stuff." She sat and thought and then asked a great question: *"How did this happen? How did a deadly drug get made out to be OK like that?* At school, they mostly talk about non-alcohol drugs as killers. It's weird. If a kid gets caught drinking, they don't get nearly as bent as they do when he gets caught with weed. I never heard a teacher say that alcohol kills more kids than all the other drugs *added together,* which it does. Is that maybe because the teachers drink, too?"

Karin was a young woman transformed. She was so liberated by her brief sobriety that she had gone on a rampage against the insanity of alcohol abuse among her friends, getting into serious arguments with some. She had even approached the drug and alcohol counselor at her school about putting on a different kind of awareness program, one that would be run only by the kids, ". . . like that boy in the movie. Kids will only listen if it's done by other kids." She was back into Friday night risk-taking behaviors on the playground, but this time it was a *sober* Karin confronting the pushers, adults who sell alcohol to children, some as young as *10.* She told me that when the jerks laughed at her, she slowly held up her cell phone and offered to turn them in to the cops. "I got 9-1-1 on speed dial . . ." she had said, ". . . you assholes wanna' see?" They stopped laughing. I knew the face that she had probably used. Dirty Harry was now a teen prohibitionist.

She said all of this without a trace of bragging or fishing for compliments. I think that kudos would only have annoyed her. When I asked what this was all about, she became quieter. "I can't explain it all to you," she said, "except to say that I have to, like, be on the offensive against this or she . . . it will kill me. Please don't ask anymore."

For the rest of the session we spoke about sobriety and what an incredibly tough thing that was for kids today. She waved off my suggestions about considering rehab. "Want to take a guess how many rehabs my father's been to?" she asked. "I think that people only stop drinking when they decide. That's why I didn't come back here for a month. No one can do that for anybody else. I need to do this on my own."

The following week when I saw Karin's face in the waiting room, it was clear that Dirty Harry had lost a round. She walked slowly into the office, looking crestfallen and ashamed, and refusing to talk. Guessing that I knew her thoughts, I began to talk about the "journey" of sobriety with its wins and losses. Appropriately annoyed, she cut me off. "I *know* all that stuff," she said, "you don't understand . . . you don't understand *why* it's so bad that I drank on Friday . . ." She paused and took a deep breath. "Drinking, for me, is not like it is for other kids who have problems. You see . . . there's another part of this . . . that's hard to say. It's like letting a monster out of a closet."

She grabbed her pillow hard, this time holding it close, while speaking very quietly. "The drunk part of me wants me dead. My friends tell me that I don't seem to care what happens to me when I'm drunk. Twice they . . . they had to pull me off of the train tracks when the train was coming. They said I was fighting with them and screaming that I wanted to die. I have some memories of that, but not much—just pieces. Then . . . on Friday . . . after my friends brought me home, I fell asleep and . . . I had this . . . I guess, *dream* that I was going to shoot myself. When I woke up, as I got out of bed, I stepped on my father's gun. It was right there . . . on the floor next to my bed."

Karin sat and stared at the pillow for a long time, then looked up at me. "That's why I can't drink. There's this . . . *bitch* . . . inside of me who wants me dead. *I* don't want to die—I want to live—now maybe for the first time, really. I want to be somebody and do something important. I want to beat this bitch and help other kids beat her, too. In my neighborhood, alcohol runs *everything* . . . like it's the Mafia or something. We're all, like, slaves to it. Kids talk about how they're gonna' leave and go do this or do that, how they're gonna' get out and be a person, and do important things but, you know what? Hardly *anybody* escapes. Yeah, some go away to college or the army for a year or two but almost all of them come back home *and become drunks just like their parents.* Most never leave the neighborhood, like it's got walls around it or something. It's *crazy!* I'M NOT GONNA LET THAT BITCH WIN, OK?!"

She slumped back down. "Anyway, that's what I was thinking about during my Sunday hangover. That . . . and that the bitch is tougher than me. So . . . I guess I need to go away to rehab. Like, now, OK?"

Karin went into a residential treatment program, which was very hard for her pride to accept. But just like Dirty Harry, she was a warrior for her beliefs, and would do whatever she needed to win. When I called her counselor for a 4-week update, she told me that Karin had thrown herself into her program "110 percent" and had become a resident leader, earning their top-level ranking. She worked passionately at helping some very despondent kids learn to fight their own "bitches," working harder and longer than even some of the paid staffers. After meeting her father and learning of her struggles, the counselor told me that, given where she came from, Karin was incredible, that she was ". . . like some bright star from a dark, dark sky."

She finished her residential rehab and was released to a day-treatment program to help her ease back into her dangerous real world, to see if she could make it there. "Hey, Doc, this is Dirty

Harry," her confident voice rang out from my answering machine. "I'm good. I feel like I'm really ready. Once I finish day-treatment, I'll call for an appointment. God, I've got, like, a million things to tell you about. Peace up, Doc."

Three days later I stood frozen as I listened to a phone message from Karin's sobbing counselor. "She's *dead . . .*" she said haltingly, *"Karin's dead . . . she got drunk and shot herself last night. I can't believe it . . . it makes no freakin' sense . . . she was doing great—she was a STAR!* I'm . . . sorry to tell you like this but I thought . . . I'm sorry, I'm just so goddamn sorry . . ."

At the funeral, there must have been a hundred kids, some of whom who were sobbing and pouring out their souls to whoever would listen. A group of three girls trembled and cried, and told me about Karin's last night. They said that the kids on the playground were "hassling the crap" out of Karin for not drinking, and that she got right back in their faces, calling them losers and saying they were going nowhere. That got the jerks so mad that they began taunting her, laughing and telling her that her boyfriend had cheated on her while she was away. They told her that they had clued him in about her drunken sexual acting out, something Karin was trying to keep secret. Then they lied and told her that he had said terrible things about her, calling her a slut and a whore.

Karin was devastated, they said. She went off to a corner to call her boyfriend to ask him and he admitted that he was now seeing someone else, that he just couldn't handle what he had heard about her. She hung up before he could tell her that he had not called her any names. She cried real hard, something they said they had never, ever seen Karin do. Then she marched back across the playground and yanked a beer out of one jerk's hands. She poured most of it on his head, and then drank the rest as the kids clapped and hooted. Then she drank and drank until she passed out, with the crowd cheering her on. In some bizarre "victory" parade, they carried her back home and knocked on her door, but no one was there. So they left her on her living room couch to sleep it off.

Then, somewhere in the darkness, Karin was murdered by the evil within her, killed by a drunken bitch armed with a gun from

Dad, loaded with some bullets from jerks, and abetted by an insid-
ious denial from all of us.

After the funeral, I went back to my empty office and sat across
from the waiting room chair where she used to sit, the one in the
corner where no one could see her. I felt a profound sadness, the
kind of sadness where time seems to slow down only for you,
where everyone else seems to be moving too fast and talking too
loud. Where you feel your life energy waning because something
marvelous and wonderful is suddenly ripped away forever, leaving
a dark void where beauty and hope once shone.

I recalled how she would sit there, her dark eyes shining, smiling her strange half-smile, the one that seemed to laugh at the
world, and at you, and herself, and at life in all of its bittersweet
irony. In my mind's eye, the picture of her face came alive, and I
could hear her voice sheepishly say, "Hey, Doctor Bradley. So . . .
what's new?" "*Damn*, Karin," I answered out loud. "What the hell
happened? You were doing great at rehab. It sounded like you
really had a shot at your dreams."

"I'm so sorry about all this," she answered, "I really am. That's,
like, the worst part of being dead. You see all these people hurting
so bad and you can't tell them anything to help them feel better.
That's why I'm talking to you now. I need you to tell everyone what
happened so nobody thinks that it's their fault.

"*I* was doing great—me, the *sober* Karin—not the drunken bitch.
I thought I had her locked away. But I got cocky. I thought I could
handle that scene in the park. You know me—Dirty Harry? I wasn't
there to drink. I was there to make a difference. To challenge the
jerks, to make some kids think about what's really going on with
their lives, maybe to help only one kid escape the booze and the
insanity of that neighborhood. Even saving one kid would be
enough." Karin smiled her sad/sweet smile again and shook her
head. "But it's a rough place; I couldn't even save me.

"Tell my boyfriend that this wasn't about him breaking up with
me. I feel so bad that I left him with that awful thought. Don't tell
him this part, but I didn't love him enough to kill myself over breaking up. Actually, you can tell him that. What pushed me over the

edge was when I thought that he had called me a slut and a whore, which he didn't. You see, he was, like, the only nice guy I ever met. So I felt like no nice guy could ever love me because of the nasty stuff I'd done—or actually that the bitch inside of me had done. Everything suddenly seemed . . . *hopeless*, you know, like what's the point? But now that I'm dead, I *know* the point. I can see that if I didn't drink that night, I could have been a great counselor or something and maybe had a great life. I could have broken that crazy chain of crazy people in my family, you know, where parents hand down insanity from one generation to another?

"My dad, he . . . he also called me names like that because of what I had done. He couldn't even come to my funeral because he thinks that he killed me. He didn't, but you'll never convince him of that. But don't be mad at him. He has issues, you know? He came from a hellhole where he used to get beat real bad all the time. He wasn't the greatest father in the world, but he never beat me and he didn't desert me. He was just trying to do a little better than his own parents did with him. You know, maybe I could have had kids and raised them right, with a mom and a dad who aren't crazy, who just love their families. Maybe I could have started a new chain of people who know how to live and love each other. What a waste, huh, Doc? Anyway, get out your notepad because there are some things I need you to tell kids and parents.

"First, tell the kids about suicide. Tell them I said that it sneaks up on you like a creep in the park, that you think you're all cool and suddenly one bad thing happens and then you want to throw your life away. And that only after you're dead do you see how stupid it is, and how you don't just kill yourself, but you also blow away everybody who loves you. Tell kids to just stay alive for a while, maybe two days, and talk to somebody, and then things will seem OK again. You can always kill yourself later if you want, but you can't *un-kill* yourself. Bullets never change their minds.

"Second, tell kids that they *have to* talk about stuff that bothers them. Teenagers think that counseling is just bullshit, you know? But if I had been able to talk about how much that "slut" and "whore" stuff hurt me, then maybe I wouldn't have reacted so badly to the jerks, and then maybe I'd still be alive and everyone around me wouldn't be so torn up. And maybe I'd be making a difference in the world.

"Finally, tell parents to think—*really think* before they say nasty stuff to their kids. Adults have no idea how soft teenagers really are inside because we can act all tough and everything. Screaming and yelling and putting kids down never breaks a crazy chain—it just makes it stronger. Only things like patience and kindness and compassion can create a new line of strong people, like a beautiful golden chain that can live on forever. Ask parents what it is that they want to leave behind when they're gone, how they want to be remembered. Do they want their legacy to be about rage and pain and damaged children? Or do they wish that sometime, perhaps even a century from now, some lucky kid who messes up will have a parent who *doesn't* go nuts. That they'll have a mom or dad who just lovingly helps them grow stronger, all because a hundred years before someone they never even knew loved them enough to create a priceless gift of wisdom, a beautiful golden chain to be treasured and handed down forever.

"Anyway, I guess our time is up. I gotta go. I see your new client is coming up the walk. She looks pretty strung out. Boy, do I ever know *that* look. Hey—tell her about me, OK? Tell her all about how I messed up and how close I came to making it out of the insanity. Tell her not to be stupid like me, but to believe that—no, to just *trust* that she can have a life if she wants to. Say that *I* told you to tell her that.

"Tell everybody you can that I was here, that I was alive, and that my life meant something. Don't let them just forget about me, OK? Help me to still make a difference in this insane world. Make me a link in their chains. That would be really cool."

Then Karin smiled a good smile, turned away, and slowly faded into the soft, warm sunlight that enfolded her chair.

"Peace up, Doc," she whispered. *"Peace up."*

⌒

As I sat at my computer and debated whether to add Karin's story to this book, a colleague's e-mail interrupted my musings with a screen alert that read, "HAVE YOU SEEN

THIS!?" Attached was new research from the American Medical Association that noted the following: 40% of America's 8th graders drink; 67% of teens have stolen alcohol from their homes; 32% claimed to have been freely given alcohol by their parents; 24% said that they drank at parties along with parents who drank with them; 26% of the responding parents admitted to allowing their teenagers to drink alcohol. The article went on to note that this largely voluntary poisoning of children by their own parents continues in spite of the overwhelming research connecting teen drinking with crime, violence, sexual activity, and irreversible damage to the adolescent brain structures that regulate memory and academic achievement functions.

What the study did not include was one statistic that Karin did not believe until she looked it up for herself: Kids who abuse alcohol have over nine times a greater risk for completing suicide than those who don't. Alcohol is not the feel-good, all American teen pasttime that we love to pretend it is. For many teens it is a wildly toxic depressant that unleashes monsters like Karin's "bitch" to murder them in the dark of the night.

I did what she asked that day. I told that next client about Karin. She listened intensely, riveted when I told her what I thought Karin might have to say, or, perhaps what Karin did say. The client said that it helped a lot, since she also had been thinking about suicide, and that it was hard to talk about that to anyone who didn't understand. She said that Karin understood.

Ever since that day, I've told Karin's story to many hurting kids. Most listen very closely and quietly, as if they are hearing a strangely familiar young voice offering them a wisdom that an adult cannot. It's almost as if Karin is in the room talking with them, gently weaving herself into their golden chains—the ones that can run on forever.

Thanks, Karin, for making a difference.

Peace up.

20

LET THERE BE EMPATHY

Michael's Story

This final adolescent hero is not a hero at all, just a survivor who always wished that he was a hero. He made the cut for this book based solely upon his verbal skills. Like a soldier with a hidden camera, Michael lived in the trenches of adolescence and documented that "war" from his viewpoint as a 17-year-old looking back over his recent teen years. Of course, this is just his experience, not what all or perhaps even most kids live, but his war stories lend a color and texture to the more common and ordinary adolescent experience of those of us who never made it onto a list of heroes.

I can't say how or where I met Michael without disclosing his identity, and he's not quite ready to do that yet. He says that one day, perhaps soon, he might feel secure enough to reveal himself as the person attached to these reminiscences. I found his fear of disclosure familiar and compelling, a reminder of how adolescence can be so difficult for so many that even adults can become reluctant to remember who we truly were and what we truly thought then. And yet, as adults, we become so intolerant of teens who screw up just as we did—and they do so within a world that's much more insane. No wonder so many of them won't talk to us.

What follows are Michael's words exactly as he presented them to me, a kind of a free-flowing "stream of adolescent consciousness." For the teen reader, I hope that his thoughts bring a little comfort. For the adult reader, I hope they bring a little honesty—and a lot of empathy. With those gifts, maybe a few more kids can talk with a few more adults. And maybe we can shut up and actually listen.

~

So, you want me to just, like *talk*, about being a teenager, saying everything that pops into my head? Nothing personal, but this "telling-it-like-it-is" stuff is hard to do, you know? I mean, I hear grown-ups talking all the time about their back-in-the-day teen years, about how great they were and how much fun they had and stuff. Lots of them talk about how hard-working and moral they were, you know, *"not like kids today."* I get really confused and feel sort of insane when I hear them talk like that, like I'm the only pervert-weirdo-misfit-coward-loser that ever lived.

I don't know. Maybe grown-ups forget what it was really like, or maybe they turn it into something else to make themselves feel better. I know *I* do that a lot. But I'll try not to do that here.

OK, let's see . . . you want me to just talk straight-up about being a teenager, about whatever pops into my head . . . *Damn!* OK, you asked for it. The first thing is sex. We're all obsessed with it—the boys are, anyway. I couldn't tell you about the girls. They're confusing. They act all sexy but it's different for them, somehow. But the boys—it's most of what we talk about. And when we're not talking about it, we're sure as hell thinking about it. But we don't *really* talk about it, you know . . . man, this is hard to explain . . .

The world, it, like, tells you nonstop to have all the sex you can, and then there's hell to pay if you do and you get caught. Well, mostly for the girls. They're, like, in a really bad spot. Boys are all cool if they have sex, and girls are whores. I feel sorry for them, but I still chase them . . . and . . . and I lie to them, sometimes. Most guys do, you know . . .

Wait a minute. I promised to be straight up. OK. The embarrassing truth is that the first time I could have had sex, *I didn't*. I couldn't tell any of my friends this, 'cause they thought that I did have sex on that night, and that made me look cool. I lied to them.

I was dating this girl and she was willing to have sex, but I knew that it would make her feel bad. She wasn't, like, really in love with me, and she had lots of emotional problems. We were just playing at being in love, you know? Anyway, when the opportunity was finally there, *I turned it down.* But I wasn't being noble or moral or whatever—that stuff had nothing to do with it. *I was just playing at being a hero.* Please don't look at me weird, but that's the truth. I told her that I loved her too much to do that to her. *And that was a lie; I was only acting.* Look, I didn't love her. I didn't even like her all that much. I was just trying to act like somebody else, like some hero-guy who wouldn't take advantage of a girl. If it had been another girl, who didn't have problems, I have no idea what I would have done. I think I still would have pretended, and turned her down. I don't know. Is that crazy or what?

I was always doing stuff like that—trying to act like somebody else. I guess it was because I couldn't stand who I was—yeah, that's it. I hated who I was. I still do lots of times. That's how so many kids start to drink and smoke, you know: *posing.* In 9th or 10th grade my friend and I used to score some beer from the gangsters and drink it with our hoagies. We loved getting hoagies on Friday nights and eating them in the woods. We got the beer because, well, that's what you do to be cool. You want to hear something funny? *I hated the taste of beer.* It *ruins* the hoagies. I *love* black cherry soda with my hoagies—that's the best. But there we were, gagging down these beers, ruining our hoagies, trying to act cool. It's the same with smoking cigarettes and those little cigar things. They're *really gross*, like, *foul*, and there we were, nauseous half the time, smoking like chimneys. What a bunch of nitwits! It's all about the act, you know?

Speaking of bad acting—this is really embarrassing—my friend and I, we never liked rock music all that much. We're more into jazz for some reason—which is another thing I can't tell other kids—they'd laugh. Anyway, the only place to see jazz is in jazz clubs, which are all 21-and-over places. My friend and I—God, I can't say this—anyway, we'd get these fake mustaches to try and sneak in. Mostly, it never worked. But one time, there was this huge black bouncer, and he looked at us, and at our bogus IDs, and I could see that he was trying hard not to laugh at these two insane white boys. And he said, "OK gentlemen. Y'all get in on two conditions: The first is that you don't drink. I'll be watching, so don't make me come over there. The second is," and here he broke out laughing out loud, "you *GOT* to take off those *JIVE* mustaches. Man, you gonna' run all the good-lookin' women out the place." His name was Jerome. For some reason, I remember him.

Friends are another place where I act a lot. I never had any cool friends at all until high school, and then I mostly had only semi-cool friends. When I got those—man, that must be what doing heroin is like. *That felt fantastic!* And so I'd act there, too, you know? Pretending that I agreed with them on almost everything, even lots of times when I didn't. I was too scared to say what I felt *even to my friends* who probably would stick with me even if they knew that I liked jazz, for example, and hated Pink Floyd. Nobody is allowed to hate Pink Floyd. Or if they were passing around the name of some girl that was "easy," and I'd think that was kinda' crummy, I wouldn't say anything then either. You see, to belong to a group—any group—to not be hangin' out alone—that's an incredible thing to a loser kid like me who was always excluded. I would have sold my soul to keep that. So I'd shut up. And act.

I used to get picked on a lot, and beaten up sometimes, so I tried to act like a tough guy who could fight. But I couldn't fight. That's another crazy game guys have to play—the fighting game. It's like poker. You pretend that you've got great cards, like, four kings, like you're *real bad*. You bluff a lot hoping the other guy will fold before you have to show what you've got. But, man, if he doesn't fold—that's horrible—for me, anyway. I'd always have like two 2's, and then they'd kick my ass almost every time.

That's why I'm joining the Army. I tell everyone about how patriotic I am and stuff, but that's not really true. That's just another act I put on. I'm mostly joining to get real big and bad so I can kick all *their* asses—no, that's not it, exactly—I don't want to beat them up, I just want them to respect me and think that I'm real tough and cool and then not mess with me. Yeah, that's more it—that's what I want when I come back from the war—if I come back.

Not all guys are afraid or bad at fighting, I think. Actually, I don't know about the afraid part—maybe everybody is. My best friend, he's a monster. He's, like, 6 feet 2 inches, goes about 250 pounds, and is as strong and hairy as a gorilla. He's a great fighter, and no one, I mean *nobody*, hardly, ever messes with him. But one time, after this bad fight where he had to really hurt this crazy dude who wouldn't quit, he went around the corner, away from all the kids who were cheering him on. I followed him and I found him . . . *crying! He was crying like a little kid.* He was really pissed when he saw me there. That was the only time I remember him ever yelling at me. He screamed that he would beat the shit out of me if I ever told anybody.

But I wasn't scared, you know? Something told me to just sit down next to him. I didn't know what to say, so I didn't say anything. He just cried and cried like a baby, for, I don't know, maybe 15 minutes? It seemed like a real long time. Another kid came around the corner and I, like, snapped out on him, acting all bad so he'd leave and not see my friend crying.

You know, that's when my friend became my *best* friend, now that I think about it. Until just now I never understood why he hung out with me so much after that night. He was a cool kid, you know, with lots of money, the best car in school, and pretty girls, and I was this skinny loser kid with a ratty old car. But ever since that night, he took care of me like I was his brother. He defended me from the jerks lots of times. I never knew what to say to him to try to act as cool as he was. I always felt stupid around him, but he, like, you know . . . *loved* me—*just for letting him cry!* I guess that's an important thing. Weird.

He was the guy who tried to teach me how to drive a stick shift car. A job got posted at school for a drugstore delivery boy but it said that only kids who knew how to drive a stick should apply. So my buddy took me out and gave me this crash course so I could pass the stick shift test. I really needed that job. My father got laid off and we had, like, no money. So my friend let me tear up his clutch learning how to shift, and I did OK. Then he drove me to the drugstore, and the owner, Carmen, asked if I could drive a stick. I lied and told him that was all I drove. So he took me to the delivery car and said, "Show me. Drive down the street a ways, and come back."

The street was a busy highway, and I was a little nervous. But I, like, almost had a heart attack when I got in the car and saw that the shift pattern in his Volkswagen was *completely different* from the one in my friend's sports car. Carmen asked if there was a problem, and instead of telling the truth, I said everything was cool. Carmen stood there watching as I pulled away. I found first gear and "revved out"— no problem. Second was tough. I managed it, but the transmission made a crunching noise. Third was great. I was flying now, so I revved it all the way to impress Carmen and slammed the shifter back for fourth. But I missed fourth, and jammed it in second by mistake. When I let out the clutch, the car, like, *screamed!* The wheels skidded, the rear fishtailed, smoke came up from the tires, and people had to swerve all around me because I had gone from, like, 60 miles-per-hour to 10 in one second. Then I was so messed up I couldn't do anything right. I kept stalling out right there in the middle of the road, in Carmen's car with ROSA PHARMACY and his phone number right there for everybody to see. It was a killer-hot day, and people were screaming and throwing fingers. It was bad.

I finally limped the car back to the drugstore, and I was waiting to get screamed at, or maybe arrested, and there was Carmen, *laughing his ass off.* I mean, he had tears coming out of his eyes, he was laughing so hard. I was mumbling about how I was sorry and all, and Carmen put his hand on my shoulder, still laughing, and he said, "Son, any man brave enough to do what you just did, that's a man who needs a job." He hired me right there. He kept laughing the rest of the afternoon. He'd be working on something, then he'd look up and see me, and just bust out laughing all over again. He drove with me for the first few deliveries 'til I got that stick shift down. You know, that first day, I almost blew up his car and all, and . . . *he never yelled at me.*

I can't really explain why, but because of that, I made myself the best worker Carmen ever had. He actually told people that for years and years, that I was the best. Like I said, I'm not a fighter, but I think I would have fought a robber with a gun for him. He was, like, the first grown-up I ever knew who seemed to know how hard it is being a kid.

I'll never forget him.

I learned a lot in that job, more than my Catholic mother would have wanted me to learn. One of my weekly deliveries was to a motel where a prostitute worked a few months out of every year for a few years. Carmen's eyes would always light up when that phone call would come in. He loved sending me there. I was this real serious, naïve Irish-Catholic kid, and I'd have to deliver this huge bottle of douche powder to room 8 at the Springfield Motel. All the guys would line up to wave as I left. Carmen would always yell, "Don't hurry back. We'll understand if you're late." That was, like, the high point of his week.

What I learned is that prostitutes aren't always like what people think. The one in Room 8, she weighed about, I don't know, 300 pounds? And she would always answer the door in a see-through nightie-thing. Man, I'd see a lot more than I ever wanted to see—a *whole lot* more. But she was real nice, and always invited me inside. There was usually some guy, like, passed out on the bed. I'd always say I had to get back to work and she'd say, *"Maybe next time, shugah. Y'all give Carmen a big kiss from Lottie. You tell him I said, 'Y'all get a LOT with Lottie.'"* Can you believe that? Her name was actually Lottie. She liked seeing me blush.

She was really weird, but you know what? She always gave me a huge tip. I learned that rich people, the ones in the big houses? They'd give you nothing and treat you like dirt, like you were born to wait on them. And the poor people, the ones who had nothing, like Lottie? They'd usually tip great and they mostly acted nicer. I guess that's because they knew what it's like to be poor. The rich people, they mostly acted like they were better than you because they had some money. If I had to pick one of them to hang out with, I'd pick Lottie—trust me, *not* for sex, but because, as messed up as she was, I remember her as a better person than the rich ones.

Oh—a sort of hero thing happened to me at Carmen's. He had this loser pharmacist, a drunk, who would fill in on some days. I think it was his brother-in-law or something. He gave an old lady the wrong strength of insulin, which could have killed her. I knew because I always delivered to this lady and I could see the color of the label through the bag. Anyway, when I got back to the store and checked the prescription, it *was* the wrong strength. I told the drunk pharmacist about it and he just waved me off. So I called Carmen, and he came to the store and checked and went nuts. He called the lady and *lied* to her, saying that the drug company put the wrong bottles in the wrong labels or whatever.

That was the first time I realized that adults screw up, too, and they lie to cover it up just like teenagers do. I know it sounds dumb, but that was a big revelation for me. That was the first time I was, like, *really there* and saw what had happened for myself. And it made me worry that maybe adults do this all the time, and that none of them have all the answers like they pretend they do. I think that's when I first saw that people aren't like, *all* good or *all* bad; they're some of both. Carmen lied his ass off to that lady, but he did it right there in front of me. Then, without being ashamed or anything, he turned to me and shook my hand and said, "You did a hell of a thing. She's a confused old lady. She might have used that insulin, and it might have killed her. Thank you." I didn't know what to say.

That happens a lot when you're a kid. You get all full of huge thoughts and feelings, and you can never seem to find the right words. And even when you can, you're too scared to because . . . I guess you get so afraid of sounding like you're dumb or a sex maniac or immoral or whatever if you really say what you're thinking. That's when people stare at you like you're stupid or have an attitude, and they yell, *"Say something!"* They think that you're silent because you're rude, but mostly it's because you, like, blank out. You don't stop feeling things, but you can't find the words that match.

I used to watch Carmen a lot. He was different from most adults I know, or maybe he was just more up-front with me. He could be real rude and crude, you know? Like, there was a real pretty girl who used to come into the store who Carmen swore was the niece of a rich, famous singer. He kept trying to fix me up with her so that I'd have an easy life. He'd make me go wait on her and then he'd sneak around to the aisle behind her so only I could see him and he'd do this motion where he'd push one of his arms back and forth through a loop that he'd make with his other arm, grinnin' like a wild man. He'd call that the "Boffa da Boff," or something like that. I have no idea if that's really Italian or whatever, but I'm pretty sure I know what it means. He told me that he did that stuff to me because I was always too serious, and that cute girls love even ugly guys who can make them laugh. I wonder if that's true.

I know he doesn't sound so great, but Carmen really cared about the kids who worked for him. When I got offered this other job, I told Carmen about it and he asked what they paid. When I told him, his eyes bugged out, and then he said, "You can't turn that down. That's twice what I could ever pay you. You have to take that." I think he knew that if he wanted to, he could make me feel so guilty that I'd stay with him. But he wouldn't do that to me, even though he looked real sad on the day I left.

I was sad, too. I, like . . . cried . . . a little. Weird. It was just a dumb job, you know? And Carmen, he could be a liar and a cheat and yet he watched out for me. On that last day, when he saw me standing there, like, getting upset, he yelled, "What's 'amtta wich' you? Get the hell out of here!" But he wasn't mad, he was trying to help me out. Guys can't say goodbye, you know?

Later, when I used him as a reference for my Army scholarship, he called and asked me to stop in to see him. When I stopped by he took me in the back, where it's quiet, and asked if I knew what I was doing—not like I was dumb or anything, but just asking to be sure that this was what I wanted. He told me something that none of the guys ever knew about him, that he had been a Marine in Korea. He didn't say it like it was a great thing. He just said it like he knew what he was talking about. I never saw him so serious. He told me to think real hard before I signed up, and that if I wanted, he would be happy to recommend me, but that if I was going just to pay for school, that maybe there were other ways. I kept waiting for the gag, you know, but he was dead serious. He said that the Army was OK if there was no war going on, but that war was—how did he say it? Oh yeah, that, "It ain't like they show you on TV." That's all he said.

That was another time when I didn't know what to say and I just stood there. He just stood there, too, saying nothing for a long time. Then he shook my hand, real sad and solemn-like, and he said, "Good luck, son. Keep your dumb Irish head down." I didn't know what he meant by that. That was the last time I ever saw him.

I couldn't tell him this, but even standing there, I knew the real reason I was joining the Army was my acting thing. I was trying to become somebody else—somebody better. Since I can remember, I wanted to be somebody else. When I was a little kid, I'd always be dressing up in Army or cowboy stuff or whatever. Teenagers do that same thing, you know, but with clothes that you never notice. Even the cool kids, they worry a lot about looking just right. They won't admit it, of course, but everyone knows that they do, just like the uncool kids.

Why is it that kids have to look just a certain way or other kids tear them down? Is it that way with grown-ups? One of my teachers, when he was getting razzed about his dumb haircut, he just stood there and smiled and waited 'til the kids were done, and then he said, "Children, the best thing about growing old and ugly is that you don't have to give a damn anymore." That pretty much shut everybody up.

He's not old or ugly. He's actually one of the cool teachers. Cool teachers aren't what you think. They're not the ones who let kids run wild. They're the ones who . . . well, I don't know . . . I guess they're the ones who don't take what kids do personally. And they, like, *listen* to the kids. Even when kids are saying stupid stuff, they don't jump down their throats. And because they do that, the kids want to behave more for them, and be like them. It's weird.

I sort of stalked that teacher back in ninth grade . . . like I was trying to learn something by watching him. His name was Mr. King. He never yelled or insulted kids or put them down like the other teachers. He just acted . . . I don't know . . . *cool*. Not cool like a kid, but cool like an adult—calm and in charge. If some kid started to act out with him, he'd just stay calm and do what he had to do. When he had to he'd still give demerits and stuff but he always seemed, like, *apologetic* about it, always giving kids a chance to get back under control or do what they were supposed to do. He never got in their faces to act like he's all tough or whatever. Hardly anyone ever gave him a rough time. The bad-ass teacher, Mr. Giambi? He's this tough ex-marine who screams and yells and goes nose-to-nose with kids all the time. But kids are *always* doing dumb stuff in his class. Weird.

And . . . I know, the other thing I liked about Mr. King was that he'd talk with *all* the kids. Lots of teachers, you know, will only talk to the cool kids, and they ignore the others. Mr. King, he'd ask each kid "what's up" whether the kid was the football star or a loser like me. I know it's silly, but that made me feel really good, like maybe I wasn't as much of a nerd. He's another guy I'll never forget. I used to wonder if I'd still feel like a loser if he was . . . you know, like . . . my father or something . . .

I guess I have to talk about my parents, now, huh? That's really hard. I'd rather not. They . . . they do the best they can, and I mean that . . . sort of, but . . . they're messed up. They both have serious problems. Look, I can't go there, right now, OK? I, like, love them, you know, even though they're really messed up and they act like they hate me or don't care sometimes. But it feels wrong to talk bad about them.

The worst thing of all that happens to kids is parents fighting. When kids are small, everyone knows that it's bad for parents to fight in front of them. But when kids become teenagers, a lot of parents don't know or don't care what happens inside of older kids when they see their parents, like, *hating* each other.

That's a tough feeling to describe. Just the other day they were screaming and yelling, and my mom was crying, and I stood there watching, and they . . . they didn't care, you know? Like it was all about them . . . like, because I'm older I don't count anymore, and they can act all crazy if they want. Teenagers aren't allowed to do that, you know. If we scream and yell, some adult always gets in our faces. We get detention or arrested or grounded. But lots of parents think that they're allowed to do all kinds of lousy things. They don't get detention. Maybe they should.

My feeling while I watch my parents fight? Hhmmm . . . I'd say . . . *alone. All alone. Like the most alone feeling you can have.* Like, you're ten feet away from them, but a million miles away.

It gets like that even when they're not fighting and everything is quiet and they're just leaving you alone—completely alone, like they don't want to be involved in your life anymore, like . . . they don't care. That's . . . *empty* . . . like outer space is empty? Like no one's there to bother you or nag you, and *you get panicked because you know that you can't survive.* I know teenagers act like they want to be cut loose but most know they're not really ready. I'm not, anyway. My parents are so messed up that I can do pretty much whatever I want, and my friends are jealous. I act like . . . there's that word again . . . I *act* like I'm real grown up and mature, but I'm not—*I'm a little kid inside. I don't know what's up, or how things work, or why I'm joining the Army, or if there's a really a God, or if it's OK to have sex with a girl you don't love, or if two people can stay married forever and love each other, or . . .* or a million other things I need to ask somebody about.

That makes me think about people I've known—like Jerome, that bouncer. And Carmen, and Lottie. They were people I think I could have asked tough questions . . . no, that's not true. I can't see myself *asking* those hard questions, but at least I would have listened when they talked about themselves, and about whatever. I guess I would have learned stuff by listening in and watching their lives. *Why is that?*

That's some group, huh? A bouncer, a liar, and a prostitute. Aren't you supposed to talk to, like, your father or your priest, or maybe the president of the United States—you know, like, the perfect people, or at least the people who think they're perfect? There was also my teacher, Mr. King. If I ever had the chance, I think I could talk straight up with him. As far as I know, he never does anything crazy . . . but it's like he would understand if *you* did crazy stuff—because maybe *he* used to? Or at least he doesn't act all perfect as if he never thought about doing crazy things. I think that's it: I guess all of those people would just listen without judging me.

It's funny. When I think about it, those are people who probably wouldn't have said very much. But they would have listened, I think. I . . . just . . . I don't know, it might have been nice if my father, or even my mother, was on that list. Maybe things would be different for me. Maybe I wouldn't have to *act* so much. Maybe if they told me that they were proud of me, *especially* when there was very little to be proud of, like when I've screwed something up, then maybe I'd be more OK with myself?

I think that's how teenagers mostly learn, you know, by watching adults? I don't really listen much anymore when somebody tries to give me advice. For a while now I've felt like I have to figure out everything on my own or it sort of doesn't count, you know? Like if I just do what I'm told, then I'm not my own person or something. But I watch adults like crazy, especially when they don't know that I'm there, like I'm a spy or something, seeing how they handle things. And then I make these, like, *notes* in my head about how *I* want to be when I'm grown up. Or maybe how I want to be now.

So I guess it makes a huge difference what kinds of people are around kids, doesn't it? I mean if most kids are like me and just copy what adults *do* and not listen much to what they *tell* kids to do, then...then I guess it's a real important job being an adult when kids are watching. And I guess it's a scary job being a teenager because you're going to get shaped a lot by whichever grown-ups happen to be around you. Weird.

Anyway, thanks for listening to all this. When I started talking, I really didn't think I had anything to say. I always feel like that, particularly when I've got a lot to say. I don't know exactly why, but having said all that makes me feel a little better, especially because you just sat and listened without asking me a million questions or telling me what to do. It's like you really wanted to know what being a kid feels like, and that you just cared about how I feel instead of trying to fix me. For some reason that makes me feel better and . . . *smarter.*

Weird.

~

The last I heard of Michael, he was doing OK, but he still struggles with himself a lot. He says that he never really got over his adolescence, but now he feels more like 18 than 13. He thinks that's progress.

Perhaps predictably, he chased a bizarre sampling of careers before he finally stuck with one. He was an Army officer, a law school student, and even had a brief shot at being a disc jockey. He says those careers were all products of his acting, of him trying to be somebody else. So none worked out, as Michael puts it, "luckily for him."

Where did he end up? Believe it or not, he's a psychologist and author who specializes in, yeah, you guessed it . . . adolescence. As the song goes, "Ain't life strange?"

He says that he's happy now, that he loves what he does, and that he has the best family in the world. He tells me that all of the good things in his life arrived only after he stopped acting.

His name is Dr. Michael Bradley, and he is the author of this book.

AFTERWORD

Twenty lives ago, in the introduction, I spoke of my hope that these teenagers might teach and inspire all of us, adults and adolescents alike. My secret wish was that these heroes might help ease a widespread fear that has infected far too many of us, a fear that the character of our teens cannot stand up to the challenges of our world. Those same fears are shared by some very brilliant people—highly esteemed, widely-read educators and authors who have long-pondered the heart and soul of the next generation. One writes:

> "I see no hope for the future of our people if they are dependent on the frivolous youth of today, for certainly all youth are reckless beyond words . . . When I was young, we were taught to be discreet and respectful of elders, but the present youth are exceedingly disrespectful and impatient of restraint."

Another asks:

> "What is happening to our young people? They disrespect their elders, they disobey their parents. They ignore the law. They riot in the streets inflamed with wild notions. Their morals are decaying. What is to become of them?"

The first writer despaired for the teens of his day, 2800 years ago. That was Hesiod, and he lived in the 8th century, B.C. The second worrier wrung his hands 400 years later. That was Plato, in the 4th century, B.C. The fact is that every generation sees its teens grow into adults amazingly similar to their predecessors. Yet every generation sees many of its adults become despondent about their successors.

Grown-ups often suffer a strange form of adult amnesia that seems to wipe out the memories of what adolescence was truly like, and of how they truly were as teenagers. Like rampaging revisionist historians, they become severely judgmental of teens who seem forever unable to be as wise, respectful, and hard-working as the adults were when they were kids; except, of course, the grown-ups forget that they were mostly just as wise, respectful, and hard-working.

Are there some differences between generations of teens? Certainly. Are those differences more pronounced today than ever before? Perhaps. But as with books that are judged by their covers, these are external, window-dressing differences that only reflect distinctions in the world that surrounds adolescents, and not differences in their hearts and souls.

Teen naysayers point to the high numbers of adolescents doing destructive things and ask, "Why are so many teens doing these things?" I point to the same numbers and ask, "Why are so *few* teens doing these things?" For adults have confronted these children with an *adult* culture that is out of control, self-indulgent, and saturated with suggestions to act out, and have cast them adrift in a world that offers few role models to show better paths. Today's teens, I argue, might be *more* heroic than past generations since *they've been challenged so terribly*. Yes, they do more sex and drugs than most adults did at fourteen. But before virtuous grown ups start wagging their righteous tongues, they might consider that the raciest TV shows of that time were "Peyton Place" and "I Dream of Jeannie." Poor competition for "Sex in the City" or "Desperate Housewives," don't you think? And drugs? Well, back then, kids had to know someone who knew someone who . . . you know. Now, weed and alcohol are often more accessible to teens than are cigarettes. Marijuana is marketed in most homerooms, and beers are offered *and shared* by a fourth of today's "virtuous, righteous" parents.

Yet faced with this over-the-edge world to navigate, most kids still turn out fine—and many turn out to be much more than fine; many are role models that even adults can look to as symbols of an amazing generation of kids who, in spite of the crazy world they've been thrown into, are people of heroic character and wisdom. That's because just like the teens in this book, *every* person has the potential to be a hero, to become better than what they have seen, better than what they have been shown. Finding that heroic potential is the challenge of teenagers. Nurturing it is the duty of adults.

Whether yours is the quest of the adult or the adolescent, it is my hope that the kids you just met might help you. Their tales offer so many profound insights about heroic hearts and souls that you probably have already found the ones that are most important for you. I gathered a few that I'd like to share since they haunt me daily in my work with teens. They appear in my mind's eye at critical times as ghostly countenances of wisdom, helping me to listen better.

The angry sneer of Dante, the defiant marijuana addict, is my reminder about who heroes are, and how they come to be. Most are not born as perfect people, full of confidence, insight, and character. Some, like Dante, screw up so much that I'm too often tempted to stop searching for the heroic winners that always live hidden deep inside of the furious, failing losers.

Ronald's cool, steely gaze, the one that saved my bacon in prison, helps me to see adolescents as they really are: complex human beings with profound and often heroic thoughts and emotions that mostly remain hidden, sometimes even under the cold colors of a brutal gang.

Susan's hard scowl, which once so coldly stared past her dying mother, helps me to remember that cruelty is often our favorite mask for fear, our safest expression of hurt. And her trembling, tear-stained face, the one that heroically acknowledged her love for her mom, reminds me of the tenacity of adolescent courage, surviving strong even in the battered hearts of broken children.

The soft smile of Matthew, the cancer warrior and president of *The Order of the Cool Time*, holds for me what true heroism is all about: small, simple, daily acts of courage that any of us can do to make a huge difference in the lives of others, even when we ourselves are hurting or scared. He reminds me that heroes live inside all of us, patiently waiting for the day when we finally find the courage to share, or care, or even just smile when we don't have to. He warns me about how cowardly easy it is to be cold and self-centered, and how heroically hard it can be to give a damn.

And then there's Angie, the girl who was brutalized by her father. Her face makes me feel the hardening, humiliating pain of a child wounded by a parent. It warns me about how easily I can hurt kids by being a "tough" adult, burying their heroic voices under mudslides of my grown-up judgment, anger, and frustration. Her tear-stained smile is an amazing revelation of the astonishing healing that can fill up a room when the rage finally skulks out.

There is one last picture that I hold in the most sacred part of my mind: a collage of all twenty of these heroes, but with faces older than the ones that I knew. Each is paired with a small child. The twenty are smiling peacefully and knowingly, all sharing some eternal secret of serenity. For each holds invisible, invincible treasures that they will magically gift to their own children: heroic hearts and souls that will be passed like blazing torches of hope from one generation to the next, pushing back hard upon the darkness, forever.

Michael J. Bradley, Ed.D. *is an award-winning author and a practicing adolescent psychologist with 30 years of experience. He lives and works not far from Philadelphia.*